Farnsworth's Classical English Metaphor

Farnsworth's

CLASSICAL

 DAVID R. GODINE · *Publisher · Boston*

ENGLISH METAPHOR

by WARD FARNSWORTH

For Annie and Sam

First published in 2016 by
DAVID R. GODINE · *Publisher*
Post Office Box 450
Jaffrey, New Hampshire 03452
www.godine.com

LIBRARY OF CONGRESS

CATALOGING-IN-PUBLICATION DATA

Farnsworth, Ward, 1967–
Farnsworth's Classical English metaphor / Ward Farnsworth.
    pages   cm
ISBN 978-1-56792-548-7 (alk. paper) — ISBN 1-56792-548-0 (alk. paper)
1. Metaphor. 2. Semantics. 3. English language—Terms and phrases. I. Title.
II. Title: Classical English metaphor.
P325.5.M47F35 2015
808.8'015—dc23
2015024981

FIRST EDITION 2016
Printed in the United States of America

CONTENTS

PREFACE

SOME YEARS AGO I made a study of how great writers and speakers of English have used ancient rhetorical devices as aids to eloquence. Improbably enough, the resulting book – *Classical English Rhetoric* – attracted a readership, drew some kind reviews, and went through several printings. Now the publisher has kindly consented to this sequel. Its topic is the art of comparison. The chapters that follow aim to show how metaphor has been put to use by masters of the art. The first book was about patterns for the arrangement of words; this one is mostly about patterns of thought. The change in focus is rewarding but calls for a different kind of attention. Whereas in *Classical English Rhetoric* one could see themes and resemblances on the verbal surface of the illustrations, in this book one also needs to look through the words to the comparative ideas they express. The goal is not just to see what the authors said. It is to see what they saw.

Despite the greater emphasis on ideas rather than words, this can be considered another book about rhetoric – that is, about the use of language to persuade or otherwise affect an audience. This book and its predecessor draw on the prose of similar times and places, and both were inspired in part by texts on rhetoric that were written for students of the subject in ancient Greece and Rome. Rhetoric now has a bad name; to many people it has come to mean bombast. I wish to help with the rehabilitation of the word, however, and to encourage its use in the honorable way that was common until recently – the sense of "rhetoric" that made it something for Lincoln to study and for Churchill to write about, and that caused it to be considered one of the liberal arts.

This book also involves matters that are of interest entirely apart from whatever rhetorical value they might have. They concern how our minds convert what we cannot directly say or perceive into what we can. Metaphor may be viewed as a language that we use to interpret and explain things to ourselves as well as to others. This book outlines an elementary vocabulary and grammar of one dialect of that language. The result may be useful to those who wish to improve their fluency in order to better communicate, but also to those who enjoy the language for its own sake. For rhetorical purposes – in other words, as a way of speaking to an audience – the noticeable use of metaphor must be sparing to be effective, and is wholly unsuitable for some occasions. But as a tool for thought and a subject for study, metaphor is available and interesting nearly all the time.

A metaphor can make unfamiliar things familiar, invisible things visible, and complicated things easier to understand. It can, as Aristotle said, give life to lifeless things. It can produce amusement by putting a subject into unexpected company. It can create feeling by borrowing it from the source to which the subject is compared. It can make a point riveting and memorable by the beauty of the comparison's fit. It can make an insult or a compliment immortal. It can attract attention by the element of surprise. And it can do all this with wondrous economy, invoking a mass of imagery and meaning in a sentence or a single word.

A metaphor can serve as an aid to persuasion. A claim made by metaphor is not an immediate appeal to reason; it is an appeal to intuition, inviting the reader to directly perceive a similarity and its truth. Sometimes the appeal is implied rather than explicit, as when the comparison is woven into the choice of words rather than declared openly – and it may then be more effective for its subtlety. Decisions are made, and arguments won and lost, in the imagination and heart as often as in the mind, so the skilled practitioner of rhetoric uses comparisons to engage all those faculties. In *The Scaffolding of Rhetoric* (1897), Churchill spoke of the resulting power of analogy, by which he meant to include metaphor:

> In spite of the arguments of the cynic the influence exercised over the human mind by apt analogies is and has always been immense. Whether they translate an established truth into simple language or whether they adventurously aspire to reveal the unknown, they are among the most formidable weapons of the rhetorician. The effect upon the most cultivated audience is electrical.

Lincoln likewise understood the levers of human decision and action, and left none of them unattended. He thus attacked slavery and the threat of secession not just with reason but with a metaphor borrowed from scripture: "A house divided against itself cannot stand."

These benefits of metaphor might be compared to other alternatives to the literal use of words. The author of a scientific argument in prose may pause to offer a mathematical model. The model is an alternative way to state a point; it simplifies and convinces. A metaphor can do the same (it, too, states an equation); and while it cannot prove a claim in the way that a mathematical model can, it may do more to persuade. Or put aside equations and think about the ways that literal language may be combined with pictures to express an idea. It is natural to imagine a spectrum: at one end is a photograph or painting, then a movie with words, then perhaps a graphic novel (fewer pictures, more words), then a book with periodic illustrations, then unadorned text. Metaphor can be viewed as belonging on this spectrum, too, but its placement is hard to pin down. It uses words but creates pictures. It can have features associated with any of the other items – the beauty of a painting, the drama of a short film, the clarity of a line drawing, the humor of a cartoon. Yet a metaphor is less conspicuous than any of those devices, and can be more powerful, because it masquerades as text.

Metaphors can serve deeper ends. Many important subjects cannot be described literally, at least not well. States of mind are like this, as are the sources and effects of language and other arts and many elements of spiritual life. They don't just require pictures in order to be understood. They require comparisons, because they cannot be depicted literally in images or in words. A subject tends to defeat literal description when it is inaccessible to the senses; our words for what we can see are more extensive and refined than our words for what is intangible. Other truths and observations cannot be captured through a literal use of words simply because words and reality aren't coextensive. The range and subtlety and feeling of what we wish to say outruns the labels that our language provides for the purpose. Comparisons free us from those limits. They allow a writer to use words not as labels to name a thing but as links that attach it to what we have known or seen or can imagine. The link summons pictures and other associations in the reader's mind and rallies them to the descriptive purpose. A metaphor may, in short, express something that otherwise cannot quite be said or shown, and provide a way to understand it – possibly the only way.

Metaphors may serve, finally, as repositories of wisdom. Not always; many successful ones are merely picturesque, or useful, or funny. As we shall see, however, the finest creators of metaphor tend also to be the keenest students of humanity and of nature; that is much of *why* their metaphors are so fine. Metaphors also expose resemblances, and may suggest deeper affinities, between subjects that seem unrelated, the perception of which is another talent of the wise. The connoisseur of comparisons tends to see everything as a reminder or example of something else, and notices how particular things epitomize general ones: the military elephants of yore, for the harm that friends may do to their allies (ch. 3); the eye, on account of how it dilates and contracts (ch. 6); old Phalaris, because he turned the tables, and they were turned on him (ch. 10); fire, for countless features of its action and the behavior of people in response to it (*passim*). This book is partly a catalogue of such archetypes, as identified by those who have seen and stated them best.

Having said enough about the value of metaphor, let me now say what this book means to do with the subject. It is, first, a study of where figurative comparisons come from and what effects they have. The sources of effective metaphor are infinite in detail but not in type. Metaphors are built from families of material that may be examined distinctly – animals, nature, architecture, and other sources we will explore. The effects of metaphor are likewise various in their nuances but capable of being ordered. Sometimes metaphors make their subjects visible; sometimes they simplify; sometimes they are drawn for the sake of caricature. And some of those purposes are more readily served by one kind of metaphor than another, depending in turn on the subject in question. This book explores some patterns that have run between all these points in the work of talented writers: how materials from source X have been used to describe family of subjects Y and accomplish purpose Z.

Second, this book hopes to provide a better and different collection of comparisons than has yet been available to the student of them. Good metaphors are not usually the result of calculation and planning; they are made intuitively, just as they are consumed, and often well up from sources that seem half-conscious (as perhaps they are; we dream in metaphors). The process of educating the intuition and imagination is best carried out with light doses of theory and long immersion in examples. The book thus supplies illustrations in heaping quantities. It puts related cases near each other to invite comparisons of comparisons, to inspire the eye, and to suggest, in a short space, the range of uses that a given metaphorical idea may have.

Third, I have emphasized the utility of metaphor but the attractions of the subject can be simpler. Metaphors allow an indirect or sideways approach to many matters of philosophical or psychological interest; they also can teach a certain way of appreciating the world. But even when they do not offer those advantages, they can be delightful in themselves – a wholesome source of insight and entertainment that need not be further justified. The book may serve as a museum for those with a taste for such pleasures: a partial OED of metaphor, if you are the kind who approaches the OED to browse. That is a chief aim of this project and the most likely way it may be enjoyed. In the event that its pedagogical aims go unfulfilled or aren't shared by the reader, they still serve as an excuse for spending time with the examples, which are fun and interesting to think about.

Readers who wish to get on with the substance can skip to the first chapter, with an admonition that the book is better approached arbitrarily than by going straight through. It is devised for the wandering reader. For those interested in a more detailed account of what this book includes and excludes, here are a few notes by way of explanation.

1. As noted at the outset, this is a sequel to *Classical English Rhetoric*, which discussed many rhetorical techniques but set aside metaphor and simile for their own treatment here. The two books follow the same model. This one, like the other, draws heavily on literature and oratory from the eighteenth and nineteenth centuries, though we will range a bit earlier and later as circumstances warrant. There is a mix of material from fiction and non-fiction, and from British, Irish, and American sources; we will see comparisons from speeches and arguments, essays and letters, novels and plays. Some gifted and canonical writers and talkers appear often. We should seek to learn from the best, which means Johnson and Melville and various other distinguished faculty in the permanent college of rhetoric. But we will hear from many other brilliant observers as well, including some who may be less familiar. Another goal of this book, besides those already mentioned, is to call attention to the work of some writers whose genius for comparison is not sufficiently known.

    In sum, this is mostly a book about the use of figurative comparisons in English prose (though we will make occasional allowances, such as verse from Shakespeare or examples from the King James translation of the Bible – and there is a little French on the cover because the picture is apt). And it is the prose of certain times and places. This choice of scope has meant the sacrifice of many other worthy sources. Cases of metaphorical achievement might easily be drawn from poetry, most obviously, or from other languages or eras, sometimes with different results. Metaphors help to define the cultures in which they are spoken. If the use of metaphor in our own time is chronicled someday, comparisons to plots and characters from movies, television shows, and sports will no doubt be prominent. But this book is long enough as it is, and in my judgment the sources treated here deserve examination of their own. In many respects they represent a golden age of rhetorical achievement.

There is an additional reason why older sources have an advantage for our purposes. Some of the traditions that we shall see depend on the author's familiarity with animals, or nature, or mythology. Many people who use words in public live further from those subjects and know less about them than their counterparts did one or two hundred years ago. Their audiences know less about them, too, partly because they live different sorts of lives, partly because the aims of formal education have changed, and partly because writers want to reach a wider range of people than they once did. All this has caused some of the themes illustrated in this book to become endangered. Certain applications may even be considered extinct. To appreciate what those traditions made possible, it is well to seek instruction from writers who were on closest terms with them. We have to go back a bit.

The writers considered here also have something to teach about style. This book is less focused on phrasing than its predecessor was, but the success of a comparison still depends in significant part on the choice and order of the words used to state it. A metaphor tries to create a little event in the mind of the reader – a mental picture, a surprise, a new idea, or all these at once. Getting it right takes a sense of timing and a skill with the paintbrush that has become more scarce. Or so it seems to me; but even if what earlier writers knew about words was no better than what anyone knows today, and even if some features of their styles seem unavailable to us now, their knowledge and instincts were different, and the differences create a chance to learn.

Citations to Shakespeare in the text don't mention his name. I am betting that readers will know who wrote *Hamlet* when they see it named, and so for his other plays. In any event, a citation to a source without an author is usually to Shakespeare or to the Bible.

2. The title of the book and some of the comments just made have used the word "metaphor" to refer to figurative comparisons in general. The word will bear that meaning but is also commonly used in a more specific way: a metaphor is a comparison, often implied, in which one thing is equated with another ("all the world's a stage"), whereas a simile makes the comparison explicit by saying that one thing is like another or using similar language ("he doth bestride the narrow world/Like a Colossus"). The differences between metaphor and simile are discussed in chapters 13 and 14, but most of the book presents those two kinds of comparisons side by side without fussing over the distinction between them. This may surprise readers who were taught in school to regard the difference between metaphor and simile as the most important point to know about comparisons. That distinction can have definite practical significance, but I do not regard it as the most important idea about our subject; it was a distinction largely ignored in ancient times. Starting with those last two chapters will do no harm, however, if that is where the curiosity of the reader lies; they could as easily have been at the start of the book as at the end. My own interest in the matters discussed there is unlimited, but then my patience for every division of this subject is greater than average.

    Occasional comparisons in this book might be considered neither metaphors nor similes because they are not sufficiently figurative in character. A figurative comparison proposes a similarity or identity between two things that appear different in kind, such as a politician and a pig; a comparison of two pigs would not be figurative. We will not trouble ourselves much about that line between those categories here, or about other issues in the theory and philosophy of metaphor. There is a vast and excellent literature on those topics already, and the aim of this book is to do some things not yet done. Let us take as our topic the rhetorical use of comparisons, which typically will have a non-literal component, and be content also to learn from less figurative but effective cases as they may appear from time to time in the pages that follow.

3. Many metaphors are bound up in the etymology of individual words or idioms so common that their figurative character has been forgotten: "running late," "catching a plane," and so forth. We will not be concerned with this category, however worthwhile it may be. Some argue that most or all language is metaphorical at bottom, or that most understanding arises from metaphor – still more propositions that have received impressive treatment elsewhere and are outside our scope here. Nor is this book concerned with highly extended metaphors; there are examples from *Moby-Dick* but the whale is not among them. Our concern is with comparisons that are intermediate in scale – the kind put forward in nothing longer than a paragraph. This focus has its drawbacks. It can cause something less than the full context of a comparison to be presented. To see the entire significance of a metaphor, and to fully judge its fit, may take pages or chapters or a book, and here the sentence is our principal unit of measure. But sentences still provide much to consider, and confining ourselves to brief examples will let each of our subjects be seen from several angles in a short space.

4. I have in general abstained from commenting on individual illustrations. Explanations of metaphors, I have come to feel, are perilously similar to explanations of jokes. Indeed, the metaphor and the joke are cousins with similarities in their frequent use of surprise, in the collisions they create between things with different proportions and status, and in the ways that the truths they express, and the reactions they provoke, can be, as already noted, half-conscious and deceptively profound. Philosophers have noted other similarities as well, but here I am especially concerned with a practical one: a metaphor usually repays contemplation better than it repays analysis or (as in E. B. White's remark) dissection. The first chapter and the introductions to the others in this book will therefore offer general claims and ideas. In most cases the selection and arrangement of the

examples that follow must largely speak for themselves, perhaps with a few observations before or after each set.

5. The theory of this book has been stated but the execution of it is loose. Sometimes examples appear where consideration of them seems most convenient even if they are outside the strict topic of the chapter or heading; they may then be introduced with a "cf." – meaning "compare (this related example)." This will give no trouble to the reader who understands the organization as just a means to an end: seeing and understanding the range of wonders that rhetorical artists have worked with comparisons. It is an unruly subject that calls for a flexible approach. Maybe a more fitting simile than a museum is a safari in which we will veer from the path as needed to get good views. Any order will do, or almost any: as noted earlier, the book really is not written to be read from front to back; it is meant to invite dedicated but arbitrary perusal (though the first chapter does provide some orientation for the rest). More important than the sequence is the pace, which is best kept leisurely. A well-conceived metaphor usually takes more time to appreciate than a literal sentence, and is worth it.

For comments, suggestions, examples, and good counsel, I wish to thank Kamela Bridges, Daniel Dickson-LaPrade, Bryan Garner, David Godine, David Greenwald, Andrew Kull, Richard Lanham, Michael Lusi, Susan Morse, Brian Perez-Daple, Christopher Ricks, Wayne Schiess, Thomas Stumpf, Jeffrey Walker, and the many rhetoric students, research assistants, and librarians over the years who have contributed to the book in one way or another. Carl W. Scarbrough created the jacket and designed the text with his usual and consummate skill.

Austin, July 2015

Farnsworth's Classical English Metaphor

Chapter One
SOURCES & USES OF COMPARISONS

This chapter will summarize some traditional uses and sources of metaphor and introduce patterns that run between those points. For the sake of overview, let us begin with the uses, or effects, of a figurative comparison. Perhaps no two metaphors are identical in their precise consequences. On a longer view, however, a metaphor usually serves one or more of these general purposes, examples of which will follow shortly:

·   Making an unfamiliar subject familiar by comparing it to what the audience knows better.

·   Throwing a familiar subject into a surprising perspective (in effect the opposite of the first purpose just mentioned).

·   Giving visible form to something inherently invisible, or otherwise making an abstraction available to the senses.

·   Caricaturing the subject by drawing a comparison that exaggerates some of its features, whether for the sake of ridicule or elevation.

·   Simplifying a complex subject.

Most good comparisons do more than one of these things, but on inspection one purpose or another often will seem paramount. Such an inspection typically is not conducted, of course; we rarely respond to a good metaphor by asking what function it serves. We admire the justice of the comparison, and find our perception and understanding improved by it, without pausing to notice how it worked. The workings vary considerably, though, and the student of our subject may find it instructive to think about them.

I described those purposes of metaphor as general. By "general" I mean to distinguish the consequences just listed – making a subject simpler, or more familiar, or more visible – from the specific and substantive comment the author means to make. To take a well-known example:

The Merchant of Venice, 4, 1

> PORTIA. The quality of mercy is not strain'd;
> It droppeth as the gentle rain from heaven
> Upon the place beneath.

The comparison makes an intangible quality available to the senses. It also makes a claim about the nature of mercy. A comparison to a blizzard would have had similar general effects; it likewise would have made the subject available to the eyes, ears, and skin. But the specifics of what it said about mercy would have been different. The specific aims of metaphor – the particular things that their authors mean to say about their subjects – tend to be individual to each case; they do not lend themselves to systematic discussion. The general aims of metaphor, however, are limited and recurring, and can more productively be made the subject of analysis. And rather than referring vaguely to general and specific effects, it may be more exact to distinguish between the *structural consequences* of a comparison (shrinking the subject, making it visible, and so on) and the *claim* the author makes about its subject (the difference between the gentle rain and a blizzard).

Now turn to the material from which metaphors are made. Any metaphor or simile has two ends, or elements: the subject or "target" of it (the thing described) and the source (the thing invoked, to which the subject is compared). The sources from which comparisons are made can be considered as families: they generally may be taken from –

· The animal kingdom.

· Nature (apart from animals).

· Human behavior, circumstances, and institutions.

· Stories of various kinds, as from history, myth, or literature.

· Man-made objects: machines, architecture, tools, etc.

Those categories might have been carved out differently; there is no reason in principle why animals might not be considered as part of nature, or why human behavior could not be considered part of the same family of material as mythology or literature that depicts it – or, for that matter, part of the animal kingdom. And each category could also be subdivided easily enough. But the divisions just sketched are convenient and tend to separate types of material that have produced different traditions and have been put to different use.

I have suggested that the uses of metaphors and the sources of metaphors are both infinite in detail but not in type; and that while any ordering of those types may be arbitrary in the end, we can draw some lines between them that are intuitive and functional. It remains to consider the interaction between those two sides of the inquiry: the ways in which writers combine the sources of comparisons and the uses of them. The resulting combinations might seem random at first glance, but with study it is possible to identify patterns, or traditions, to which those skilled in the art have returned, and to consider why. For caricaturing humans, the classic sources of material are animals and mythology and people in extreme circumstances; for giving visible form to an abstraction, nature and man-made things are more likely to serve; and we shall see other tendencies, many of them more specific.

The rest of this chapter provides an illustrated and more detailed outline of the themes just listed and claims just made. The chapters to come will then explore them more completely.

1. *Uses of comparisons.* To return to our first theme: the effects of comparisons vary in their specifics, but their typical and general goals are capable of summary.

a. *Comparison to make the subject familiar.* Achieving familiarity is a standard purpose of comparison. The speaker wants to describe a face, or an idea, or an experience that the reader hasn't encountered directly (the subject of the comparison); so the speaker says that it resembles a source the reader *has* encountered or can imagine more easily. Telling others of a subject foreign to their experience can be done in literal terms, but the audience is more likely to be affected and enlightened if the thing is compared to what they know or can summon to mind.

Hazlitt, *Mr. Gifford* (1825)

The using an elliptical mode of expression (such as he did not use to find in Guides to the English Tongue) jars him like coming suddenly to a step in a flight of stairs that you were not aware of.

Henry James, *The Ambassadors* (1903)

The air of supreme respectability – that was a strange blank wall for his adventure to have brought him to break his nose against.

Dickens, *David Copperfield* (1850)

I led him up the dark stairs, to prevent his knocking his head against anything, and really his damp cold hand felt so like a frog in mine, that I was tempted to drop it and run away.

The experiences and feelings of the speaker are not known directly to the reader but are illustrated by things familiar: the feeling of a frog in the hand. But is it so familiar? Many people have never held a frog or broken their noses, yet the comparisons succeed anyway. They work because the feeling of a frog or a broken nose is familiar to the imagination even if not readily available to the memory (which may, after all, be considered a branch of the imagination). Many comparisons work this way. They make a subject familiar by likening it to a source that is easier to imagine even if the reader knows it no more directly.

b. *Comparison for the sake of perspective.* Increasing the familiarity of the thing described is often one aim of a metaphor or simile, but sometimes a comparison works the other way around: it throws a too-familiar subject into a surprising perspective, causing the reader to see it from a different point of view. It is taking the reader for a balloon ride, or looking at the subject through one end or the other of a telescope. The effect may be to shrink the significance of the subject, or to cause it to seem enlarged, or to otherwise let an old thing be seen anew. We might regard this as making a familiar subject unfamiliar. Some examples of comparisons that serve this perspective-giving purpose by making their human subjects, or certain features of them, seem small:

> As flies to wanton boys are we to th' gods.
> They kill us for their sport.

King Lear, 4, 1

> I suppose no man can violate his nature. All the sallies of his will are rounded in by the law of his being, as the inequalities of Andes and Himmaleh are insignificant in the curve of the sphere.

Emerson, *Self-Reliance* (1841)

> My bet is that we have not the kind of cosmic importance that the parsons and philosophers teach. I doubt if a shudder would go through the spheres if the whole ant heap were kerosened.

Holmes, Jr., letter to Lewis Einstein (1909)

Oliver Wendell Holmes Jr. and Sr. were both prolific producers of metaphor, and they each appear a number of times in the chapters to follow. The younger Holmes –

the one who served on the Supreme Court – was the more underrated of the two in literary ability. His comparisons tended to be notable for their pungency, as we shall see again.

c. *Comparison to make the subject visible.* A comparison often makes an intangible subject available to the senses. Appeals to any of the five senses are possible, and some comparisons invoke several of them; by far the most frequent and important sensory effect of a comparison, however, is to make the subject visible, with uses of the other senses often present but subsidiary. Thus a simile may give visible form to an abstraction:

Chesterton, *The Giant* (1910)

And this is really all that we can do when we fight something really stronger than ourselves; we can deal it its death-wound one moment; it deals us death in the end. It is something if we can shock and jar the unthinking impetus and enormous innocence of evil; just as a pebble on a railway can stagger the Scotch express.

Or to invisible features of inner life:

Wollstonecraft, *A Vindication of the Rights of Woman* (1792)

The conduct and manners of women, in fact, evidently prove that their minds are not in a healthy state; for, like the flowers which are planted in too rich a soil, strength and usefulness are sacrificed to beauty; and the flaunting leaves, after having pleased a fastidious eye, fade disregarded on the stalk, long before the season when they ought to have arrived at maturity.

Or to the effects of language:

Johnson, *Lives of the English Poets* (1781)

No poem should be long of which the purpose is only to strike the fancy, without enlightening the understanding by precept, ratiocination, or narrative. A blaze first pleases, and then tires the sight.

Making those subjects available to the senses, and especially to the eyes, is one of the great repeating purposes of metaphor, and this book will spend a chapter on each of them. We respond strongly to what we see, and things can be seen as vividly in the mind's eye as they can in the world – sometimes more vividly. Images also inspire feeling, and good metaphors are felt as well as observed. If one wants an audience to respond to an abstract proposition or to what otherwise cannot be seen, one does well to convert it to visible form by making a comparison.

d. *Comparison for the sake of caricature*. A quite different purpose of comparison is to caricature the subject – that is, to exaggerate some feature of it, whether for the sake of reduction, elevation, or mere emphasis.

> Mrs Pipchin hovered behind the victim, with her sable plumage and her hooked beak, like a bird of ill-omen.

Dickens, *Dombey and Son* (1848)

> There are few things more disheartening and disgusting than when you are walking the streets of a strange village on the Sabbath, to hear a preacher shouting like a boatswain in a gale of wind, and thus harshly profaning the quiet atmosphere of the day.

Thoreau, *A Week on the Concord and Merrimack Rivers* (1849)

> [I]t was plain that the whale alongside must be what the fishermen call a blasted whale, that is, a whale that has died unmolested on the sea, and so floated an unappropriated corpse. It may well be conceived, what an unsavory odor such a mass must exhale; worse than an Assyrian city in the plague, when the living are incompetent to bury the departed.

Melville, *Moby-Dick* (1851)

In none of these cases does the comparison make an invisible subject visible or otherwise available to the senses in a new way. Granted, in the case from Dickens the comparison lets the reader see a face that was otherwise visible only in the mind's eye of the author; and so, perhaps, for each of the others. But for purposes of this book we would call that a case of making something familiar that the reader has not seen – a face. It is not an instance of giving visible form to an abstract thing inherently unavailable to the senses. Thoreau compares one noise to another, and Melville compares one smell to another. While both comparisons are picturesque, their primary purpose is to exaggerate. They compare the subject to a source with common properties but more extreme.

The examples just shown were similes. Sometimes, of course, a comparison of this kind takes the form of a metaphor, and the exaggeration or caricature just amounts to renaming the subject, as in this specimen:

Sheil, argument for the defense in the trial of John O'Connell (1844)

> Shake the whole constitution to the centre, and the lawyer will sit tranquil in his cabinet; but touch a single thread in the cobwebs of Westminster-hall, and the exasperated spider crawls out in its defense.

(Sheil claimed that William Pitt the Elder devised this metaphor first; whoever may be entitled to credit for its invention, its use in the argument of a criminal trial suggests higher standards for rhetoric in that setting than we have since come to expect.)

Caricature of the type just shown is a major and recurring purpose of comparison. Sometimes a literal account of a subject does not speak sufficiently for the impression it creates, nor is the effect conveyed by adjectives. It can only be brought home by comparison to something extreme. The listener knows that the subject described wasn't really quite as hooked or as loud or as dreadful as the source of the comparison but understands it to have seemed that way. And whatever the listener may know as a matter of reason, new associations are now attached to the subject and may not come off easily. The audience who imagines the subject also imagines bits of what it was compared to, and likely forms a combined picture – a composite (the lawyer as spider). The picture may contain strange proportions and juxtapositions, which can serve as foundation blocks of another rhetorical resource: comedy.

Exaggerated comparisons may be further divided into those that elevate their subjects and those that diminish them – the difference between caricaturing a person by comparison to Atlas or to a reptile. The latter category is especially handy, as metaphor is a potent instrument for the delivery of insult and invective. These applications require care. The victim's complete recovery is by no means assured; when the results are clever they may enjoy a longevity out of all proportion to their accuracy, if any, as in Johnson's unjust but well-remembered case:

> Next day, Sunday, July 31, I told him I had been that morning at a meeting of the people called Quakers, where I had heard a woman preach. JOHNSON. "Sir, a woman's preaching is like a dog's walking on his hinder legs. It is not done well; but you are surprised to find it done at all."

Boswell, *Life of Johnson* (1791)

Let us be mindful of Beerbohm's appreciative sensibility:

> After an encounter with him they never again were quite the same men in the eyes of their fellows. Whistler's insults always stuck – stuck and spread round the insulted, who found themselves at length encased in them, like flies in amber.
>
> You may shed a tear over the flies, if you will. For myself, I am content to laud the amber.

Beerbohm, *Whistler's Writing* (1909)

e. *Comparison to simplify.* A comparison can give simpler form to a subject that is complicated. In theory a comparison might also do the opposite, but in practice that is rare; simplifying a complex idea has advantages that do not arise from giving complexity to an idea that is simple. Simplification may have pedagogical value, as it can bring clarity to a point that is hard to understand. Another frequent rhetorical consequence of simplicity is to make a claim more persuasive. Complexity begets confusion and resistance. A simplifying comparison soothes the mind and makes an idea easier to accept; the listener's judgment about the merits of a claim may be favorably influenced by the relief and pleasure of having a satisfying way to think about it. Pleasure may be had, too, and sometimes good humor, in seeing an inflated subject summed up in a humble way. Johnson had a gift for such usages.

Johnson, in Boswell's *Life* (1791)

A country governed by a despot is an inverted cone. Government there cannot be so firm, as when it rests upon a broad basis gradually contracted, as the government of Great Britain, which is founded on the parliament, then is in the privy council, then in the King.

Boswell, *Life of Johnson* (1791)

We talked of the education of children; and I asked him what he thought was best to teach them first. JOHNSON. "Sir, it is no matter what you teach them first, any more than what leg you shall put into your breeches first. Sir, you may stand disputing which is best to put in first, but in the meantime your breech is bare. Sir, while you are considering which of two things you should teach your child first, another boy has learnt them both."

Boswell, *Life of Johnson* (1791)

We talked of the numbers of people that sometimes have composed the household of great families. I mentioned that there were a hundred in the family of the present Earl of Eglintoune's father. Dr. Johnson seeming to doubt it, I began to enumerate. "Let us see: my Lord and my Lady two." JOHNSON. "Nay, Sir, if you are to count by twos, you may be long enough." BOSWELL. "Well, but now I add two sons and seven daughters, and a servant for each, that will make twenty; so we have the fifth part already." JOHNSON. "Very true. You get at twenty pretty readily; but you will not so easily get further on. We grow to five feet pretty readily; but it is not so easy to grow to seven."

Comparisons that simplify almost always also serve other purposes, too, such as making their subjects visible or exaggerating some feature of them. In a sense all of the examples just shown may be said to involve carica-ture, as they compare their subjects to sources that might be considered more extreme. But the sources also are simpler than their subjects. An increase in simplicity can be hard to define when comparing pictures of two things that are different in kind, as always is the case with a met-aphor. In general, however, we may regard a comparison as simplifying its subject when the source has fewer vari-ables and can be understood more easily or immediately. The examples just shown fit that description. (Granted, references to an inverted cone have become less acces-sible since the advent of the ice-cream cone, experience with which calls the natural position of a cone into question.)

2. *Sources of comparisons.* The source material from which metaphors and similes may be drawn is limitless in detail but can be reduced without much violence to the five categories mentioned at the start of the chapter and set out below. While any of these categories can be used to advance any of the goals just considered, some serve certain purposes more readily than others.

a. *Comparisons to animals.* A first great tradition uses animals to describe people for the sake of caricature, usu-ally with unflattering results. The bird of ill-omen offered by Dickens a moment ago was an example.

Conrad, *Lord Jim* (1900)

He reminded one of everything that is unsavoury. His slow laborious walk resembled the creeping of a repulsive beetle, the legs alone moving with horrid industry while the body glided evenly.

Burke, *Reflections on the Revolution in France* (1791)

Along with its natural protectors and guardians, learning will be cast into the mire and trodden down under the hoofs of a swinish multitude.

As we shall see in more detail in Chapter 2, animals lend themselves to these uses because they look and act like grotesque versions of people. Most features of human appearance and behavior have rough but exaggerated analogues in the animal kingdom; animals are structurally like humans but with different proportions in all ways. These similarities also make animals an apt source of material for putting humans into a surprising perspective, as shown in the comparison Holmes drew earlier between humanity and an ant heap. Animals occasionally but less often give visible form to abstractions, as we shall see from time to time.

Comparisons to animals are good practice for the student of metaphor and simile. The appearances and doings of most of the people one encounters in daily life can be made the subject of such silent comparisons, as is the author's own habit.

b. *Comparisons to nature.* By "nature" we mean here to exclude animals, for the rest of nature tends to serve different comparative purposes. Nature is less frequently used to caricature human appearances but is immensely helpful for giving visible form to abstractions and other invisibilities. The most frequent advantage of animals, in the making of metaphors, is their structural resemblance to humans. Nature has other comparative virtues: properties of growth, intricacy of action, and images of force that are simple and evocative. Abstractions and inner states often are complex in ways that make those features of nature ideal for illustration.

Waverley had, indeed, as he looked closer into the state of the Chevalier's court, less reason to be satisfied with it. It contained, as they say an acorn includes all the ramifications of the future oak, as many seeds of tracasserie and intrigue as might have done honour to the court of a large empire.

Scott, *Waverley* (1814)

Under the whole heavens there is no relation more unfavorable to the development of honorable character, than that sustained by the slaveholder to the slave. Reason is imprisoned here, and passions run wild. Like the fires of the prairie, once lighted, they are at the mercy of every wind, and must burn, till they have consumed all that is combustible within their remorseless grasp.

Douglass, *My Bondage and My Freedom* (1855)

Under the heading of nature we might include, too, human biology, which provides excellent visible comparisons to inner states.

[C]opy their politeness, their carriage, their address, and the easy and well-bred turn of their conversation; but remember that, let them shine ever so bright, their vices, if they have any, are so many spots which you would no more imitate, than you would make an artificial wart upon your face, because some very handsome man had the misfortune to have a natural one upon his: but, on the contrary, think how much handsomer he would have been without it.

Chesterfield, letter to his son (1748)

Comparative uses of nature are examined in Chapters 3, 4, and 5. Human biology receives its own consideration in Chapter 6.

c. *Comparisons to human activity.* Many fine comparisons are drawn from human behavior and roles. This pattern is commonly used for the sake of caricature: a person is compared to another who is more extreme. But a metaphor drawn from behavior also may serve the cause of familiarity or simplicity.

Emerson, *Lecture on the Times* (1841)

Those who are urging with most ardor what are called the greatest benefit of mankind are narrow, self-pleasing, conceited men, and affect us as the insane do. They bite us, and we run mad also.

Dickens, *Great Expectations* (1861)

In these dialogues, my sister spoke to me as if she were morally wrenching one of my teeth out at every reference; while Pumblechook himself, self-constituted my patron, would sit supervising me with a depreciatory eye, like the architect of my fortunes who thought himself engaged on a very unremunerative job.

Darwin, *On the Origin of Species* (1859)

[W]hen a new insect first arrived on the island, the tendency of natural selection to enlarge or to reduce the wings, would depend on whether a greater number of individuals were saved by successfully battling with the winds, or by giving up the attempt and rarely or never flying. As with mariners shipwrecked near a coast, it would have been better for the good swimmers if they had been able to swim still further, whereas it would have been better for the bad swimmers if they had not been able to swim at all and had stuck to the wreck.

A caricature compares the commonplace form of a thing to the epitome or extreme form of the same. Comparisons to human activity for the purpose are thus drawn most often from its fringes – from the doings of people who are at some distance from the conventional center of human affairs by their nature (the madman, the child, the disabled) or by circumstance (the shipwrecked sailor). The skilled eye, the eye of a Dickens, is able to see the extreme possibilities in a wider range of less obvious circumstances: the ways in which an architect may, in the right circumstance, epitomize a certain kind of skepticism.

The meaning of a source in the lexicon of metaphor may diverge from its meaning in the world. The line just shown from Emerson is an example. The insane do not bite others and cause them to run mad also (today the metaphor would probably borrow from horror movies); and to recur to previous examples, the stench of a plague in old Assyria, or the effect of a pebble on the Scotch Express, may have a tenuous relation to fact. We will see more such cases in every chapter. Makers of metaphor traffic heavily in lore. And there is a larger point to observe as well: the strength of the image in a metaphor typically arises less from its factual rigor than from its vividness; indeed, the mind tends to treat vividness as evidence of accuracy – a bad habit, but valuable for makers of metaphors to understand.

As the illustration from Darwin shows, comparisons to human behavior can also simplify a subject in valuable ways. Sometimes these comparisons also function in a manner that might be considered the opposite of caricature. Instead of comparing a common thing to an extreme one, they compare a thing more contentious or obscure to a source that is more common. The comparison dymystifyies the subject. Johnson's simplifications often work this way and can be artful for their homeliness, as we saw earlier in the chapter: comparing a decision about education to a decision about which leg to put in the trousers first.

Under the heading of human behavior and roles we also might include, finally, human institutions: the use of governments, religions, markets, and other such entities as sources of metaphor.

BRUTUS. ... Between the acting of a dreadful thing *Julius Caesar*, 2, 1
And the first motion, all the interim is
Like a phantasma, or a hideous dream:

The Genius and the mortal instruments
Are then in council; and the state of man,
Like to a little kingdom, suffers then
The nature of an insurrection.

Sources of this kind are sometimes invoked for the sake of visibility. The institution borrowed for the purpose – a kingdom – may itself be an abstraction, but the incidents associated with it (here, images of insurrection) give perceptible form to an inner state that had no visibility of its own. Institutions may also be borrowed to describe other abstractions; the author means to trade on the reader's sense of familiarity with one of them in order to explain another, and so to drive home a conceptual argument, as in this case:

Abrams v. United States (1919)
(Holmes, dissenting)

But when men have realized that time has upset many fighting faiths, they may come to believe even more than they believe the very foundations of their own conduct that the ultimate good desired is better reached by free trade in ideas – that the best test of truth is the power of the thought to get itself accepted in the competition of the market, and that truth is the only ground upon which their wishes safely can be carried out. That, at any rate, is the theory of our Constitution.

Some traditional uses of human activities as sources of comparison are examined in chapters 7, 8, and 9.

d. *Comparisons to stories*. Under this heading go both mythology and history; those sources might be separated, of course, but they frequently do similar work in comparisons. Both tend to be used for the sake of caricature. The reason can be viewed by considering what makes a story memorable and famous, whether it be historical or mythical. It is often because the story epitomizes something resonant and recurring in human behavior or experience. Metaphor draws out those prime features of a tale and uses them to illuminate the meaning of a new case.

We saw earlier that comparisons to animals serve a similar purpose. They caricature human appearances and activity. But mythical and historical comparisons throw a different light onto their subjects. They more easily elevate or lend grandeur to them, and may put a subject into a more contemplative and dignifying posture even when the comparison is unflattering.

> In the Pythian fury of his gestures – in his screaming voice – in his directness of purpose, Fox would now remind you of some demon steam-engine on a railroad, some Fire-king or Salmoneus, that had counterfeited, because he could not steal, Jove's thunderbolts; hissing, bubbling, snorting, fuming; demoniac gas, you think – gas from Acheron must feed that dreadful system of convulsions. But pump out the imaginary gas, and, behold! it is ditch-water.

de Quincey, *Schlosser's Literary History of the Eighteenth Century* (1880)

> The South means to repress with decisions of the Supreme Court; they might as well, like Xerxes, try to subdue the waves of the ocean by throwing chains into the water.

Schurz, speech at St. Louis (1860)

The materials in this general category are wide-ranging. They can include any comparisons drawn to stories in history or literature or, for that matter, to the movies or television shows mentioned in the preface, though those particular sources won't detain us here. We will make a sample study in Chapter 10 of some parts of this field: uses of mythology, fable, and classical history.

e. *Comparisons to man-made things.* Another family of material for metaphor comes from human invention.

> The forms of beauty fall naturally around the path of him who is in the performance of his proper work; as the curled shavings drop from the plane, and borings cluster round the auger.

Thoreau, *A Week on the Concord and Merrimack Rivers* (1849)

Holmes, *The Autocrat of the Breakfast-Table* (1858)

[J]ust as a written constitution is essential to the best social order, so a code of finalities is a necessary condition of profitable talk between two persons. Talking is like playing on the harp; there is as much in laying the hand on the strings to stop their vibrations as in twanging them to bring out their music.

The usual purpose of comparisons to the manufactured world, as these examples show, is similar to the most common use of nature (for notice that both sources are intricate and impersonal): they can give visible form to abstractions or other invisibilities, or make complex systems easier to understand, or both. We will take a chapter-long look at this family of material with emphasis on one distinguished aspect of it: architecture (Chapter II). The most reliable sources of metaphor tend to be the features of the world we know best, and dwellings are among the most familiar of all human creations.

There are exceptions to every generalization just made. Animals and mythology are most often invoked to exaggerate a feature of human appearance or behavior, not to give visibility to an abstraction or the workings of the mind – but all combinations occur sometimes, and at various points the chapters that follow will step away from their primary themes to notice some of those secondary ones. Nor do I mean to suggest that examples within the traditions we will examine are any better than examples outside them, which are often splendid. I only mean to say that the traditions exist and are interesting.

The study of patterns and traditions might seem dangerous if they are thought to invite the formulaic creation of metaphors, or repetition of what has been seen and said before. They don't. The skilled practitioner works in them with originality and spontaneity, just as when working within traditions of architecture or music or any other art. The chapters that follow supply the proof; we will see outstanding makers of comparisons borrowing similar material for broadly similar purposes, but with each producing their own singular effects. The relationship between the study of examples and the avoidance of cliché might best be captured by considering, as if they were part of a conversation, three passages from writers who understood the issue well:

> Wit, you know, is the unexpected copulation of ideas, the discovery of some occult relation between images in appearance remote from each other; an effusion of wit, therefore, presupposes an accumulation of knowledge; a memory stored with notions, which the imagination may cull out to compose new assemblages.

Johnson, *The Rambler* no. 194 (1752)

> He who loves music will know what the best men have done, and hence will have numberless passages from older writers floating at all times in his mind, like germs in the air, ready to hook themselves on to anything of an associated character. Some of these he will reject at once, as already too strongly wedded to associations of their own; some are tried and found not so suitable as was thought; some one, however, will probably soon assert itself as either suitable, or easily altered so as to become exactly what is wanted; if, indeed, it is the right passage in the right man's mind, it will have modified itself unbidden already.

Note Books of Samuel Butler (1912)

> Never use a metaphor, simile or other figure of speech which you are used to seeing in print.

Orwell, *Politics and the English Language* (1946)

Chapter Two

THE USE OF ANIMALS
TO DESCRIBE HUMANS

Animals provide a marvelous basis for comparison to human appearances and other traits. They occasionally are used in other ways as well, but these applications are sufficiently important to merit a chapter to themselves. The reasons may be stated briefly.

a. Animals frequently can be viewed as caricatures of people. They usually have the same physical structure but in different proportions – eyes and ears and arms and legs, but arranged in ways that would seem freakish on a human. And the same might be said for many of their other qualities: like people, animals may be fat or loud or fearsome, but the fattest animal is fatter than a fat man, and so on with most traits, making animals a natural source of comparison when one wants to exaggerate a human quality or suggest its extreme form.

b. Humans generally wish to view themselves as higher or better than (other) animals, and go to much trouble in their habits and manners and laws to reinforce the difference. Thus comparison to an animal tends predictably to make its human subject ridiculous or contemptible, and is a mighty device for the achievement of insult and abuse.

c. The appearances and behaviors of most animals are familiar, and this makes them efficient helps to description. They can be invoked in very few words to produce a strong connotation or image.

Few of the comparisons to follow require the reader to know any of the relevant facts about the animals named. They include enough explanation, or are vivid enough in themselves, to permit enjoyment by anyone. But they do require the *author* to know some animal facts, which is one reason why comparisons of the kind displayed in this chapter have become less common. Literate people, readers and writers both, live at a farther remove from animal life than they once did, or read less about it, and so know less of it.

Readers of the predecessor volume to this one will recall that most rhetorical schemes – that is, patterns for the arrangement of words – can be named with old terms from Greek or Latin. We have not inherited similar terms for the various families or uses of metaphor. I have mostly decided not to burden the reader with new nominees, but the aficionado of classical languages may find it diverting to devise them. This chapter, for example, might be regarded as presenting a technique called *theriosis* – literally, beastification. (The word *theriomorphosis* already exists and conveys the same idea, but is too cumbersome to put forward with a straight face.) The Greek word for nature is *physis*, so comparisons to nature would be cases of *physiosis*, etc.

1. *Physical resemblances.* The faces of most animals roughly resemble the faces of humans, but with features that are arranged and proportioned differently. They are like faces seen in a curved mirror at a carnival; the eyes are larger, or farther apart. They make fine sources of caricature.

> Another of Master Simon's counselors is the apothecary, a short and rather fat man, with a pair of prominent eyes, that diverge like those of a lobster.

Irving, *Bracebridge Hall* (1822)

> The old lady with the red face and the black eyebrows looked at us for a moment with something of the apoplectic stare of a parrot.

Chesterton, *The Club of Queer Trades* (1905)

> For the first time in our long connection I observed Jeeves almost smile. The corner of his mouth curved quite a quarter of an inch, and for a

Wodehouse, *My Man, Jeeves* (1919)

moment his eye ceased to look like a meditative fish's.

The mouths of animals have more range than ours do in size and elasticity, and so likewise provide fodder for caricature.

Borrow, *Lavengro* (1851)

Presently there were nods and winks in the direction of the bell-rope; and, as these produced no effect, uncouth visages were made, like those of monkeys when enraged; teeth were gnashed, tongues thrust out, and even fists were bent at me.

Melville, *Mardi* (1849)

These regions passed, we came to savage islands, where the glittering coral seemed bones imbedded, bleaching in the sun. Savage men stood naked on the strand, and brandished uncouth clubs, and gnashed their teeth like boars.

Chesterton, *The Club of Queer Trades* (1905)

The old man gaped helplessly like some monstrous fish.

Or motion: a tendency merely suggested or half-visible in human movement is invariably presented in more exaggerated form by some member of the animal kingdom.

Fielding, *Joseph Andrews* (1742)

To complete the whole, he had a stateliness in his gait, when he walked, not unlike that of a goose, only he stalked slower.

Beerbohm, *The House of Commons Manner* (1909)

Be smooth-tongued, and the Englishman will withdraw from you as quickly as may be, walking sideways like a crab, and looking askance at you with panic in his eyes. But stammer and blurt to him, and he will fall straight under the spell of your transparent honesty.

Chesterton, *Manalive* (1912)

Sometimes he would tickle the nose of his eldest child (he had two children); sometimes he would hook the rake on to the branch of a tree, and hoist himself up with horrible gymnastic jerks, like those of a giant frog in its final agony.

These comparisons tend to be unflattering to their subjects. They force the reader to create a mental picture of a hybrid, and sometimes to attribute more of the animal to the human subject than the author explicitly invited. The theater of the mind has rules of its own.

2. *Sounds.* Humans are notable for their ability to speak words. When they make other sounds they more closely resemble animals, and so lend themselves to comparison.

> Two of the enemy's men entered the boat just where this fellow stood in the foresheets; he immediately saluted them with a ladle full of the stuff, boiling hot which so burned and scalded them, being half-naked that they roared out like bulls, and, enraged with the fire, leaped both into the sea.

Defoe, *Further Adventures of Robinson Crusoe* (1719)

> "Certainly not!" shouted Mr. Pickwick. "Hurrah!" And then there was another roaring, like that of a whole menagerie when the elephant has rung the bell for the cold meat.

Dickens, *The Pickwick Papers* (1837)

> His phrase was greeted by a strange laugh from a student who lounged against the wall, his peaked cap down on his eyes. The laugh, pitched in a high key and coming from a so muscular frame, seemed like the whinny of an elephant.

Joyce, *A Portrait of the Artist as a Young Man* (1916)

By the same token, human speech, when it does take the form of words, can be compared to the noises of animals to put the speaker into a bestial light.

> "Where's the girl?" says he, with a voice as loud as the braying of a jackass.

Kipling, *The Man Who Would Be King* (1888)

> Women with hoarse voices and harsh laughter had called after him. Drunkards had reeled by, cursing and chattering to themselves like monstrous apes.

Wilde, *The Picture of Dorian Gray* (1890)

Beerbohm, *Hilary Maltby and Stephen Braxton* (1919)

Quivering with rage, I returned to my bedroom. "Intolerable," I heard myself repeating like a parrot that knew no other word.

The tone of a voice:

Meredith, *The Ordeal of Richard Feverel* (1859)

Her voice sounded to him like that of a broken-throated lamb, so painful and weak it was, with the plaintive stop in the utterance.

Conrad, *Chance* (1913)

His voice was thin like the buzzing of a mosquito.

3. *Resemblances in character and ability*. Many human traits can be found in purer form in animals. Strength and tenacity are common examples; and these some-times are cases where a comparison to an animal will elevate its subject rather than reducing it in stature.

Holmes, *The Professor at the Breakfast Table* (1859)

Harry, champion, by acclamation, of the college heavy-weights, broad-shouldered, bull-necked, square-jawed, six feet and trimmings, a little sci-ence, lots of pluck, good-natured as a steer in peace, formidable as a red-eyed bison in the crack of hand-to-hand battle!

Eliot, *Daniel Deronda* (1876)

And she had found a will like that of a crab or a boa-constrictor, which goes on pinching or crushing without alarm at thunder.

Ignorance, insensitivity, and other brute traits likewise find their epitome in animals, which can make less flat-tering reference points for human versions of the same.

The Diary of Samuel Pepys (1667)

... the Duke of Albemarle, who takes the part of the Guards against us in our supplies of money, which is an odd consideration for a dull, heavy blockhead as he is, understanding no more of either than a goose....

Douglass, *My Bondage and My Freedom* (1855)

To talk to those imps about justice and mercy, would have been as absurd as to reason with bears and tigers. Lead and steel are the only arguments that they understand.

Ready in gibes, quick-answer'd, saucy, and
As quarrelous as the weasel.

Cymbeline, 3, 4

With the possible exception of the last, those examples involved general references to animals not distinguished for their wit. The comparison can be made more specific by putting the creature into a particular circumstance.

Empire has happened to them and civilization has happened to them as fresh lettuces come to tame rabbits. They do not understand how they got, and they will not understand how to keep.

Wells, *An Englishman Looks at the World* (1914)

They may even be suffering quite terribly by it. But they are no more mastering its causes, reasons, conditions, and the possibility of its future prevention than a monkey that has been rescued in a scorching condition from the burning of a house will have mastered the problem of a fire. It is just happening to and about them.

Wells, *War and the Future* (1917)

He went home as a horse goes back to his stable, because he knew nowhere else to go.

The Education of Henry Adams (1918)

A human behavior or quality of character may be diminished precisely *because* it is shared by animals.

BOSWELL. "But will you not allow him a nobleness of resolution, in penetrating into distant regions?" JOHNSON. "That, Sir, is not to the present purpose: we are talking of sense. A fighting cock has a nobleness of resolution."

Boswell, *Life of Johnson* (1791)

'Tis no great valor to perish sword in hand, and bravado on lip; cased all in panoply complete. For even the alligator dies in his mail, and the swordfish never surrenders.

Melville, *Mardi* (1849)

Holmes, Jr., *Natural Law* (1918)

No doubt behind these legal rights is the fighting will of the subject to maintain them, and the spread of his emotions to the general rules by which they are maintained; but that does not seem to me the same thing as the supposed a priori discernment of a duty or the assertion of a preexisting right. A dog will fight for his bone.

4. *Prospects for improvement*. Humans may have dispositions that are hard to change; such immutability is clearer in the case of animals, and may be illustrated accordingly.

Thoreau, *Walden* (1854)

I confess, that practically speaking, when I have learned a man's real disposition, I have no hopes of changing it for the better or worse in this state of existence. As the Orientals say, "A cur's tail may be warmed, and pressed, and bound round with ligatures, and after a twelve years' labor bestowed upon it, still it will retain its natural form."

Holmes, Jr., *The Path of the Law* (1897)

If the typical criminal is a degenerate, bound to swindle or to murder by as deep seated an organic necessity as that which makes the rattlesnake bite, it is idle to talk of deterring him by the classical method of imprisonment. He must be got rid of; he cannot be improved, or frightened out of his structural reaction.

A related application is the analogy to what is inevitable in animals to describe what is inevitable in humans, or some particular type of them.

Chesterton, *Thomas Carlyle* (1903)

[T]he cosmopolitan is basing his whole case upon the idea that man should, if he can, become as God, with equal sympathies and no prejudices, while the nationalist denies any such duty at the very start, and regards man as an animal who has preferences, as a bird has feathers.

But what is the anarchistic ex-professor's own theory? – for a professor must have a theory, as a dog must have fleas.

Mencken, *Criticism of Criticism of Criticism* (1919)

Animals capable of training are brought along by methods cruder than education, the lore of which can provide matter for and effective and humiliating comparisons.

Foolish fellows! (said Dr. Johnson), don't they see that they are as much dependent upon the Peers one way as the other. The Peers have but to oppose a candidate to ensure him success. It is said the only way to make a pig go forward, is to pull him back by the tail. These people must be treated like pigs.

Boswell, *Life of Johnson* (1791)

Indeed, one day when Adams was pleading with a Cabinet officer for patience and tact in dealing with Representatives, the Secretary impatiently broke out: "You can't use tact with a Congressman! A Congressman is a hog! You must take a stick and hit him on the snout!"

The Education of Henry Adams (1918)

In short, all experience shows that almost all men require at times both the spur of hope and the bridle of fear, and that religious hope and fear are an effective spur and bridle, though some people are too hard-mouthed and thick-skinned to care much for either, and though others will now and then take the bit in their teeth and rush where passion carries them, notwithstanding both.

James Fitzjames Stephen, *Liberty, Equality, Fraternity* (1873)

5. *Instinctive life.* We have seen that humans may be compared to animals on the basis of traits that we imagine they share – courage, ignorance, etc. We turn now to a more specific set of comparisons: those involving instinctive behavior. Sometimes such comparisons are made to humans generally.

[L]et them have what instructions you will, and ever so learned lectures of breeding daily inculcated

Locke, *Some Thoughts Concerning Education* (1693).

into them, that which will most influence their carriage, will be the company they converse with, and the fashion of those about them. Children (nay, and men too) do most by example. We are all a sort of chameleons, that still take a tincture from things near us....

Shaw, *Man and Superman* (1903)

If we were reasoning, farsighted people, four fifths of us would go straight to the Guardians for relief, and knock the whole social system to pieces with most beneficial reconstructive results. The reason we do not do this is because we work like bees or ants, by instinct or habit, not reasoning about the matter at all.

St. John, note on Locke's *Conduct of the Understanding* (1854)

In fact, men think in packs as jackals hunt.

Or the point may be more particular – a claim not about humans in general, but about certain of them, or a distinct pattern of human behavior; and these subjects may in turn be compared not to animals generally, but to animals in certain circumstances and the instincts they display.

Goldsmith, *The Traveler* (dedication) (1764)

Like the tiger, that seldom desists from pursuing man after having once preyed upon human flesh, the reader who has once gratified his appetite with calumny makes ever after the most agreeable feast upon murdered reputations!

Johnson, *A Project for the Employment of Authors* (1756)

That the number of authors is disproportionate to the maintenance, which the public seems willing to assign them; that there is neither praise nor meat for all who write, is apparent from this, that, like wolves in long winters, they are forced to prey on one another.

Bolingbroke, letter to William Windham (1717)

In the House of Commons his credit was low and my reputation very high. You know the nature of that assembly: they grow, like hounds, fond of the man who shews them game, and by whose halloo they are used to be encouraged.

Mrs. Tulliver had lived thirteen years with her husband, yet she retained in all the freshness of her early married life a facility of saying things which drove him in the opposite direction to the one she desired. Some minds are wonderful for keeping their bloom in this way, as a patriarchal goldfish apparently retains to the last its youthful illusion that it can swim in a straight line beyond the encircling glass.

Eliot, *The Mill on the Floss* (1860).

Cf.:

I'm capable of a great jerk, an effort, and then a relaxation – but steady every-day goodness is beyond me. I must be a moral kangaroo!

Gaskell, *Wives and Daughters* (1866)

The instinct for vengeance and self-protection is a common subject for comparisons of this kind.

They hold together like bees; offend one, and all will revenge his quarrel.

Kingsley, *Westward Ho!* (1855)

Vengeance imports a feeling of blame, and an opinion, however distorted by passion, that a wrong has been done. It can hardly go very far beyond the case of a harm intentionally inflicted: even a dog distinguishes between being stumbled over and being kicked.

Holmes, Jr., *The Common Law* (1888)

Ants are as completely Socialistic as any community can possibly be, yet they put to death any ant which strays among them by mistake from a neighboring ant-heap. Men do not differ much from ants, as regards their instincts in this respect, wherever there is a great divergence of race, as between white men and yellow men.

Russell, *Proposed Roads to Freedom* (1920)

The human instinct for mating and ritual is another often compared to animal life.

Trollope, *Can You Forgive Her?* (1864)

That some repent no one can doubt; but I am inclined to believe that most men and women take their lots as they find them, marrying as the birds do by force of nature, and going on with their mates with a general, though not perhaps an undisturbed satisfaction. . . .

Chesterton, *Simmons and the Social Tie* (1910)

Boys, like dogs, have a sort of romantic ritual which is not always their real selves. And this romantic ritual is generally the ritual of not being romantic; the pretence of being much more masculine and materialistic than they are.

War elephants and their instincts have been pressed into laudable rhetorical service. They have a minor but irreplaceable role in the lexicon of metaphor.

Swift, *The Battle of the Books* (1697)

The generals made use of him for his talent of railing, which, kept within government, proved frequently of great service to their cause, but, at other times, did more mischief than good; for, at the least touch of offence, and often without any at all, he would, like a wounded elephant, convert it against his leaders.

Dickens, *Threatening Letter to Thomas Hood from An Ancient Gentleman* (1844)

What the condition of this country will be, when its standing army is composed of dwarfs, with here and there a wild man to throw its ranks into confusion, like the elephants employed in war in former times, I leave you to imagine, sir.

Lord Stowell, in Boswell's *Life of Johnson* (1791) (on why Lord North did not want Johnson as an ally in Parliament)

He perhaps thought, and not unreasonably, that, like the elephant in the battle, he was quite as likely to trample down his friends as his foes.

More flattering results are possible when the instincts of a creature are productive.

For the empirical, like the ant, only collects and uses; the rational, like the spider, spins from itself. But the practice of the bee is midway, which draws materials from the flowers of both garden and field, but transmutes and digests them by a faculty of its own. Nor is the work of true philosophy different....

Bacon, *Thoughts and Observations Concerning the Interpretation of Nature* (1620)

Or consider Henry Adams' discussion of grisaille – painting in shades of gray:

Grisaille is a separate branch of colour-decoration which belongs with the whole system of lighting and fenetrage, and will have to remain a closed book because the feeling and experience which explained it once are lost, and we cannot recover either. Such things must have been always felt rather than reasoned, like the irregularities in plan of the builders; the best work of the best times shows the same subtlety of sense as the dog shows in retrieving, or the bee in flying, but which tourists have lost.

Adams, *Mont-Saint-Michel and Chartres* (1904)

Where a human trait or behavior is ambiguous (it might be the expression of something high or low), comparison to an animal can distinguish the possibilities.

The few odd minutes I have had to spare I have given to Plato, recurring to his *Symposium* after fifty years; with a translation alongside I find the Greek easy. My successive reflections have been these: How natural the talk. But it is the "first intention" common to the classics. They have not a looking glass at each end of their room, and their simplicity is the bark of a dog, not the simplicity of art.

Holmes, Jr., letter to Frederick Pollock (1911)

6. *Hybrid cases.* Because animals and humans are superficially similar, it is easy to impute human qualities and

feelings to animals – and then to turn the resulting picture around, with a person compared to an animal said to have certain of its (human) traits. In effect the animal is anthropomorphized, then compared back to the human to make the latter more vivid. Some cases of this kind involve human attributes assigned broadly to certain types of creatures.

Stevenson, *The Sire de Maletroit's Door* (1882)

His countenance had a strongly masculine cast; not properly human, but such as we see in the bull, the goat, or the domestic boar; something equivocal and wheedling, something greedy, brutal, and dangerous.

Eliot, *Daniel Deronda* (1876)

Mr. Lush felt a triumph that was mingled with much distrust; for Grandcourt had said no word to him about her, and looked as neutral as an alligator; there was no telling what might turn up in the slowly-churning chances of his mind.

Melville, *Redburn* (1849)

He had a round face, too, like a walrus; and with about the same expression, half human and half indescribable.

Human qualities also may be associated not just with a whole species but with a particular animal in a comparison – to invoke not the lowliness of the dog generally, but the more particular disposition of the dog that has been kicked. The conduct or inner state of the animal is described with words that normally apply to people, making the result partly human and causing the comparison to feel closer.

Boswell, *Journal of a Tour to the Hebrides* (1785)

I told him, he was not sensible of the danger, having lain under cover in the boat during the storm: he was like the chicken, that hides its head under its wing, and then thinks itself safe.

Emily Brontë, *Wuthering Heights* (1847)

Don't get the expression of a vicious cur that appears to know the kicks it gets are its desert, and yet hates all the world, as well as the kicker, for what it suffers.

[T]he house of Smallweed, always early to go out and late to marry, has strengthened itself in its practical character, has discarded all amusements, discountenanced all storybooks, fairy tales, fictions, and fables, and banished all levities whatsoever. Hence the gratifying fact that it has had no child born to it and that the complete little men and women whom it has produced have been observed to bear a likeness to old monkeys with something depressing on their minds.

Dickens, *Bleak House* (1853)

More extreme cases – not necessarily metaphorical, but in place here – enjoyably hypothesize what an animal would think or say if it could.

Somebody quoted to him with admiration the soliloquy of an officer who had lived in the wilds of America: "Here am I, free and unrestrained, amidst the rude magnificence of nature, with the Indian woman by my side, and this gun, with which I can procure food when I want it! What more can be desired for human happiness?" "Do not allow yourself, sir," replied Johnson, "to be imposed upon by such gross absurdity. It is sad stuff; it is brutish. If a bull could speak, he might as well exclaim, 'Here am I with this cow and this grass; what being can enjoy greater felicity?"

Boswell, *Life of Johnson* (1791)

In the two new volumes Johnson says, and very probably did, or is made to say, that Gray's poetry is dull, and that he was a dull man! The same oracle dislikes Prior, Swift, and Fielding. If an elephant could write a book, perhaps one that had read a great deal would say, that an Arabian horse is a very clumsy ungraceful animal.

Walpole, letter to Miss Berry (1791)

Mill, *Utilitarianism* (1863)

It is better to be a human being dissatisfied than a pig satisfied; better to be Socrates dissatisfied than a fool satisfied. And if the fool, or the pig, is of a different opinion, it is because they only know their own side of the question. The other party to the comparison knows both sides.

7. *Insults; loathsomeness.* Many of the examples already seen have diminished their human subjects, depicting them as slow-witted or incorrigible. But we nevertheless should give further consideration to comparisons made more directly for the sake of insult and disparagement. Most insults are metaphors, as when the person made the subject of them is compared to an orifice or appendage. There is an old tradition, however, of abuse accomplished by comparisons to animal life; these devices allow the speaker to retain more dignity and use more imagination, and they have a distinct potency of their own. Insects are a natural source for the purpose, as they tend to be puny as well as odious.

Webster, *The White Devil* (1612)

You diversivolent lawyer, marke him; knaves turn informers, as maggots turn to flies; you may catch gudgeons with either.

Phillips, argument in *Guthrie v. Sterne* (1815)

If I am instructed rightly, he is one of those vain and vapid coxcombs, ... one of those fashionable insects, that folly has painted, and fortune plumed, for the annoyance of our atmosphere; dangerous alike in their torpidity and their animation; infesting where they fly and poisoning where they repose.

Chesterton, *French and English* (1909)

If the Frenchman saw our aristocracy and liked it, if he saw our snobbishness and liked it, if he set himself to imitate it, we all know what we should feel. We all know that we should feel that that particular Frenchman was a repulsive little gnat.

Instructive applications to critics:

> He will soon flit to other prey, when you disregard him. It is my way: I never publish a sheet, but buzz! out fly a swarm of hornets, insects that never settle upon you, if you don't strike at them and whose venom is diverted to the next object that presents itself.

Walpole, letter to the Earl of Hertford (1764)

> The last sort I shall mention are verbal critics – mere word-catchers, fellows that pick out a word in a sentence and a sentence in a volume and tell you it is wrong. ... Littleness is their element, and they give a character of meanness to whatever they touch. They creep, buzz, and fly-blow. It is much easier to crush than to catch these troublesome insects; and when they are in your power your self-respect spares them.

Hazlitt, *On Criticism* (1821)

To armies:

> The Eastern armies were indeed like insects; in their blind, busy destructiveness, in their black nihilism of personal outlook, in their hateful indifference to individual life and love, in their base belief in mere numbers, in their pessimistic courage and their atheistic patriotism, the riders and raiders of the East are indeed like all the creeping things of the earth.

Chesterton, *The Empire of the Insect* (1910)

> I see advancing upon all this, in hideous onslaught, the Nazi war machine, with its clanking, heel-clicking, dandified Prussian officers, its crafty expert agents, fresh from the cowing and tying down of a dozen countries. I see also the dull, drilled, docile brutish masses of the Hun soldiery, plodding on like a swarm of crawling locusts.

Churchill, London radio broadcast (1941)

Reptiles and amphibians also provide first-rate source material for invective.

Twain, *Life on the Mississippi*
(1888)

But when he came home the next week, alive, renowned, and appeared in church all battered up and bandaged, a shining hero, stared at and wondered over by everybody, it seemed to us that the partiality of Providence for an undeserving reptile had reached a point where it was open to criticism.

Dickens, *The Pickwick Papers*
(1837)

"I consider you, sir," said Mr. Pott, moved by this sarcasm, "I consider you a viper. I look upon you, sir, as a man who has placed himself beyond the pale of society, by his most audacious, disgraceful, and abominable public conduct. I view you, sir, personally and politically, in no other light than as a most unparalleled and unmitigated viper."

Coleridge, letter to Henry
Martin (1794)

I sent for Bowles's Works while at Oxford. How was I shocked! Every omission and every alteration disgusted taste, and mangled sensibility. Surely some Oxford toad had been squatting at the poet's ear, and spitting into it the cold venom of dullness.

A few examples will suggest the range of other animals widely used for damning description.

Melville, *Mardi* (1849)

Were they worthy the dignity of being damned, I would damn them; but they are not. Critics? – Asses! rather mules! – so emasculated, from vanity, they can not father a true thought. Like mules, too, from dunghills, they trample down gardens of roses: and deem that crushed fragrance their own.

Memoirs of Daniel O'Connell
(1836)

[T]hat genuine lick-spittle of royalty, Sir Benjamin Bloomfield, who like the jackal, had preceded his royal master and patron to cater to his love of pomp and show, was designated as the distinguished stranger, and on his health being drank, the band struck up 'Welcome here again.'

Walpole, letter to Hannah
More (1795)

Adieu! thou excellent woman! thou reverse of that hyena in petticoats, Mrs. Wolstoncroft, who to this day discharges her ink and gall on Marie Antoinette, whose unparalleled sufferings have not yet stanched that Alecto's blazing ferocity.

A related tradition employs creatures not precisely to injure their subjects but to suggest the reaction they provoke. People and animals both can inspire revulsion, but unpleasant animals do it more easily and in a manner familiar to every reader. Insects and reptiles again are standard sources.

[Y]ou don't love me, then? It was only my station, and the rank of my wife, that you valued? Now that you think me disqualified to become your husband, you recoil from my touch as if I were some toad or ape.

Charlotte Brontë, Jane Eyre (1847)

… men of ideas instead of legs, a sort of intellectual centipede that made you crawl all over.

Thoreau, Walden (1854)

"I want every boy to be keen."
    "We are, sir," said Psmith, with fervor.
    "Excellent."
    "On archaeology."
    Mr. Downing – for it was no less a celebrity – started, as one who perceives a loathly caterpillar in his salad.

Wodehouse, Mike and Psmith (1909)

8. *Status.* So far we have examined comparisons between people and one type of creature or another. But the relations between different animals can also help illuminate the status of a subject or the relations between two of them. Thus uses of the grand or domineering animal, some of which do not bring out the best in their authors but reflect their times:

But Dr. Johnson has much of the *nil admirari* in smaller concerns. That survey of life which gave birth to his *Vanity of Human Wishes* early sobered his mind. Besides, so great a mind as his cannot be

Boswell, Journal of a Tour to the Hebrides (1785)

moved by inferior objects: an elephant does not run and skip like lesser animals.

Boswell, *Life of Johnson* (1791)

Johnson defended the oriental regulation of different castes of men, which was objected to as totally destructive of the hopes of rising in society by personal merit. He shewed that there was a principle in it sufficiently plausible by analogy. "We see (said he) in metals that there are different species; and so likewise in animals, though one species may not differ very widely from another, as in the species of dogs, – the cur, the spaniel, the mastiff. The Bramins are the mastiffs of mankind."

Holmes, Jr., letter to Harold Laski (1928)

With your belief in some apriorities like equality you may have difficulties. I who believe in force (mitigated by politeness) have no trouble – and if I were sincere and were asked certain *whys* by a woman should reply, "Because Ma'am I am the bull."

These examples serve as exceptions to the typical pattern in which comparisons to animals reduce the stature of a human subject. With adjustment, though, even an animal of high status can, if impaired, put the subject of a comparison into a diminished light.

James Fitzjames Stephen, *Liberty, Equality, Fraternity* (1873)

"Make all men equal so far as laws can make them equal, and what does that mean but that each unit is to be rendered hopelessly feeble in presence of an overwhelming majority?" The existence of such a state of society reduces individuals to impotence, and to tell them to be powerful, original, and independent is to mock them. It is like plucking a bird's feathers in order to put it on a level with beasts, and then telling it to fly.

Martin, *Wendell Phillips* (1890)

The orator almost always spoke without notes. On the few occasions when he used them they were an evident embarrassment: it was like an eagle walking.

Hastings. Besides, the King hath wasted all his rods
  On late offenders, that he now doth lack
  The very instruments of chastisement;
  So that his power, like to a fangless lion,
  May offer, but not hold.

                                                 2 Henry IV, 4, 1

Good effects can be had by introducing two animals and identifying the subject of the comparison with one of them rather than the other: like *this* animal, not *that* one.

And I will shoot Mr. Wood and his deputies through the head, like highwaymen or house-breakers, if they dare to force one farthing of their coin upon me in the payment of an hundred pounds. It is no loss of honour to submit to the lion, but who, with the figure of a man, can think with patience of being devoured alive by a rat.

                                               Swift, *Letter to Mr. Harding the Printer* (1724)

I know he has endeavoured to show himself master of the art of swift writing, and would persuade the world that what he writes is *ex tempore* wit, and written *currente calamo*. But I doubt not to show, that though he would be thought to imitate the silkworm, that spins its web from its own bowels, yet I shall make him appear like the leech, that lives upon the blood of other men, drawn from the gums; and, when he is rubbed with salt, spues it up again.

                                               Langbaine, *An Account of the Dramatic Poets* (1691) (on Edward Ravenscroft)

The same style of comparison helps to distinguish different sorts of people: one is elevated while the other is reduced.

In short, a man who has great knowledge, from experience and observation, of the characters, customs, and manners of mankind, is a being as different from, and as superior to, a man of mere book and systematical knowledge, as a well-managed horse is to an ass.

                                               Chesterfield, letter to his son (1753)

Boswell, *Life of Johnson* (1791)

Nay, (said Johnson,) he has given him some smart hits to be sure; but there is no proportion between the two men; they must not be named together. A fly, Sir, may sting a stately horse and make him wince; but one is but an insect, and the other is a horse still.

Burke, *Reflections on the Revolution in France* (1791)

Because half a dozen grasshoppers under a fern make the field ring with their importunate chink, whilst thousands of great cattle, reposed beneath the shadow of the British oak, chew the cud and are silent, pray do not imagine that those who make the noise are the only inhabitants of the field; that, of course, they are many in number, or that, after all, they are other than the little, shriveled, meager, hopping, though loud and troublesome, insects of the hour.

9. *Perspective*. Animals are a leading source of comparison for putting humans into striking perspective. From a well-chosen angle, we seem as animals do from our usual vantage point.

James Fitzjames Stephen, *Liberty, Equality, Fraternity* (1873)

I should certainly not agree with Mr. Mill's opinion that English people in general are dull, deficient in originality, and as like each other as herrings in a barrel appear to us.

Ruskin, *Fors Clavigera* (1884)

[M]ore may be observed of England at this time, – namely, that she has no "social structure" whatsoever: but is a mere heap of agonizing human maggots, scrambling and sprawling over each other for any manner of rotten eatable thing they can get a bite of.

Holmes, Jr., letter to Harold Laski (1925)

But I look at men through Malthus's glasses – as like flies – here swept away by a pestilence – there multiplying unduly and paying for it.

It may be, that in the sight of Heaven, you are more worthless and less fit to live than millions like this poor man's child. Oh God! to hear the Insect on the leaf pronouncing on the too much life among his hungry brothers in the dust!

Dickens, *A Christmas Carol* (1843)

The separation of the animal kingdom from human life also creates a chance for perspective of another kind: animals have their own tastes and relations that are as compelling to them as ours are to us.

Shall I punish the robber? Shall I curse the profligate? As soon destroy the toad, because my partial taste may judge him ugly; or doom to hell, for his carnivorous appetite, the muscanonge of my native lakes! Toad is not horrible to toad, or thief to thief.

Kingsley, *Alton Locke* (1849)

The creator and arbiter of beauty is the heart; to the male rattlesnake the female rattlesnake is the loveliest thing in nature.

Bierce, *A Cynic Looks at Life* (1912)

Likewise the moral indifference of the animal world.

I suppose we must punish evil-doers as we extirpate vermin; but I don't know that we have any more right to judge them than we have to judge rats and mice, which are just as good as cats and weasels, though we think it necessary to treat them as criminals.

Holmes, *Elsie Venner* (1861)

Nor, at the time, had it failed to enter his monomaniac mind, that all the anguish of that then present suffering was but the direct issue of former woe; and he too plainly seemed to see, that as the most poisonous reptile of the marsh perpetuates his kind as inevitably as the sweetest songster of the grove; so, equally with every felicity, all miserable events do naturally beget their like.

Melville, *Moby-Dick* (1851)

Comparisons for the sake of perspective can also be put into the service of more ambitious efforts at philosophy. (Sometimes they amount to analogies rather than metaphors – literal parallels, in other words, not figurative identities.) The classic application is to observe how poorly animals understand what is higher than themselves, and to consider the probability that humans are in a similar position. This is a tradition of thought and comparison that runs back at least to Plato's *Phaedo*.

Melville, *Moby-Dick* (1851)

Methinks that in looking at things spiritual, we are too much like oysters observing the sun through the water, and thinking that thick water the thinnest of air.

Locke, *An Essay Concerning Human Understanding* (1690)

He who will not set himself proudly at the top of all things, but will consider the immensity of this fabric and the great variety that is to be found in this little and inconsiderable part of it which he has to do with, may be apt to think that, in other mansions of it, there may be other and different intelligent beings, of whose faculties he has as little knowledge or apprehension as a worm shut up in one drawer of a cabinet hath of the senses or understanding of a man....

Walpole, letter to the Earl of Strafford (1784)

We are poor silly animals: we live for an instant upon a particle of a boundless universe, and are much like a butterfly that should argue about the nature of the seasons and what creates their vicissitudes, and does not exist itself to see one annual revolution of them!

Holmes, Jr., *Law and the Court* (1913)

I think it not improbable that man, like the grub that prepares a chamber for the winged thing it never has seen but is to be – that man may have cosmic destinies that he does not understand.

I believe rather that we stand in much the same relation to the whole of the universe as our canine and feline pets do to the whole of human life. They inhabit our drawing-rooms and libraries. They take part in scenes of whose significance they have no inkling. They are merely tangent to curves of history the beginnings and ends and forms of which pass wholly beyond their ken. So we are tangents to the wider life of things. But, just as many of the dog's and cat's ideals coincide with our ideals, and the dogs and cats have daily living proof of the fact, so we may well believe, on the proofs that religious experience affords, that higher powers exist and are at work to save the world on ideal lines similar to our own.

William James, *Pragmatism* (1907)

Chapter Three

THE USE OF NATURE
TO DESCRIBE ABSTRACTIONS

We have seen how well animals can be used to caricature the appearance or behavior of humans. The most common function of metaphor, and the richest source of material for it, changes when the subject of the comparison is not a person but is instead an abstraction – government, for example, or public opinion, or good or evil. A metaphor is then likely to serve a different purpose: the subject has no form that is directly perceptible to the senses, and the comparison allows it to be seen or heard or felt, and perhaps understood more clearly. A comparison to what is known also satisfies the appetite of the mind to assimilate what it does not understand into what it can. As Churchill put it:

Churchill, *The Scaffolding of Rhetoric* (1897)

The ambition of human beings to extend their knowledge favours the belief that the unknown is only an extension of the known: that the abstract and the concrete are ruled by similar principles: that the finite and the infinite are homogeneous.

For giving visible form to an abstraction, animals tend to be less effective than they were for the purposes of caricature that we saw in the last chapter. Abstract subjects of the kind just mentioned do not look like animals. They do not look like anything. And the traits and behavior of an abstraction may be complicated in ways that a mere reference to personality cannot capture, and for which, indeed, an image of personality may not be wanted. (We will see a few exceptions later in this chapter, however, and more of them in Chapter 12.)

A more typically valuable source of material for

making abstractions visible thus comes from nature – by which we mean, here, nature of the non-sentient variety: the rest beyond the animal kingdom. Nature provides powerful images of cause and effect, of laws of growth, and of relationships more subtle and complex than animal life can easily supply. The use of nature to make abstractions visible is too wide and varied to be canvassed completely in this space, but we can view some distinguished applications.

1. *Political life and opinion* are dynamic subjects, and so invite comparisons to parts of nature that display growth, force, or motion. The variety of materials commonly used for the purpose makes it useful to resort to outline form.

a. *Comparisons to plants.*

> Let them take arms. The remedy is to set them right as to facts, pardon, and pacify them. What signify a few lives lost in a century or two? The tree of liberty must be refreshed from time to time with the blood of patriots and tyrants. It is its natural manure.

Jefferson, letter to William Stephens Smith (1787)

> A government thus founded on the broad basis of human nature, like a tree which is suffered to retain its native shape, will flourish for ages with little care or attention. But like this same tree, if distorted into a form unnatural and monstrous, will require the constant use of the pruning knife, and all the art and contrivance of a skilful operator, to counteract the efforts of nature against the violence which has been offered her.

Stevens, *Americanus III* (1787)

> I always regarded the hereditary Chamber established by Louis the Eighteenth as an institution which could not last.... It belonged neither to the old France nor to the new France. It was a mere exotic transplanted from our island. Here it

Macaulay, speech in the House of Commons (1831)

had struck its roots deep, and having stood during ages, was still green and vigorous. But it languished in the foreign soil and the foreign air, and was blown down by the first storm. It will be no such easy task to uproot the aristocracy of England.

Cf.:

Chesterton, *The Man Who Thinks Backwards* (1912)

History is like some deeply planted tree which, though gigantic in girth, tapers away at last into tiny twigs; and we are in the topmost branches. Each of us is trying to bend the tree by a twig: to alter England through a distant colony, or to capture the State through a small State department, or to destroy all voting through a vote.

b. *Air* has two classic metaphorical uses. Since it is a necessary support of other things in nature – fire, for example, or breath – it may be invoked to describe similar relationships of dependency between abstract forces or principles.

Madison, Federalist 10 (1787)

Liberty is to faction, what air is to fire, an ailment without which it instantly expires. But it could not be a less folly to abolish liberty, which is essential to political life, because it nourishes faction, than it would be to wish the annihilation of air, which is essential to animal life, because it imparts to fire its destructive agency.

Whitman, *Democratic Vistas* (1871)

As circulation to air, so is agitation and a plentiful degree of speculative license to political and moral sanity.

Southey, *Sir Thomas More: Or, Colloquies on the Progress and Prospects of Society* (1824)

All classes are now brought within the reach of your current literature, that literature which, like a moral atmosphere, is as it were the medium of intellectual life, and on the quality of which, according as it may be salubrious or noxious, the health of the public mind depends.

In human experience, air also serves as a surrounding atmosphere and can therefore be used to epitomize pervasiveness elsewhere.

> Religion lies over them like an all-embracing heavenly canopy, like an atmosphere and life-element, which is not spoken of, which in all things is presupposed without speech.

Carlyle, *Past and Present* (1843)

Cf.:

> Life, so far as she troubled to conceive it, was a circle of rich, pleasant people, with identical interests and identical foes. In this circle, one thought, married, and died. Outside it were poverty and vulgarity for ever trying to enter, just as the London fog tries to enter the pine-woods pouring through the gaps in the northern hills.

Forster, *A Room with a View* (1908)

Weather, as a source of comparison, has some uses similar to those just seen: it can describe necessary conditions for the growth or health of other things.

> I hold it that a little rebellion now and then is a good thing, & as necessary in the political world as storms in the physical.

Jefferson, letter to James Madison (1787)

Or the quality of weather can represent the quality of an event, as by supplying pictures of turbulence.

> In a word, the damages of popular fury were compensated by legislative gravity. Almost every other part of America in various ways demonstrated their gratitude. I am bold to say, that so sudden a calm recovered after so violent a storm is without parallel in history.

Burke, Speech on American Taxation (1774)

Weather also is a help to describe whatever arises without reason and cannot be controlled.

Emerson, *Politics* (1844)

We might as wisely reprove the east wind or the frost, as a political party, whose members, for the most part, could give no account of their position, but stand for the defense of those interests in which they find themselves.

c. *Fire* has vast metaphorical applications, as we shall see in various chapters of this book. As applied to political experience, its destructive power readily suggests forms of strife.

Hazlitt, *On Vulgarity and Affectation* (1821)

I can endure the brutality (as it is termed) of mobs better than the inhumanity of courts. The violence of the one rages like a fire; the insidious policy of the other strikes like a pestilence, and is more fatal and inevitable.

Fire is useful not only for images of its workings but for the range of human reactions to it.

Paine, *The American Crisis* (1783)

Hitherto you have experienced the expenses, but nothing of the miseries of war. Your disappointments have been accompanied with no immediate suffering, and your losses came to you only by intelligence. Like fire at a distance you heard not even the cry; you felt not the danger, you saw not the confusion.

Sheil, argument for the defense in the trial of John O'Connell (1844)

He told you that the country was traversed by incendiaries who set fire to the passions of the people; the whole fabric of society, according to the Attorney-General, for the last nine months has been in a blaze; wherefore then did he stand with folded arms to gaze at the conflagration?

These comparisons go well with architectural metaphors: the burning edifice as the image of a political institution in crisis.

The beginnings of confusion with us in England are at present feeble enough; but with you we have seen an infancy still more feeble growing by moments into a strength to heap mountains upon mountains, and to wage war with Heaven itself. Whenever our neighbour's house is on fire, it cannot be amiss for the engines to play a little on our own.

Burke, Reflections on the Revolution in France (1791)

In proportion, therefore, as a nation, a community, or an individual (possessing the inherent quality of greatness) is involved in perils and misfortunes, in proportion does it rise in grandeur; and even when sinking under calamity, makes, like a house on fire, a more glorious display than ever it did in the fairest period of its prosperity.

Irving, Knickerbocker's History of New York (1809)

d. *Water* is likewise an essential resource for natural simile. Its flow or path can suggest the progress of human events.

As a great river may be traced back until its fountainhead is found in a thread of water streaming from a cleft in the rocks, so a great national movement may sometimes be followed until its starting-point is found in the cell of a monk or the studies of a pair of wrangling professors.

Holmes, John Lothrop Motley—A Memoir (1879)

Or, as in this example from Emerson, subtler properties of water may be exploited – the relation between its movement and its parts.

Society is a wave. The wave moves onward, but the water of which it is composed does not. The same particle does not rise from the valley to the ridge. Its unity is only phenomenal. The persons who make up a nation to-day, next year die, and their experience with them.

Emerson, Self-Reliance (1841)

Tides, currents, and floods are particularly helpful for depicting social and political forces. They can epitomize forces that carry people forward or that rise and threaten their containers.

Julius Caesar, 4, 3

Brutus. The enemy increaseth every day;
We, at the height, are ready to decline.
There is a tide in the affairs of men
Which taken at the flood leads on to fortune;
Omitted, all the voyage of their life
Is bound in shallows and in miseries.
On such a full sea are we now afloat,
And we must take the current when it serves,
Or lose our ventures.

Bacon, *Of Vicissitude of Things* (1625)

The great accessions and unions of kingdoms, do likewise stir up wars; for when a state grows to an over-power, it is like a great flood, that will be sure to overflow.

Macaulay, *Sir James Mackintosh* (1835)

[T]he motion of the public mind in our country resembles that of the sea when the tide is rising. Each successive wave rushes forward, breaks, and rolls back; but the great flood is steadily coming in.

Wells, *War and the Future* (1917)

The true superman comes not as the tremendous personal entry of a star, but in the less dramatic form of a general increase of goodwill and skill and common sense. A species rises not by thrusting up peaks but by the brimming up as a flood does.

e. *Volcanoes* and their emanations have some properties not found elsewhere. They can give visual form to abstractions that have the character of an outburst, then self-destruction, or dormancy, or the potential for recurrence.

Ames, speech at Massachusetts Ratifying Convention (1788)

A democracy is a volcano, which conceals the fiery materials of its own destruction.

Old religious factions are volcanoes burnt out; on the lava and ashes and squalid scoriae of old eruptions grow the peaceful olive, the cheering vine, and the sustaining corn.

Burke, Speech on the Petition of the Unitarian Society (1792)

Does he suppose that the prosecutions to which he has now resorted will serve instead of Exchequer bills, and intimidate people into the payment of tithes? If he does, I can tell him that he is mistaken; I can tell him, that these prosecutions are only playing with the ashes thrown from the volcano, while the volcano itself is boiling for another eruption, which is likely, for aught I know, to overwhelm those who are amusing themselves by looking at its former devastations.

O'Connell, speech on tithes (1832)

Many other natural wonders, and natural disasters, have distinctive features that seem to match patterns found elsewhere in life. The action of an avalanche is another example: its accumulated potential, its small beginnings, and its force and destructive capacity once started.

But he would try Gaul first; and into Gaul he poured, with all his Tartar hordes, and with them all the Teuton tribes, who had gathered in his progress, as an avalanche gathers the snow in its course.

Kingsley, *The Roman and the Teuton* (1864)

It wants to have a House of Commons which is not weighted with nominees of the landed class, but with representatives of the other interests. And as to contending for a reform short of that, it is like asking for a bit of an avalanche which has already begun to thunder.

Eliot, *Middlemarch* (1872)

A panic, like an avalanche, is a thing much easier to start than stop.

Wells, *An Englishman Looks at the World* (1914)

The people in my supposed world know this and if, for any reason, they want to kill a civilisation,

Note Books of Samuel Butler (1912)

stuff it and put it into a museum, they tell it something that is too much ahead of its other ideas, something that travels faster than thought, thus setting an avalanche of new ideas tumbling in upon it and utterly destroying everything.

f. *Animals* should be considered briefly. Our principal concern in this chapter is nature outside the animal kingdom, for nature is borrowed more often to give visible form to abstractions. But sometimes political sentiments or events are of a character that does call for a comparison to animal life, as when the forces involved are so active or violent as to demand animate form.

Julius Caesar, 3, 1

ANTONY. ...And Caesar's spirit ranging for revenge,
With Ate by his side come hot from hell,
Shall in these confines with a monarch's voice
Cry 'Havoc!' and let slip the dogs of war....

Henry V, prologue

Then should the warlike Harry, like himself,
Assume the port of Mars; and at his heels,
Leash'd in like hounds, should famine, sword,
       and fire,
Crouch for employment.

2 Henry IV, 1, 1

NORTHUMBERLAND. ...The times are wild;
       contention, like a horse
Full of high feeding, madly hath broke loose
And bears down all before him.

2. *Truth, falsehood, and knowledge.* It is edifying to observe what materials for comparison recur in the work of different writers to describe the same sorts of subjects, and to consider why. For the motions of political and social life, comparisons to the active and flowing side of nature recommended themselves: fire, water, avalanches, etc. Truth is an abstraction with different properties and so has lent itself to images more solid and stationary.

Truth scarce ever yet carried it by vote anywhere at its first appearance: new opinions are always suspected, and usually opposed, without any other reason but because they are not already common. But truth, like gold, is not the less so for being newly brought out of the mine. It is trial and examination must give it price, and not any antique fashion; and though it be not yet current by the public stamp, yet it may, for all that, be as old as nature, and is certainly not the less genuine.

Locke, *An Essay Concerning Human Understanding* (1690)

Truth is tough. It will not break, like a bubble, at a touch; nay, you may kick it about all day, like a football, and it will be round and full at evening.

Holmes, *The Professor at the Breakfast Table* (1859)

Truth independent; truth that we *find* merely; truth no longer malleable to human need; truth incorrigible, in a word; such truth exists indeed superabundantly – or is supposed to exist by rationalistically minded thinkers; but then it means only the dead heart of the living tree, and its being there means only that truth also has its paleontology and its "prescription," and may grow stiff with years of veteran service and petrified in men's regard by sheer antiquity.

William James, *Pragmatism* (1907)

Water has been an effective source of comparison when the subject is the extent of knowledge at large.

[K]nowledge is like a water that will never arise again higher than the level from which it fell; and therefore to go beyond Aristotle by the light of Aristotle is to think that a borrowed light can increase the original light from whom it is taken.

Bacon, *Valerius Terminus: On the Interpretation of Nature* (1603)

It is asserted that this is the age of Superficial Knowledge; and amongst the proofs of this assertion we find Encyclopædias and other popular abstracts of knowledge particularly insisted on.

de Quincey, *Superficial Knowledge* (1824)

But in this notion and its alleged proofs there is equal error – wherever there is much diffusion of knowledge, there must be a good deal of superficiality: prodigious extension implies a due proportion of weak intension; a sea-like expansion of knowledge will cover large shallows as well as large depths.

Comparisons of truth to light are sufficiently well known, from scripture and elsewhere, as perhaps to require little illustration, but examples of a few less familiar applications may be of interest.

Macaulay, *Milton* (1825)

There is only one cure for the evils which newly acquired freedom produces; and that cure is freedom. When a prisoner first leaves his cell he cannot bear the light of day: he is unable to discriminate colours, or recognise faces. But the remedy is, not to remand him into his dungeon, but to accustom him to the rays of the sun. The blaze of truth and liberty may at first dazzle and bewilder nations which have become half blind in the house of bondage. But let them gaze on, and they will soon be able to bear it.

de Quincey, *The Pagan Oracles* (1842)

[T]he light of absolute truth on moral or on spiritual themes is too dazzling to be sustained by the diseased optics of those habituated to darkness.

Johnson, *The Rambler* no. 156 (1751)

Of the great principles of truth which the first speculatists discovered, the simplicity is embarrassed by ambitious additions, or the evidence obscured by inaccurate argumentation; and as they descend from one succession of writers to another, like light transmitted from room to room, they lose their strength and splendour, and fade at last in total evanescence.

To most of us, living willingly in a sort of intellectual moonlight, in the faintly reflected light of
truth, the shadows so firmly renounced by Mr.
Henry James's men and women, stand out endowed
with extraordinary value....

Conrad, *Henry James* (1905)

Some other metaphorical uses of light will be shown in
chapters to come. Meanwhile the natural images of falsehood have been various.

CORIOLANUS. ... And mountainous error be too
    highly heap'd
For truth to o'erpeer.

Coriolanus, 2, 2

The God in whom we believe is a God of moral
truth, and not a God of mystery or obscurity. Mystery is the antagonist of truth. It is a fog of human
invention that obscures truth, and represents it in
distortion. Truth never invelops itself in mystery;
and the mystery in which it is at any time envel-
oped, is the work of its antagonist, and never of
itself.

Paine, *The Age of Reason* (1795)

The man erred; and his error terminates in itself.
But an error of principle does *not* terminate in
itself; it is a fountain; it is self-diffusive; and it has
a life of its own.

de Quincey, *Superficial
Knowledge* (1824)

3. *Virtue and vice; good and evil.* Virtues and vices have
beginnings and can become larger in scale with time, a
pattern that seems so much like growth as to invite use
of that word without much sense of metaphor. Plant life
has therefore been a favorite source of imagery for illustration of those subjects, with variation in the details
according to which end of the polarity is under discussion. Thus some uses of flowers, fruits, and other plant-
ings to depict aspects of character:

Paine, *Rights of Man* (1791)

Whatever wisdom constituently is, it is like a seedless plant; it may be reared when it appears, but it cannot be voluntarily produced.

Addison, *The Spectator* no. 592 (1714)

Envy and cavil are the natural fruits of laziness and ignorance.

Eliot, *Silas Marner* (1861)

He glanced at his son as he entered the room, and said, "What, sir! haven't you had your breakfast yet?" but there was no pleasant morning greeting between them; not because of any unfriendliness, but because the sweet flower of courtesy is not a growth of such homes as the Red House.

Berkeley, *Alciphron, or The Minute Philosopher* (1732)

And suppose that in man after a certain season, the appetite of lust or the faculty of reason shall shoot forth, open, and display themselves as leaves and blossoms do in a tree; would you therefore deny them to be natural to him, because they did not appear in his original infancy?

Cf.:

Stevenson, *Aes Triplex* (1878)

So soon as prudence has begun to grow up in the brain, like a dismal fungus, it finds its first expression in a paralysis of generous acts. The victim begins to shrink spiritually; he develops a fancy for parlours with a regulated temperature, and takes his morality on the principle of tin shoes and tepid milk.

The use of the root:

1 Timothy 6:10

For the love of money is the root of all evil: which while some coveted after, they have erred from the faith, and pierced themselves through with many sorrows.

Thoreau, *Walden* (1854)

There are a thousand hacking at the branches of evil to one who is striking at the root, and it may be that he who bestows the largest amount of time and money on the needy is doing the most by his mode of life to produce that misery which he strives in vain to relieve.

Or the weed:

> The richest genius, like the most fertile soil, when uncultivated, shoots up into the rankest weeds; and instead of vines and olives for the pleasure and use of man, produces, to its slothful owner, the most abundant crop of poisons.
>
> Hume, *The Stoic* (1748)

> Suspicion and persecution are weeds of the same dunghill, and flourish together.
>
> Paine, *The American Crisis* (1783)

> The atmosphere of the camp and the smoke of the battle-field are morally invigorating; the hardy virtues flourish in them, the nonsense dies like a wilted weed.
>
> Hawthorne, *Chiefly About War Matters* (1862)

Cf.:

> It often happens, that extirpating the love of glory, which is observed to take the deepest root in noble minds, tears up several virtues with it; and that suppressing the desire for fame is apt to reduce men to a state of indolence and supineness.
>
> Addison, *The Freeholder* no. 39 (1716)

Shakespeare, for whom nature and the garden were constant sources of metaphor, invoked the weed in this way often.

> KING HENRY IV. Most subject is the fattest soil
>   to weeds;
> And he, the noble image of my youth,
> Is overspread with them....
>
> 2 *Henry IV*, 4, 4

> DUKE. ...Twice treble shame on Angelo,
>   To weed my vice and let his grow!
>
> *Measure for Measure*, 3, 2

Hamlet, I, 2

HAMLET. ... How weary, stale, flat, and unprofitable,
Seems to me all the uses of this world!
Fie on't! oh fie, fie! 'Tis an unweeded garden,
That grows to seed; things rank and gross
in nature
Possess it merely.

Water can depict qualities or action more insidious than those viewed earlier in the chapter:

Addison, *The Spectator* no. 316 (1711)

Indolence is a stream which flows slowly on, but yet undermines the foundation of every virtue.

Hume, *The Skeptic* (1742)

As a stream necessarily follows the several inclinations of the ground, on which it runs; so are the ignorant and thoughtless part of mankind actuated by their natural propensities. Such are effectively excluded from all pretensions to philosophy....

Virtues also have been traditionally compared to natural solids. Notice the similarity to comparisons used to describe truth.

Bacon, *Of Beauty* (1625)

Virtue is like a rich stone, best plain set....

Chesterfield, letter to his son (1747)

Virtue and learning, like gold, have their intrinsic value but if they are not polished, they certainly lose a great deal of their luster; and even polished brass will pass upon more people than rough gold.

Chesterton, *Tolstoy and the Cult of Simplicity* (1903)

If human beings could only succeed in achieving a real passive resistance they would be strong with the appalling strength of inanimate things, they would be calm with the maddening calm of oak or iron, which conquer without vengeance and are conquered without humiliation.

The interaction between virtue and vice has been attractively suggested by chemical comparisons.

There he sat, with his beaming eye on Mrs V., and his shining face suffused with gladness, and his capacious waistcoat smiling in every wrinkle, and his jovial humour peeping from under the table in the very plumpness of his legs; a sight to turn the vinegar of misanthropy into purest milk of human kindness.

Dickens, *Barnaby Rudge* (1841)

[V]ice and virtue blindly mingled, form a union where vice too often proves the alkali.

Melville, *Mardi* (1849)

[V]irtue, which is, as it were, the fine polish to the wheels of society, necessarily pleases; while vice, like the vile rust, which makes them jar and grate upon one another, is as necessarily offensive.

Smith, *The Theory of Moral Sentiments* (1759)

4. *Fortune and misfortune* tend to be experienced as forces in motion, and so attract comparisons to aspects of nature with those properties.

The great and mighty reverses of fortune, like the revolutions of nature, may be said to carry their own weight and reason along with them: they seem unavoidable and remediless, and we submit to them without murmuring as to a fatal necessity.

Hazlitt, *On Great and Little Things* (1821)

I was by nature a good and affectionate son, but as I took my way into the great world from which I had been so long secluded I could not help remembering that all my misfortunes had flowed like a stream from the niggard economy of my parents in the matter of school luncheons....

Bierce, *The Hypnotist* (1893)

I was firm and immovable in my purpose; but yct agitated by anticipation of uncertain danger and troubles; and if I could have foreseen the hurricane and perfect hail-storm of affliction which soon fell upon me, well might I have been agitated.

de Quincey, *Confessions of an English Opium Eater* (1821)

5. *Life*. Nature also provides images useful for the description of large features of human life, and especially of its transitory, bounded, or constrained character.

James 4:14

Whereas ye know not what shall be on the morrow. For what is your life? It is even a vapour, that appeareth for a little time, and then vanisheth away.

Johnson, *The Rambler* no. 187 (1751)

"O life!" says he, "frail and uncertain! where shall wretched man find thy resemblance, but in ice floating on the ocean? It towers on high, it sparkles from afar, while the storms drive and the waters beat it, the sun melts it above, and the rocks shatter it below."

James Fitzjames Stephen, *Liberty, Equality, Fraternity* (1873)

The life of the great mass of men, to a great extent the life of all men, is like a watercourse guided this way or that by a system of dams, sluices, weirs, and embankments. The volume and the quality of the different streams differ, and so do the plans of the works by which their flow is regulated, but it is by these works – that is to say, by their various customs and institutions – that men's lives are regulated.

Webster, argument in *Vidal et al. v. Girard's Executors* (1844)

This first great commandment teaches man that there is one, and only one, great First Cause, one, and only one, proper object of human worship. This is the great, the ever fresh, the overflowing fountain of all revealed truth. Without it, human life is a desert, of no known termination on any side, but shut in on all sides by a dark and impenetrable horizon.

Charlotte Brontë, *Villette* (1853)

I like to see flowers growing, but when they are gathered, they cease to please. I look on them as things rootless and perishable; their likeness to life makes me sad.

I wax impatient sometimes to think how much time it takes to do a little fragment of what one would like to do and dreams of. Life is like an artichoke; each day, week, month, year, gives you one little bit which you nibble off – but precious little compared with what you throw away.

Holmes, Jr., letter to Frederick Pollock (1887)

6. *Science and mathematics*. This chapter is the appropriate place to briefly notice the use of principles from mathematics and physics to depict abstractions or other invisibilities. Ideas from geometry, for example, can provide comparisons to simplify a point; they are conceptually pure and are easy to visualize.

[H]is first flight of fancy commonly transports him to ideas of what is most perfect, finished, and exalted, till, having soared out of his own reach and sight, not well perceiving how near the frontiers of height and depth border upon each other, with the same course and wing he falls down plump into the lowest bottom of things, like one who travels the east into the west, or like a straight line drawn by its own length into a circle.

Swift, A Tale of a Tub (1704)

Indeed, he seemed to approach the grave as a hyperbolic curve approaches a straight line – less directly as he got nearer, till it was doubtful if he would ever reach it at all.

Hardy, Far from the Madding Crowd (1874)

That any human creature ever, under any conceivable circumstances, acted otherwise than in obedience to that which for the time being was his strongest wish, is to me an assertion as incredible and as unmeaning as the assertion that on a particular occasion two straight lines enclosed a space.

James Fitzjames Stephen, Liberty, Equality, Fraternity (1873)

Simple images of solids, typically borrowed from physics, have similar advantages: they can make an abstraction both easier to understand and easier to see. What the resulting picture lacks in colorful detail, it gains in simplicity.

Emerson, *Spiritual Laws* (1841)
His ambition is exactly proportioned to his powers. The height of the pinnacle is determined by the breadth of the base.

Hume, *A Treatise of Human Nature* (1738)
[W]e more readily contract a hatred against a whole family, where our first quarrel is with the head of it, than where we are displeased with a son, or servant, or some inferior member. In short, our passions, like other objects, descend with greater facility than they ascend.

Spencer, *The Philosophy of Style* (1852)
The illusion that great men and great events came oftener in early times than now, is partly due to historical perspective. As in a range of equidistant columns, the furthest off look the closest; so, the conspicuous objects of the past seem more thickly clustered the more remote they are.

Johnson, *Lives of the English Poets* (1781)
Tediousness is the most fatal of all faults; negligence or errors are signal and local, but tediousness pervades the whole; other faults are censured and forgotten, but the power of tediousness propagates itself. He that is weary the first hour is more weary the second; as bodies forced into motion contrary to their tendency pass more and more slowly through every successive interval of space.

Chapter Four

THE USE OF NATURE
TO DESCRIBE INNER STATES

Nothing is more familiar to human experience than thought and feeling, and nothing is less visible in itself – or, in many cases, more difficult to describe literally.

> Words cannot describe our feelings. The finer parts are lost, as the down upon a plum; the radiance of light cannot be painted.

Boswell, *Journal* (1772)

> Every time one man says to another, "Tell us plainly what you mean?" he is assuming the infal-libility of language: that is to say, he is assuming that there is a perfect scheme of verbal expression for all the internal moods and meanings of men.... He knows that there are in the soul tints more bewildering, more numberless, and more nameless than the colours of an autumn forest.... Yet he seriously believes that these things can every one of them, in all their tones and semi-tones, in all their blends and unions, be accurately repre-sented by an arbitrary system of grunts and squeals.

Chesterton, *G. F. Watts* (1904)

It thus is no surprise to find the incidents of inner life among the common subjects of metaphor and simile, which can make them perceptible and more comprehen-sible. Animal life occasionally is suitable for the purpose, too, as we shall see below, but it tends to be too crude to capture the intricacy and subtlety of inner experience. That subject is often characterized by properties like depth, turbulence, and growth, and nature provides the best pictures of them.

As we saw in the previous chapter, the most import-ant features of nature from a metaphorical standpoint are plants, fire, water, and, to a lesser extent, minerals. Those basic sources are familiar to all and highly versatile; they provide compelling images of properties and forces that recur in more complex form everywhere else in human experience. Like the commonly used words in a language, they may be used to express a wide range of ideas.

1. *The inner self generally; mind and soul.* Again, the applications of nature to these topics are sufficiently diverse to justify a brief outline.

a. When the subject is the invisible growth and life of the self, we find natural comparisons in the visible growth and life of plants.

Holmes, Jr., letter to Harold Laski (1929)

Your companions at the funeral who took part in prayer they didn't believe in merely illustrate what I am eternally repeating: that man is like all other growing things and when he has grown in a certain crevice for say twenty years you can't straighten him out without attacking his life. That is what gives the power to churches that no rational man would deem worthy of thought if he were growing free and had no past.

Thoreau, *On the Duty of Civil Disobedience* (1849)

I perceive that, when an acorn and a chestnut fall side by side, the one does not remain inert to make way for the other, but both obey their own laws, and spring and grow and flourish as best they can, till one, perchance, overshadows and destroys the other. If a plant cannot live according to its nature, it dies; and so a man.

Melville, letter to Nathaniel Hawthorne (1851)

My development has been all within a few years past. I am like one of those seeds taken out of the Egyptian Pyramids, which, after being three thousand years a seed and nothing but a seed, being planted in English soil, it developed itself, grew to greenness, and then fell to mould.

Cf.:

> The real offence, as she ultimately perceived, was her having a mind of her own at all. Her mind was to be his – attached to his own like a small garden-plot to a deer-park.

Henry James, *The Portrait of a Lady* (1881)

b. Comparisons to water follow from the sense that the subjects flow, or move – or should.

> [W]hen, seeing him justly delighted with Solander's conversation, I observed once that he was a man of great parts who talked from a full mind – "It may be so," said Mr. Johnson, "but you cannot know it yet, nor I neither: the pump works well, to be sure! but how, I wonder, are we to decide in so very short an acquaintance, whether it is supplied by a spring or a reservoir?"

Piozzi, *Anecdotes of the Late Samuel Johnson* (1786)

> The philosophy of six thousand years has not searched the chambers and magazines of the soul. In its experiments there has always remained, in the last analysis, a residuum it could not resolve. Man is a stream whose source is hidden.

Emerson, *The Over-Soul* (1841)

> The man who never alters his opinion is like standing water, and breeds reptiles of the mind.

Blake, *The Marriage of Heaven and Hell* (1793)

> Most men have no inclination, no rapids, no cascades, but marshes, and alligators, and miasma instead.

Thoreau, *A Week on the Concord and Merrimack Rivers* (1849)

In other cases the affinity arises from the transparency or opacity of mind and character.

> My faults will not be hid from you, and perhaps it is no dispraise to me that they will not: the cleanness and purity of one's mind is never better

Pope, letter to William Congreve (1714)

proved, than in discovering its own faults at first view; as when a stream shows the dirt at its bottom, it shows also the transparency of the water.

Sheil, *Lord Norbury* (1827)

At the conclusion of his charge, he made some efforts to call the attention of the jury to any leading incident which particularly struck him, but what he meant it was not very easy to conjecture; and when he sat down, the whole performance exhibited a mind which resembled a whirlpool of mud, in which law, facts, arguments, and evidence, were lost in unfathomable confusion.

Melville, *The Confidence-Man* (1857)

Always, they should represent human nature not in obscurity, but transparency, which, indeed, is the practice with most novelists, and is, perhaps, in certain cases, someway felt to be a kind of honor rendered by them to their kind. But whether it involve honor or otherwise might be mooted, considering that, if these waters of human nature can be so readily seen through, it may be either that they are very pure or very shallow.

de Quincey, *Schlosser's Literary History of the Eighteenth Century* (1880)

No waters in him turbid with new crystallizations; everywhere the eye can see to the bottom.

Cf.:

Melville, *Moby-Dick* (1851)

For as this appalling ocean surrounds the verdant land, so in the soul of man there lies one insular Tahiti, full of peace and joy, but encompassed by all the horrors of the half known life. God keep thee! Push not off from that isle, thou canst never return!

c. When speaking of static properties of a subject's character, the source imagery can change accordingly, as with these comparisons to gold or gems. (Some of the cases to follow might as easily have appeared with the illustrations of virtue in the previous chapter.)

So I learned then, once for all, that gold in its native state is but dull, unornamental stuff, and that only low-born metals excite the admiration of the ignorant with an ostentatious glitter. However, like the rest of the world, I still go on underrating men of gold and glorifying men of mica. Commonplace human nature cannot rise above that.

Twain, *Roughing It* (1872)

And it is often to be observed, that as in digging for precious metals in the mines, much earthy rubbish has first to be troublesomely handled and thrown out; so, in digging in one's soul for the fine gold of genius, much dullness and commonplace is first brought to light.

Melville, *Pierre* (1852)

The soul is a kind of rough diamond, which requires art, labour, and time to polish it. For want of which, many a good natural genius is lost, or lies unfashioned, like a jewel in the mine.

Addison, *The Spectator* no. 554 (1712)

The needle and lodestone, or natural magnet, to illustrate subtle and irresistible force or a reliable guide to direction:

But there is a limit even to this extreme refinement and scrupulousness of the Chancellor. The understanding acts only in the absence of the passions. At the approach of the loadstone, the needle trembles, and points to it.

Hazlitt, *Lord Eldon—Mr. Wilberforce* (1825)

[I]t is not for man to follow the trail of truth too far, since by so doing he entirely loses the directing compass of his mind; for arrived at the Pole, to whose barrenness only it points, there, the needle indifferently respects all points of the horizon alike.

Melville, *Pierre* (1852)

[T]here are minds so whimsically constituted, that they may sometimes be profitably interpreted by contraries, a process of which the great Tycho

Coleridge, *The Third Landing-Place* (1818)

Brahe is said to have availed himself in the case of the little Lackwit, who used to sit and mutter at his feet while he was studying. A mind of this sort we may compare to a magnetic needle, the poles of which have been suddenly reversed by a flash of lightning, or other more obscure accident of nature.

d. Other natural comparisons to describe mind, character, or related subjects:

Dickens, *Great Expectations* (1861)

[I]t is a principle of his that no man who was not a true gentleman at heart, ever was, since the world began, a true gentleman in manner. He says, no varnish can hide the grain of the wood; and that the more varnish you put on, the more the grain will express itself.

Melville, *Pierre* (1852)

But, as to the resolute traveler in Switzerland, the Alps do never in one wide and comprehensive sweep, instantaneously reveal their full awfulness of amplitude – their overawing extent of peak crowded on peak, and spur sloping on spur, and chain jammed behind chain, and all their wonderful battalionings of might; so hath heaven wisely ordained, that on first entering into the Switzerland of his soul, man shall not at once perceive its tremendous immensity; lest illy prepared for such an encounter, his spirit should sink and perish in the lowermost snows. Only by judicious degrees, appointed of God, does man come at last to gain his Mont Blanc and take an overtopping view of these Alps; and even then, the tithe is not shown; and far over the invisible Atlantic, the Rocky Mountains and the Andes are yet unbeheld. Appalling is the soul of a man!

2. *Feelings and passions*, being volatile and hard to control, are easily identified with fire and combustion.

BRUTUS. ...O Cassius, you are yoked with a lamb, *Julius Caesar, 4, 3*
That carries anger as the flint bears fire,
Who, much enforced, shows a hasty spark
And straight is cold again.

I was in a towering passion, – to which, by the way, Scott, *Rob Roy* (1817)
nothing contributes more than the having recently
undergone a spice of personal fear, which, like a
few drops of water flung on a glowing fire, is sure
to inflame the ardour which it is insufficient to
quench.

Ever and anon, too, there came a glare of red light Hawthorne, *The Scarlet Letter*
out of his eyes, as if the old man's soul were on fire (1850)
and kept on smouldering duskily within his
breast, until by some casual puff of passion it was
blown into a momentary flame.

The rise of water provides good images of feelings that
challenge the capacity of their containers.

Grief and passion are like floods rais'd in little Dryden, *Essay of Dramatic*
brooks by a sudden rain; they are quickly up, and *Poesie* (1668)
if the concernment be powr'd unexpectedly in
upon us, it overflows us: But a long sober shower
gives them leisure to run out as they came in, without troubling the ordinary current.

[W]hen we have suffered from any violent emo- Burke, *On the Sublime and*
tion, the mind naturally continues in something *Beautiful* (1757)
like the same condition, after the cause which first
produced it has ceased to operate. The tossing of
the sea remains after the storm; and when this
remain of horror has entirely subsided, all the passion, which the accident raised, subsides along
with it; and the mind returns to its usual state of
indifference.

I verily believe no poor fellow's idea-pot ever bub- Coleridge, letter to Josiah
bled up so vehemently with fears, doubts, and Wade (1786)

difficulties, as mine does at present. Heaven grant it may not boil over, and put out the fire!

Cf.:

Richardson, *Clarissa* (1748)

I think, that smooth love; that is to say, a passion without rubs; in other words, a passion without passion; is like a sleepy stream that is hardly seen to give motion to a straw.

Some other uses of nature to illustrate passion and feeling:

Dickens, *David Copperfield* (1850)

I complied, in a very uncomfortable state, and with a warm shooting all over me, as if my apprehensions were breaking out into buds.

Ouida, *Guilderoy* (1889)

Moralists say that a soul should resist passion. They might as well say that a house should resist an earthquake.

Shaw, *Back to Methuselah* (preface) (1921)

[T]he Darwinian process may be described as a chapter of accidents. As such, it seems simple, because you do not at first realize all that it involves. But when its whole significance dawns on you, your heart sinks into a heap of sand within you.

Johnson, *The Adventurer* no. 95 (1753)

It has been discovered by Sir Isaac Newton, that the distinct and primogenial colours are only seven; but every eye can witness, that from various mixtures, in various proportions, infinite diversifications of tints may be produced. In like manner, the passions of the mind, which put the world in motion, and produce all the bustle and eagerness of the busy crowds that swarm upon the earth; the passions, from whence arise all the pleasures and pains that we see and hear of, if we analyze the mind of man, are very few....

3. *Thoughts, ideas, and knowledge.* Ideas develop within the mind by a process everyone knows firsthand but nobody has seen or can describe directly. It may occur in stages that feel like growth, and so invite comparisons to plant life.

> The mind is but a barren soil; is a soil soon exhausted, and will produce no crop, or only one, unless it be continually fertilised and enriched with foreign matter.

Reynolds, *Discourses* (1774)

> What work nobler than transplanting foreign thought into the barren domestic soil? except indeed planting thought of your own, which the fewest are privileged to do.

Carlyle, *Sartor Resartus* (1834)

> Any new formula which suddenly emerges in our consciousness has its roots in long trains of thought; it is virtually old when it first makes its appearance among the recognized growths of our intellect.

Holmes, *The Autocrat of the Breakfast Table* (1858)

> Nightly I revisited the cafe, and sat there with an open mind – a mind wide-open to catch the idea that should drop into it like a ripe golden plum. The plum did not ripen. The mind remained wide-open for a week or more, but nothing except that phrase about the sea rustled to and fro in it.

Beerbohm, *A Relic* (1918)

Fire can depict another aspect of thought: its inception.

> [T]here can be no improvement but from the free communication and comparing of ideas. Kings and nobles, for this reason, receive little benefit from society – where all is submission on one side, and condescension on the other. The mind strikes out truth by collision, as steel strikes fire from the flint!

Hazlitt, *On the Aristocracy of Letters* (1821)

Johnson, letter to William
Drummond (1776)

Knowledge always desires increase: it is like fire, which must first be kindled by some external agent, but which will afterwards propagate itself.

Fire also may suggest the workings of the mind, just as we saw it used to depict passions.

Holmes, *Elsie Venner* (1861)

They have a feeble curiosity for news perhaps, which they take daily as a man takes his bitters, and then fall silent and think they are thinking. But the mind goes out under this regimen, like a fire without a draught....

Johnson, in Piozzi's *Anecdotes*
(1786)

[T]he solitary mortal is certainly luxurious, probably superstitious, and possibly mad: the mind stagnates for want of employment, grows morbid, and is extinguished like a candle in foul air.

When the subject is not the growth of an idea but the flow or progress of multiple ideas, images of motion are helpful and can be furnished by water. Again, some of these examples are similar to usages seen in the previous chapter.

Addison, *The Spectator* no. 62
(1711)

It is very hard for the mind to disengage itself from a subject on which it has been long employed. The thoughts will be rising of themselves from time to time, though we give them no encouragement; as the tossings and fluctuations of the sea continue several hours after the winds are laid.

Thoreau, *A Week on the
Concord and Merrimack Rivers*
(1849)

The current of our thoughts made as sudden bends as the river, which was continually opening new prospects to the east or south, but we are aware that rivers flow most rapidly and shallowest at these points.

Sterne, *Tristram Shandy* (1759)

[T]he thought floated only in Dr. Slop's mind, without sail or ballast to it, as a simple proposition; millions of which, as your worship knows, are every day swimming quietly in the middle of the thin juice of a man's understanding, without being carried backwards or forwards, till some little gusts of passion or interest drive them to one side.

Some other uses of nature to lend visibility to thoughts and the mind:

There is no space between consecutive thoughts, or between the never-ending series of actions. All pack tight, and mould their surfaces against each other, so that in the long run there is a wonderful average uniformity in the forms of both thoughts and actions, just as you find that cylinders crowded all become hexagonal prisms, and spheres pressed together are formed into regular polyhedra.

Holmes, *The Professor at the Breakfast Table* (1859)

From no train of thought did these fancies come; not from within, but from without; suddenly, too, and in one throng, like hoar frost; yet as soon to vanish as the mild sun of Captain Delano's good-nature regained its meridian.

Melville, *Benito Cereno* (1856)

Meditating by one's self is like digging in the mine; it often, perhaps, brings up maiden earth, which never came near the light before; but whether it contain any metal in it, is never so well tried as in conversation with a knowing judicious friend, who carries about him the true touch-stone, which is love of truth in a clear-thinking head.

Locke, letter to William Molyneux (1695)

[A]s I walked on that grass my ignorance over-whelmed me – and yet that phrase is false, because it suggests something like a storm from the sky above. It is truer to say that my ignorance exploded underneath me, like a mine dug long before; and indeed it was dug before the begin-ning of the ages.

Chesterton, *The Gardener and the Guinea* (1912)

Cf.:

Hawthorne, *The Scarlet Letter* (1850)

He now dug into the poor clergyman's heart, like a miner searching for gold; or, rather, like a sexton delving into a grave, possibly in quest of a jewel that had been buried on the dead man's bosom, but likely to find nothing save mortality and corruption.

4. *Happiness and unhappiness.* Happiness and pleasure may seem to be earned, or to move from small beginnings to completeness through planning and stages. Either way they are open to illustration by use of plants.

Chesterton, *Rostand* (1903)

"Cyrano de Bergerac" came to us as the new decoration of an old truth, that merriment was one of the world's natural flowers, and not one of its exotics.

Melville, *Mardi* (1849)

But vain, Yoomy, to snatch at Happiness. Of that we may not pluck and eat. It is the fruit of our own toilsome planting; slow it grows, nourished by many teats, and all our earnest tendings. Yet ere it ripen, frosts may nip; – and then, we plant again; and yet again.

Cf.:

Charlotte Brontë, *Villette* (1853)

No mockery in this world ever sounds to me so hollow as that of being told to cultivate happiness. What does such advice mean? Happiness is not a potato, to be planted in mould, and tilled with manure. Happiness is a glory shining far down upon us out of Heaven. She is a divine dew which the soul, on certain of its summer mornings, feels dropping upon it from the amaranth bloom and golden fruitage of Paradise.

And the comparison of happiness to a laboriously cultivated plant creates chances for spin-off comparisons, as to the field hand:

[O]n a subject so important to us all as happiness, we should listen with pleasure to any man's experience or experiments, even though he were but a plough-boy, who cannot be supposed to have ploughed very deep into such an intractable soil as that of human pains and pleasures, or to have conducted his researches upon any very enlightened principles.

de Quincey, *Confessions of an English Opium Eater* (1821)

Unhappiness has tended to provoke a wider range of natural images. Perhaps it is because happiness is simpler, or seems that way (think of Tolstoy's comment about happy and unhappy families); or maybe it is because feelings of happiness do not fill their bearer with a comparable need to be unburdened through description; or possibly something in the character of happiness makes it a more challenging subject, as in Frederick Douglass's comment:

Anguish and grief, like darkness and rain, may be described, but joy and gladness, like the rainbow of promise, defy alike the pen and pencil.

Douglass, *My Bondage and My Freedom* (1855).

[T]he unexpectant discontent of worn and disappointed parents weighs on the children like a damp, thick air, in which all the functions of life are depressed....

Eliot, *The Mill on the Floss* (1860)

Sorrow is a kind of rust of the soul, which every new idea contributes in its passage to scour away. It is the putrefaction of stagnant life and is remedied by exercise and motion.

Johnson, *The Rambler* no. 47 (1750)

[A] similar phenomenon developed itself in her humour, which was then observed to be of a sharp and acid quality, as though an extra lemon (figuratively speaking) had been squeezed into the nectar of her disposition, and had rather damaged its flavour.

Dickens, *The Life and Adventures of Martin Chuzzlewit* (1844)

Cf.:

Richard III, 1, 1

GLOUCESTER. Now is the winter of our discontent
Made glorious summer by this sun of York....

5. *Malleability.* The nature of the human mind at birth has been the subject of famous philosophical speculations and use of metaphor – so famous, indeed, that some of them seem needless to rehearse here. The notion of the mind as a blank slate, or tabula rasa, goes back to classical times, but is most associated with Locke.

Locke, *An Essay Concerning Human Understanding* (1690)

Let us then suppose the mind to be, as we say, white paper void of all characters, without any ideas. How comes it to be furnished? Whence comes it by that vast store which the busy and boundless fancy of man has painted on it with an almost endless variety? Whence has it all the materials of reason and knowledge? To this I answer, in one word, from experience.

Without debating here the accuracy or implications of Locke's idea, we may admire the rhetorical force of it, and the ingenuity of some subsequent uses of natural metaphor to describe the process by which ideas reach the mind (or don't).

Defoe, *The Family Instructor* (1715)

The child may be wrought upon. Nature, like some vegetables, is malleable when taken green and early; but hard and brittle when condensed by time and age. At first it bows and bends to instruction and reproof, but afterwards obstinately refuses both.

Smith, *The Theory of Moral Sentiments* (1759)

The opinion of other people becomes, in this case, of the utmost importance to him. Their approbation is the most healing balsam; their disapprobation, the bitterest and most tormenting poison that can be poured into his uneasy mind.

When the brain itself is disordered, by disease, by drunkenness, or by other accidents, these philosophers are of opinion, that the impressions are disfigured, or instantly erased, or not at all received; in which case, there is either no remembrance, or a confused one: and they think, that the brains of old men, grown callous by length of time, are, like hard wax, equally tenacious of old impressions, and unsusceptible of new.

Beattie, *Dissertations Moral and Critical* (1783)

The affair – I mean the affair of life – couldn't, no doubt, have been different for me; for it's at the best a tin mould, either fluted and embossed, with ornamental excrescences, or else smooth and dreadfully plain, into which, a helpless jelly, one's consciousness is poured – so that one 'takes' the form as the great cook says, and is more or less compactly held by it: one lives in fine as one can.

Henry James, *The Ambassadors* (1903)

Some additional images of ideas entering the mind are considered in Chapter 5.

6. *Death and decline*. The current chapter is the best place to treat this topic. Its fit here is rough because the subject only overlaps partly with the problem of depicting inner states. But consider how the death of plants can illustrate the end of life, or of the life-force:

In process of time, however, the old governor, like all other children of mortality, began to exhibit evident tokens of decay. Like an aged oak, which, though it long has braved the fury of the elements, and still retains its gigantic proportions, begins to shake and groan, with every blast – so was it with the gallant Peter....

Irving, *Knickerbocker's History of New York* (1809)

From my twenty-fifth year I date my life. Three weeks have scarcely passed, at any time between then and now, that I have not unfolded within

Melville, letter to Nathaniel Hawthorne (1851)

myself. But I feel that I am now come to the inmost leaf of the bulb, and that shortly the flower must fall to the mould.

Cf.:

Pope, letter to William Wycherley (1705)

Most men in years, as they are generally discouragers of youth, are like old trees, which, being past bearing themselves, will suffer no young plants to flourish beneath them.

Likewise images of cold.

Romeo and Juliet, 4, 5

CAPULET. ... Death lies on her, like an untimely frost Upon the sweetest flower of all the field.

Stevenson, *Aes Triplex* (1878)

[A]fter a certain distance, every step we take in life we find the ice growing thinner below our feet, and all around us and behind us we see our contemporaries going through.

Sometimes a writer is especially observant of some particular thing in nature and so deploys it more than once, and in more than one way, with rare and interesting acuity:

Holmes, *Elsie Venner* (1861)

[T]he old people get the coughs which give them a few shakes and their lives drop in pieces like the ashes of a burned thread which have kept the threadlike shape until they were stirred. ...

Holmes, *Elsie Venner* (1861)

Go to the nearest chemist and ask him to show you some of the dark-red phosphorus which will not burn without fierce heating, but at 500 deg. Fahrenheit, changes back again to the inflammable substance we know so well. Grief seems more like ashes than like fire; but as grief has been love once, so it may become love again.

7. *Animals to describe inner experience.* Animal life is used less often than the rest of nature to describe inner states,

but has had honorable and useful applications that we might notice here by way of postscript to the chapter. Thus the arrival and movement of ideas and thoughts can be viewed as resembling the activity of creatures.

O, full of scorpions is my mind, dear wife!	*Macbeth*, 3, 2

Suspicions amongst thoughts, are like bats amongst birds, they ever fly by twilight. Certainly they are to be repressed, or at least well guarded: for they cloud the mind....	Bacon, *Of Suspicion* (1625)

A man cannot wheedle nor overawe his Genius. It requires to be conciliated by nobler conduct than the world demands or can appreciate. These winged thoughts are like birds, and will not be handled; even hens will not let you touch them like quadrupeds. Nothing was ever so unfamiliar and startling to a man as his own thoughts.	Thoreau, *A Week on the Concord and Merrimack Rivers* (1849)

The spores of a great many ideas are floating about in the atmosphere. We no more know where all the growths of our mind came from, than where the lichens which eat the names off from the gravestones borrowed the germs that gave them birth.	Holmes, *My Hunt After "The Captain"* (1862)

Passions call for a different kind of animal depiction – the inner entity as beast:

NORFOLK. Stay, my lord, And let your reason with your choler question What 'tis you go about. To climb steep hills Requires slow pace at first. Anger is like A full-hot horse, who being allow'd his way, Self-mettle tires him.	*Henry VIII*, 1, 1

But, being moody, give him line and scope Till that his passions, like a whale on ground, Confound themselves with working.	2 *Henry IV*, 4, 4

Wells, *The New Machiavelli* (1911)

It caused me to grow up, I will not say blankly ignorant, but with an ignorance blurred and dishonoured by shame, by enigmatical warnings, by cultivated aversions, an ignorance in which a fascinated curiosity and desire struggled like a thing in a net.

Dickens, *The Life and Adventures of Martin Chuzzlewit* (1844)

Mr Mould's men found it necessary to drown their grief, like a young kitten in the morning of its existence, for which reason they generally fuddled themselves before they began to do anything, lest it should make head and get the better of them.

Animals can give form not only to thoughts and feelings but to the mind and soul; these images may allow elaboration through an account of the animal's predicament or other circumstance.

Conrad, *Lord Jim* (1900)

I would have given anything for the power to soothe her frail soul, tormenting itself in its invincible ignorance like a small bird beating about the cruel wires of a cage.

Carlyle, letter to Emerson (1840)

I find him painful as a writer; like a soul ever promising to take wing into the Aether, yet never doing it, ever splashing webfooted in the terrene mud, and only splashing the worse the more he strives!

Melville, *Moby-Dick* (1851)

There is a wisdom that is woe; but there is a woe that is madness. And there is a Catskill eagle in some souls that can alike dive down into the blackest gorges, and soar out of them again and become invisible in the sunny spaces. And even if he forever flies within the gorge, that gorge is in the mountains; so that even in his lowest swoop the mountain eagle is still higher than other birds upon the plain, even though they soar.

[A] different principle attaches to investigation in this spiritual field from investigation in any other. If a man baits a line for fish, the fish will come, even if he declares there are no such things as fishes. If a man limes a twig for birds, the birds will be caught, even if he thinks it superstitious to believe in birds at all. But a man cannot bait a line for souls.

Chesterton, *Spiritualism* (1909)

Chapter Five

THE USE OF NATURE TO DESCRIBE LANGUAGE

Words and their effects are a major subject of metaphor. Their importance needs no elaboration for a reader of this book. The value of metaphor for discussion of them is evident enough as well; for while words may be heard out loud or seen in print, the features of them that matter most tend not to be directly visible or audible. We have no well-developed literal language to describe the relationship between a word and what it is supposed to label, or the place from which words come, or the effect of words on one who reads or hears them. But a writer can create pictures of all these things that borrow from what we know and see more directly. Nature will again be the most important source in this chapter, but we will consider some others as well (animals, human biology, and some man-made materials).

1. *Words*. Comparisons from nature can assign words properties that are available to the senses: not just visibility but qualities such as temperature and feeling to the touch.

Chesterton, *Phonetic Spelling* (1915)

Now my own fear touching anything in the way of phonetic spelling is that it would simply increase this tendency to use words as counters and not as coins. The original life in a word (as in the word "talent") burns low as it is: sensible spelling might extinguish it altogether.

Thoreau, *Walking* (1862)

Where is the literature which gives expression to Nature? He would be a poet who could impress the winds and streams into his service, to speak for him; who nailed words to their primitive senses, as farmers drive down stakes in the spring....

In the highly cultured languages of England, France, and Germany, are words, by thousands, which are strictly untranslatable. They may be approached, but cannot be reflected as from a mirror. To take an image from the language of eclipses, the correspondence between the disk of the original word and its translated representative is, in thousands of instances, not annular; the centres do not coincide; the words overlap; and this arises from the varying modes in which different nations *combine* ideas.

de Quincey, *Protestantism* (1848)

The relation between a thought and the words that express it has generated lines of comparison from outside nature that we should also notice here. As seen in the example from Chesterton a moment ago, currency has served as good material for the purpose – visible, tangible, and understood by any reader. Language and coins have natural affinities by virtue of their customary character.

I conceive that words are like money, not the worse for being common, but that it is the stamp of custom alone that gives them circulation or value. I am fastidious in this respect, and would almost as soon coin the currency of the realm as counterfeit the King's English.

Hazlitt, *On Familiar Style* (1821)

Pounds, shillings and pence are recognised covenanted tokens, the outward and visible signs of an inward and spiritual purchasing power, but till in actual use they are only potential money, as the symbols of language, whatever they may be, are only potential language till they are passing between two minds.

Butler, *Thought and Language* (1890)

Currency is also an apt source of comparison because, like language, it may be debased.

Walpole, letter to Mary and Agnes Berry (1789)

It is a misfortune that words are become so much the current coin of society, that, like King William's shillings, they have no impression left; they are so smooth, that they mark no more to whom they first belonged than to whom they do belong, and are not worth even the twelvepence into which they may be changed....

Holmes, *The Autocrat of the Breakfast-Table* (1858)

When the great calamities of life overtook their friends, these last were spoken of as being *a good deal cut up*. Nine-tenths of human existence were summed up in the single word, *bore*. These expressions come to be the algebraic symbols of minds which have grown too weak or indolent to discriminate. They are the blank checks of intellectual bankruptcy; – you may fill them up with what idea you like; it makes no difference, for there are no funds in the treasury upon which they are drawn.

As applied to kind words:

Johnson, *The Rambler* no. 136 (1751)

Praise, like gold and diamonds, owes its value only to its scarcity.

Cf. this application to arguments:

Scott, *Rob Roy* (1817)

Such were the arguments which my will boldly preferred to my conscience, as coin which ought to be current, and which conscience, like a grumbling shopkeeper, was contented to accept, rather than come to an open breach with a customer, though more than doubting that the tender was spurious.

The relationship between words and the ideas they convey may also be compared to clothing and what it covers.

[P]ray attend carefully to the choice of your words, and to the turn of your expression. Indeed, it is a point of very great consequence. To be heard with success, you must be heard with pleasure: words are the dress of thoughts; which should no more be presented in rags, tatters, and dirt, than your person should.

Chesterfield, letter to his son (1750)

Language is the dress of thought: and as the noblest mien or most graceful action would be degraded and obscured by a garb appropriated to the gross employments of rustics or mechanics, so the most heroic sentiments will lose their efficacy, and the most splendid ideas drop their magnificence, if they are conveyed by words used commonly upon low and trivial occasions. . . .

Johnson, *Lives of the English Poets* (1781)

The words in which a man clothes his thoughts are like all other clothes – the cut raises presumptions about his thoughts, and these generally turn out to be just, but the words are no more the thoughts than a man's coat is himself.

Note Books of Samuel Butler (1912)

It is this necessity for working with tools which break in your hand when any really powerful strain is put upon them which so often gives an advantage in argument to the inferior over the superior, to the man who can answer to the purpose easy things to understand over the man whose thoughts split the seams of the dress in which he has to clothe them.

James Fitzjames Stephen, *Liberty, Equality, Fraternity* (1873)

2. *Style*. We have a technical vocabulary for the styles of writers, but it is abstract. Comparisons to nature can make them visual and convey other nuances.

Of the faults of Scott as an artist it is not very necessary to speak, for faults are generally and easily pointed out, while there is yet no adequate

Chesterton, *The Position of Sir Walter Scott* (1903)

valuation of the varieties and contrasts of virtue. We have compiled a complete botanical classification of the weeds in the poetical garden, but the flowers still flourish neglected and nameless.

Hazlitt, *Lord Byron* (1825)

Lord Byron's verse glows like a flame, consuming every thing in its way; Sir Walter Scott's glides like a river, clear, gentle, harmless.

Mencken, *Professor Veblen* (1919)

Tunnel under his great moraines and stalagmites of words, dig down into his vast kitchen-midden of discordant and raucous polysyllables, blow up the hard, thick shell of his almost theological manner, and what you will find in his discourse is chiefly a mass of platitudes. . . .

In addition to cases drawn strictly from nature, observe also the uses of glass for our present purpose. Instead of viewing words as the clothing of thought, they are treated as a medium through which ideas are passed with more or less clarity.

Hazlitt, *Lord Byron* (1825)

The colouring of Lord Byron's style, however rich and dipped in Tyrian dyes, is nevertheless opaque, is in itself an object of delight and wonder: Sir Walter Scott's is perfectly transparent. In studying the one, you seem to gaze at the figures cut in stained glass, which exclude the view beyond, and where the pure light of Heaven is only a means of setting off the gorgeousness of art: in reading the other, you look through a noble window at the clear and varied landscape without.

Boyle, *A Proemial Essay* (1661)

[T]o affect needless rhetorical ornaments in setting down an experiment, or explicating something abstruse in nature, were little less improper, than it were (for him that designs not to look directly upon the sun itself) to paint the eye-glasses of a telescope, whose clearness is their commendation, and in which even the most delightful colours cannot so much please the eye, as they would hinder the sight.

Animals, too, may provide images of style; their movement or character can resemble the felt experience of language.

> I hope when you write Constitutional decisions you will not emulate some of our judges who having only half a page to say take 50 pages to say it in – I was remarking yesterday to one of my brethren that we appreciate the boa constrictor but not the asp here. For my part I prefer an unpretentious little thing virulent with originality and insight to these swelling discourses padded with quotations from every accessible source.

Holmes, Jr., letter to Andrew Inglis Clark (1901)

Alas, the preference for the boa constrictor that Holmes describes prevails more completely in the legal profession today than it did in his time.

> It's pretty much the same in men and women and in books and everything, that it is in turkeys and chickens. Why, take your poets, now, say Browning and Tennyson. Don't you think you can say which is the dark-meat and which is the white-meat poet? And so of the people you know; can't you pick out the full-flavored, coarse-fibred characters from the delicate, fine-fibred ones?

Holmes, *The Poet at the Breakfast Table* (1872)

> I told him that Voltaire, in a conversation with me, had distinguished Pope and Dryden thus: – "Pope drives a handsome chariot, with a couple of neat trim nags; Dryden a coach, and six stately horses." JOHNSON. "Why, Sir, the truth is, they both drive coaches and six; but Dryden's horses are either galloping or stumbling: Pope's go at a steady even trot."

Boswell, *Life of Johnson* (1791)

Sometimes the animal is compared to the author, with the style resulting from its behavior or circumstances.

Chapman, *Robert Browning* (1898)

He writes like a lion devouring an antelope. He rends his subject, breaks its bones, and tears out the heart of it. He is not made more, but less, comprehensible by the verse-forms in which he writes.

Mencken, *Professor Veblen* (1919)

The learned professor gets himself enmeshed in his gnarled sentences like a bull trapped by barbed wire, and his efforts to extricate himself are quite as furious and quite as spectacular.

Or the force of language may be compared to human muscularity:

James Fitzjames Stephen, *Liberty, Equality, Fraternity* (1873)

I think no one will ever use words to much purpose unless he can feel and see that eloquence is eloquence and logic logic only if and in so far as the skin of language covers firm bone and hard muscle.

Percy, in Boswell's *Life of Johnson* (1791)

The conversation of Johnson is strong and clear, and may be compared to an antique statue, where every nerve and muscle is distinct and clear. Ordinary conversation resembles an inferior cast.

Walpole, letter to William Mason (1776)

The style is as smooth as a Flemish picture, and the muscles are concealed and only for natural uses, not exaggerated like Michael Angelo's to show the painter's skill in anatomy; nor composed of the limbs of clowns of different nations, like Dr. Johnson's heterogeneous monsters. This book is Mr. Gibbon's History of the Decline and Fall of the Roman Empire.

(Walpole and Johnson were friends to our subject matter, but not to each other.) Cf.:

Towne vs. Eisner, 245 U.S. 418 (1918) (Holmes, Jr.)

A word is not a crystal, transparent and unchanged, it is the skin of a living thought and may vary

greatly in color and content according to the circumstances and the time in which it is used.

3. *The power of an utterance.* We have seen that water, in
one form or another, can be used to give visible form to
nearly any abstraction. As applied to the force and effect
of speech or writing:

> That ancient sea of human passion upon which
> high words and great phrases are the resplendent
> foam is just now at a low ebb. We have even gone
> the length of congratulating ourselves because we
> can see the mud and the monsters at the bot-
> tom.... The whole of the best and finest work of
> the modern novelist (such as the work of Mr
> James) is primarily concerned with that delicate
> and fascinating speech which burrows deeper and
> deeper like a mole; but we have wholly forgotten
> that speech which mounts higher and higher like
> a wave and falls in a crashing peroration.

Chesterton, *The Position of Sir
Walter Scott* (1903)

> The effect of any writing on the public mind is
> mathematically measurable by its depth of thought.
> How much water does it draw? If it awaken you to
> think, if it lift you from your feet with the great
> voice of eloquence, then the effect is to be wide,
> slow, permanent, over the minds of men....

Emerson, *Spiritual Laws* (1841)

> I heard him. His speech was the whole of the sub-
> ject, and a concatenated, and an inspired argument
> not to be resisted. It was the march of an elephant;
> it was the wave of the Atlantic; a column of water
> 3,000 miles deep.

Grattan, speech in the Irish
Parliament (1808)

One wonders if the argument to which Grattan refers
could have been any more delightful than his apprecia-
tion of it. Unfortunately the speech that was the subject
of his praise has not survived.

The same medium can describe lesser success. The

features of water that make it a powerful way to describe eloquence can then be set aside in favor of different pictures: water not as a wave but as that which drips or spills.

Hazlitt, *The Late Mr. Horne Tooke* (1825)

Each of his sentences told very well in itself, but they did not all together make a speech. He left off where he began. His eloquence was a succession of drops, not a stream.

Carlyle, *The French Revolution* (1837)

A long-flowing Turk, for rejoinder, bows with Eastern solemnity, and utters articulate sounds: but owing to his imperfect knowledge of the French dialect, his words are like spilt water; the thought he had in him remains conjectural to this day.

Johnson, in Piozzi's *Anecdotes* (1786)

I forced him one day, in a similar humour, to prefer Young's description of "Night" to the so much admired ones of Dryden and Shakespeare, as more forcible and more general.... "This," said he, "is true; but remember that, taking the compositions of Young in general, they are but like bright stepping-stones over a miry road. Young froths and foams, and bubbles sometimes very vigorously; but we must not compare the noise made by your tea-kettle here with the roaring of the ocean."

Water is an effective source for describing language because it provides images of volume and power, clarity or turbidity. Fire is helpful on other comparative occasions because it has different properties to offer: action, heat, energy, and brightness.

Scott, *Count Robert of Paris* (1832)

The Emperor commenced this oration, with those looks described by his daughter as so piercing, that they dazzled like lightning, and his periods, if not precisely flowing like burning lava, were yet the accents of a man having the power of absolute command ...

Eloquence may set fire to reason. But whatever may be thought of the redundant discourse before us, it had no chance of starting a present conflagration.

Gitlow v. New York, 268 U.S. 652 (1925) (Holmes, Jr., dissenting)

Our themes combined:

> At a time like this, scorching irony, not convincing argument, is needed. O! had I the ability, and could I reach the nation's ear, I would, to-day, pour out a fiery stream of biting ridicule, blasting reproach, withering sarcasm, and stern rebuke. For it is not light that is needed, but fire; it is not the gentle shower, but thunder. We need the storm, the whirlwind, and the earthquake.

Douglass, Fourth of July speech, Rochester (1852)

We saw that water can be used to describe not only language that succeeds but also that which fails. So can fire, as by offering images of light without heat.

> It was thought formerly enough to have an occasionally fine passage in the progress of a story or a poem, and an occasionally striking image or expression in a fine passage or description. But this style, it seems, was to be exploded as rude, Gothic, meagre and dry. Now all must be raised to the same tantalizing and preposterous level.... A poem is to resemble an exhibition of fireworks, with a continual explosion of quaint figures and devices, flash after flash, that surprise for the moment, and leave no trace of light or warmth behind them.

Hazlitt, *Mr. T. Moore–Mr. Leigh Hunt* (1825)

4. *The source of creative work.* Some of these patterns resemble the comparisons made to depict the origins of thought and feeling in chapter 4. Thus the use of plants to suggest the cultivation and growth of art:

> Paper is cheap, and authors need not now erase one book before they write another. Instead of cultivating the earth for wheat and potatoes, they

Thoreau, *A Week on the Concord and Merrimack Rivers* (1849) cultivate literature, and fill a place in the Republic of Letters. Or they would fain write for fame merely, as others actually raise crops of grain to be distilled into brandy.

Addison, Dialogues on Medals (1721)

I know in descriptions of this nature the scenes are generally supposed to grow out of the author's imagination, and if they are not charming in all their parts, the reader never imputes it to the want of sun or soil, but to the barrenness of invention.

Hazlitt, *Mr. T. Moore – Mr. Leigh Hunt* (1825)

He stunts and enfeebles equally the growth of the imagination and the affections, by not taking the seed of poetry and sowing it in the ground of truth, and letting it expand in the dew and rain, and shoot up to heaven....

Chapman, *Michael Angelo's Sonnets* (1909)

The seeds of flowers from the Alps may be planted in our gardens, but a new kind of flower will come up; and this is what has happened over and over again to the skilled gardeners of English literature in their struggles with the Italian sonnet.

These themes also can be illustrated by images involving fire: creativity as combustion.

Emerson, *Plato; Or, the Philosopher* (1850)

Plato, especially, has no external biography. If he had lover, wife, or children, we hear nothing of them. He ground them all into paint. As a good chimney burns its smoke, so a philosopher converts the value of all his fortunes into his intellectual performances.

Byron, letter to Annabella Milbanke (1813)

I by no means rank poetry or poets high in the scale of intellect. This may look like affectation, but it is my real opinion. It is the lava of the imagination whose eruption prevents an earthquake.

Shelley, *A Defence of Poetry* (1821)

A man cannot say, "I will compose poetry." The greatest poet even cannot say it; for the mind in creation is as a fading coal, which some invisible influence, like an inconstant wind, awakens to transitory brightness; this power arises from within, like the color of a flower which fades and changes as it is developed, and the conscious portions of our natures are unprophetic either of its approach or its departure.

A watery idea:

> [T]he only question remains, whether the metric feet used by the good writers of the last age or the prosaic numbers employed by the good writers of this be preferable? And here the practice of the last age appears to me superior: they submitted to the restraint of numbers and similar sounds; and this restraint, instead of diminishing, augmented the force of their sentiment and style. Fancy restrained may be compared to a fountain which plays highest by diminishing the aperture.

Goldsmith, *The Citizen of the World* (1760)

Cf.:

> The advantages which rhyme has over blank verse are so many, that it were lost time to name them. . . . But that benefit which I consider most in it, because I have not seldom found it, is, that it bounds and circumscribes the fancy: for imagination in a poet is a faculty so wild and lawless, that, like an high-ranging spaniel, it must have clogs tied to it, lest it outrun the judgment.

Dryden, *The Rival Ladies* (dedication) (1664)

Speaking of animals, the extraction of value from them is another productive source of comparison to describe human creative output.

> Why, the owner does not know it for many years when a poet has put his farm in rhyme, the most admirable kind of invisible fence, has fairly impounded it, milked it, skimmed it, and got all the cream, and left the farmer only the skimmed milk.

Thoreau, *Walden* (1854)

Irving, *Tales of a Traveller*
(1824)

Let them suppose the author the very being they picture him from his works; I am not the man to mar their illusion. I am not the man to hint, while one is admiring the silken web of Persia, that it has been spun from the entrails of a miserable worm.

Macaulay, *Horace Walpole*
(1833)

The faults of Horace Walpole's head and heart are indeed sufficiently glaring. His writings, it is true, rank as high among the delicacies of intellectual epicures as the Strasburg pies among the dishes described in the Almanach des Gourmands. But as the pâté-de-foie-gras owes its excellence to the diseases of the wretched animal which furnishes it, and would be good for nothing if it were not made of livers preternaturally swollen, so none but an unhealthy and disorganised mind could have produced such literary luxuries as the works of Walpole.

Cf.:

Boswell, *Journal of a Tour to the Hebrides* (1785)

I mentioned Lord Monboddo's opinion, that if a man could get a work by heart, he might print it, as by such an act the mind is exercised. JOHNSON. "No, Sir; a man's repeating it no more makes it his property, than a man may sell a cow which he drives home." I said, printing an abridgement of a work was allowed, which was only cutting the horns and tail off the cow. JOHNSON. "No, Sir; 'tis making the cow have a calf."

5. *Reading or otherwise consuming words.* Words are brought into the mind through one sensory organ or another. That process can be made to resemble ingestion of a more tangible kind. Thus drinking:

Boswell, *Life of Johnson* (1791)

Addison's style, like a light wine, pleases everybody from the first. Johnson's, like a liquor of more body, seems too strong at first, but, by degrees, is highly relished. . . .

Of this our modern encyclopædias are the best proof. For whom are they designed, and by whom used? – By those who in a former age would have gone to the fountain heads? No, but by those who in any age preceding the present would have drunk at no waters at all.

de Quincey, *Superficial Knowledge* (1824)

It is the characteristic of great poems that they will yield of their sense in due proportion to the hasty and the deliberate reader. To the practical they will be common sense, and to the wise wisdom; as either the traveler may wet his lips, or an army may fill its water-casks at a full stream.

Thoreau, *A Week on the Concord and Merrimack Rivers* (1849)

As when the rays of the sun are collected into the focus of a burning glass, the smaller the spot is which receives them, compared with the surface of the glass, the greater is the splendor; or as in distillation, the less the quantity of spirit is that is extracted by the still, compared with the quantity of liquor from which the extraction is made, the greater is the strength; so in exhibiting our sentiments by speech, the narrower the compass of words is wherein the thought is comprised, the more energetic is the expression.

Campbell, *The Philosophy of Rhetoric* (1776)

Eating:

BRUTUS. What a blunt fellow is this grown to be!
He was quick mettle when he went to school.
CASSIUS. So is he now in execution
Of any bold or noble enterprise,
However he puts on this tardy form.
This rudeness is a sauce to his good wit,
Which gives men stomach to digest his words
With better appetite.

Julius Caesar, I, 2

The truth sticks in our throats with all the sauces it is served with: it will never go down until we take it without any sauce at all.

Shaw, *Saint Joan* (preface) (1923)

Melville, *Redburn* (1849)

And I think that with regard to a matter, concerning which I myself am wholly ignorant, it is far better to quote my old friend verbatim, than to mince his substantial baron-of-beef of information into a flimsy ragout of my own; and so, pass it off as original.

Addison, *The Spectator* no. 409 (1712)

Gratian very often recommends 'the fine taste' as the utmost perfection of an accomplished man.... Most languages make use of this metaphor, to express that faculty of the mind, which distinguishes all the most concealed faults and nicest perfections in writing. We may be sure this metaphor would not have been so general in all tongues, had there not been a very great conformity between that mental taste, which is the subject of this paper, and that sensitive taste which gives us a relish of every different flavour that affects the palate. Accordingly we find, there are as many degrees of refinement in the intellectual faculty, as in the sense, which is marked out by this common denomination.

An application to another form of art:

Twain, *The Innocents Abroad* (1869)

Perhaps the reason I used to enjoy going to the Academy of Fine Arts in New York was because there were but a few hundred paintings in it, and it did not surfeit me to go through the list. I suppose the Academy was bacon and beans in the Forty-Mile Desert, and a European gallery is a state dinner of thirteen courses. One leaves no sign after him of the one dish, but the thirteen frighten away his appetite and give him no satisfaction.

Compare a digestive metaphor from the animal kingdom:

de Quincey, *Style* (1829)

Time must be given for the intellect to eddy about a truth, and to appropriate its bearings. There is a sort of previous lubrication, such as the boa-constrictor applies to any subject of digestion, which is requisite to familiarize the mind with a startling or a complex novelty.

And compare these images from the world of man-made objects to distinguish different ways that ideas might enter the mind:

> Testimony is like the shot of a long-bow, which owes its efficacy to the force of the shooter; argument is like the shot of the cross-bow, equally forcible whether discharged by a giant or a dwarf.

Boyle, in Johnson's *Dictionary of the English Language* (4th ed. 1773)

> The essence of poetry is that it is an appeal to the hearer's or reader's good faith and power of perception. Logic drives its thoughts into your head with a hammer. Poetry is like light. You can shut your eyes to it if you will, but if, having eyes to open, you open them, it will show you a world of wonders.

James Fitzjames Stephen, *Liberty, Equality, Fraternity* (1873)

> One class of men must have their faith hammered in like a nail, by authority; another class must have it worked in like a screw, by argument.

Holmes, *The Pulpit and the Pew* (1881)

Cf.:

> If there are words and wrongs like knives, whose deep inflicted lacerations never heal – cutting injuries and insults of serrated and poison-dripping edge – so, too, there are consolations of tone too fine for the ear not fondly and for ever to retain their echo....

Charlotte Brontë, *Villette* (1853).

6. *Words compared to other forms of art.* Other forms of art, such as music or painting, are impressive to the senses in ways that language – especially written language – is not (though compare Wilde below). Comparisons to them may therefore make more vivid the felt impression that words can create.

Dryden, *Discourse on Epic Poetry* (1697)

[T]he words are in poetry what the colours are in painting. If the design be good, and the draft be true, the colouring is the first beauty that strikes the eye.

Wilde, *The Critic as Artist* (1891)

[T]he material that painter or sculptor uses is meagre in comparison with that of words. Words have not merely music as sweet as that of viol and lute, colour as rich and vivid as any that makes lovely for us the canvas of the Venetian or the Spaniard, and plastic form no less sure and certain than that which reveals itself in marble or in bronze, but thought and passion and spirituality are theirs also, are theirs indeed alone.

de Quincey, *Confessions of an English Opium-Eater* (preface to revised edition) (1862)

I desire to remind him of the perilous difficulty besieging all attempts to clothe in words the visionary scenes derived from the world of dreams, where a single false note, a single word in a wrong key, ruins the whole music....

Boswell, *Life of Johnson* (1791)

Mrs. Kennicot related, in his presence, a lively saying of Dr. Johnson to Miss Hannah More, who had expressed a wonder that the poet who had written Paradise Lost, should write such poor sonnets: – "Milton, Madam, was a genius that could cut a Colossus from a rock; but could not carve heads upon cherry-stones."

Chapter Six

HUMAN BIOLOGY

We turn to human biology, a subpart of nature that requires its own attention. The usual function of the body when used in a comparison is to make visible, and often to simplify, abstractions or inner states. We also will look briefly here at some related applications: medical treatment, parts of the body, etc.

1. *Vices; the inner and outer self compared.* The physical self may be used figuratively to illustrate aspects of the inner self; invisible features of character can be made visible or more tangible by comparison to externals. A popular tradition of this kind compares a vice to a disease of the flesh. Such figurative comparisons are especially inviting because they draw upon parallels that feel nearly literal. Invisible habit and visible illness may progress alike; one may cause the other; the first-hand experience of each can feel similar.

> It is with jealousy as with the gout; when such distempers are in the blood there is never any security against their breaking out, and that often on the slightest occasions, and when least suspected.

Fielding, *Tom Jones* (1749)

> The effect of power and publicity on all men is the aggravation of self, a sort of tumor that ends by killing the victim's sympathies; a diseased appetite, like a passion for drink or perverted tastes; one can scarcely use expressions too strong to describe the violence of egotism it stimulates; and Thurlow Weed was one of the exceptions; a rare immune.

The Education of Henry Adams (1918)

Emerson, *Spiritual Laws* (1841)

Our young people are diseased with the theological problems of original sin, origin of evil, predestination and the like. These never presented a practical difficulty to any man, – never darkened across any man's road who did not go out of his way to seek them. These are the soul's mumps and measles and whooping-coughs, and those who have not caught them cannot describe their health or prescribe the cure.

Extensions to infection, which provides a good source of comparison to the spread of psychological ills among people:

Bacon, *Of Envy* (1625)

[A]s infection spreadeth upon that which is sound, and tainteth it; so when envy is gotten once into a state, it traduceth even the best actions thereof, and turneth them into an ill odor.

Fielding, *An Inquiry Into the Causes of the Late Increase of Robbers* (1751)

I am not here to satirise the great, among whom luxury is probably rather a moral than a political evil. But vices no more than diseases will stop with them; for bad habits are as infectious by example as the plague itself by contact. In free countries, at least, it is a branch of liberty claimed by the people to be as wicked and as profligate as their superiors.

Dickens, *Little Dorrit* (1857)

That it is at least as difficult to stay a moral infection as a physical one; that such a disease will spread with the malignity and rapidity of the Plague; that the contagion, when it has once made head, will spare no pursuit or condition, but will lay hold on people in the soundest health, and become developed in the most unlikely constitutions: is a fact as firmly established by experience as that we human creatures breathe an atmosphere.

Snobbishness has, like drink, a kind of grand poetry. And snobbishness has this peculiar and devilish quality of evil, that it is rampant among very kindly people, with open hearts and houses. But it is our great English vice; to be watched more fiercely than small-pox.

Chesterton, *Some Policemen and a Moral* (1910)

Or the comparison may be taken in a different direction – to recovery, and the application of medical correctives.

The wounds of the conscience, like those of the body, cannot be well cured till they are searched to the bottom; and they cannot be searched without pain.

John Mason, *A Treatise on Self-Knowledge* (1745)

As a conquered rebellion strengthens a government, or as health is more perfectly established by recovery from some diseases; so anger, when removed, often gives new life to affection.

Fielding, *Tom Jones* (1749)

Many believers have described the terrible agony with which they had at one period of their lives listened to the first whisperings of scepticism.... When the disease has been driven inward by throwing in abundant doses of Paley, Butler, with perhaps an oblique reference to preferment and respectability, it continues to give many severe twinges, and perhaps it may permanently injure the constitution. But, if it has been allowed to run its natural course, and the sufferer has resolutely rejected every remedy except fair and honest argument, I think that the recovery is generally cheering.

Leslie Stephen, *An Apology for Plainspeaking* (1873)

It seemed to me that all the main representatives of the middle class had gone off in one direction or in the other; they had either set out in pursuit of the Smart Set or they had set out in pursuit of the Simple Life. I cannot say which I dislike more

Chesterton, *A Glimpse of My Country* (1910)

myself; the people in question are welcome to have either of them, or, as is more likely, to have both, in hideous alternations of disease and cure.

Cf.:

Hamlet, 4, 1

CLAUDIUS. ...It will be laid to us, whose providence
Should have kept short, restrain'd and out of haunt,
This mad young man: but so much was our love,
We would not understand what was most fit;
But, like the owner of a foul disease,
To keep it from divulging, let it feed
Even on the pith of life.

The administration of medicine has most productively been invoked for its unpleasant but sometimes necessary character.

Eliot, *Middlemarch* (1872)

When he had something painful to tell, it was usually his way to introduce it among a number of disjointed particulars, as if it were a medicine that would get a milder flavor by mixing.

Melville, *Pierre* (1852)

[T]he soul of man, thus surrounded, can not, and does never intelligently confront the totality of its wretchedness. The bitter drug is divided into separate draughts for him: to-day he takes one part of his woe; to-morrow he takes more; and so on, till the last drop is drunk.

Trollope, *North America* (1862)

Such and such like are the incidents which make an Englishman in the States unhappy, and rouse his gall against the institutions of the country; these things and the continued appliance of the irritating ointment of American braggadocio with which his sores are kept open.

Pernicious ideas also can be compared to disease, with small doses of them likened to assimilation or inoculation.

The disproportions of absurdity grow less and less visible, as we are reconciled by degrees to the deformity of a mistress; and falsehood by long use is assimilated to the mind, as poison to the body.

Johnson, *The Rambler* no. 95 (1751)

[I]t is evident that Christianity, however degraded and distorted by cruelty and intolerance, must always exert a modifying influence on men's passions, and protect them from the more violent forms of fanatical fever, as we are protected from smallpox by vaccination.

Churchill, *The Story of the Malakand Field Force* (1898

When the doctors inoculate you and the homeopathists dose you, they give you an infinitesimally attenuated dose. If they gave you the virus at full strength it would overcome your resistance and produce its direct effect. The doses of false doctrine given at public schools and universities are so big that they overwhelm the resistance that a tiny dose would provoke. The normal student is corrupted beyond redemption, and will drive the genius who resists out of the country if he can.

Shaw, *Back to Methuselah* (preface) (1921)

Before closing this section, we ought not overlook simpler uses of disease and dysfunction just for the sake of deprecation and abuse.

LEAR. ...But yet thou art my flesh, my blood,
    my daughter;
Or rather a disease that's in my flesh,
Which I must needs call mine. Thou art a boil,
A plague sore, an embossed carbuncle
In my corrupted blood.

King Lear, 2, 4

He was, in fact, precisely the ideal Englishman of our modern theory; and precisely for that reason all the real Englishmen loathed him like leprosy.

Chesterton, *Heretics* (1905)

These usages may be mixed to lively effect with other unappealing source material.

Emerson, *Swedenborg; Or, the Mystic* (1850)

He was painfully alive to the difference between knowing and doing, and this sensibility is incessantly expressed. Philosophers are, therefore, vipers, cockatrices, asps, hemorrhoids, presters, and flying serpents; literary men are conjurers and charlatans.

2. *Nations; political institutions.* The interdependent workings of the physical self make the body and its life cycle useful as a microcosm of other systems, such as political institutions or social assemblies. Thus some rhetorical uses of disease to describe ailments of a nation:

Hobbes, *Leviathan* (1651)

Another infirmity of a Commonwealth is the immoderate greatness of a town, when it is able to furnish out of its own circuit the number and expense of a great army; as also the great number of corporations, which are as it were many lesser Commonwealths in the bowels of a greater, like worms in the entrails of a natural man.

Dickinson, *Fabius III* (1788)

Another comparison has been made by the learned, between a natural and a political body; and no wonder indeed, when the title of the latter was borrowed from the resemblance. It has therefore been justly observed, that if a mortification takes place in one or some of the limbs, and the rest of the body is sound, remedies may be applied, and not only the contagion prevented from spreading, but the diseased part or parts saved by the connection with the body, and restored to former usefulness. When general putrefaction prevails, death is to be expected. History, sacred and profane, tells us, that, corruption of manners sinks nations into slavery.

Sir, this alarming discontent is not the growth of a day, or of a year. If there be any symptoms by which it is possible to distinguish the chronic diseases of the body politic from its passing inflammations, all those symptoms exist in the present case. The taint has been gradually becoming more extensive and more malignant, through the whole lifetime of two generations. We have tried anodynes. We have tried cruel operations. What are we to try now?

Macaulay, speech in the House of Commons (1831)

[M]indless forgotten nonentities governed the land; sent men to the prison or the gallows for blasphemy and sedition (meaning the truth about Church and State); and sedulously stored up the social disease and corruption which explode from time to time in gigantic boils that have to be lanced by a million bayonets.

Shaw, *Back to Methuselah* (preface) (1921)

Circulatory comparisons may illustrate the flow of various things through a society: money, power, people.

Who are you, that you should fret and rage, and bite the chains of nature? Nothing worse happens to you than does to all nations who have extensive empire; and it happens in all the forms into which empire can be thrown. In large bodies the circulation of power must be less vigorous at the extremities. Nature has said it. The Turk cannot govern Egypt and Arabia and Kurdistan as he governs Thrace; nor has he the same dominion in Crimea and Algiers which he has at Brusa and Smyrna.

Burke, *Speech on Conciliation with America* (1775)

He was very sensible that all political writers upon the subject had unanimously agreed and lamented, from the beginning of Queen Elizabeth's reign down to his own time, that the current of men and money towards the metropolis, upon one frivolous errand or another, – set in so strong, – as to

Sterne, *Tristram Shandy* (1759)

become dangerous to our civil rights, – though, by the bye, – a current was not the image he took most delight in, – a distemper was here his favourite metaphor, and he would run it down into a perfect allegory, by maintaining it was identically the same in the body national as in the body natural, where the blood and spirits were driven up into the head faster than they could find their ways down; – a stoppage of circulation must ensue, which was death in both cases.

And where bodily comparisons are possible, so are comparisons to physical ailments and then to correctives – laws, wars, etc.

Pitt, speech in the House of Commons (1766)

The boroughs of this country have properly enough been called "the rotten parts" of the Constitution. I have lived in Cornwall, and, without entering into any invidious particularity, have seen enough to justify the appellation. But in my judgment, my Lords, these boroughs, corrupt as they are, must be considered as the natural infirmity of the Constitution. Like the infirmities of the body, we must bear them with patience, and submit to carry them about with us. The limb is mortified, but the amputation might be death.

James Fitzjames Stephen, *Liberty, Equality, Fraternity* (1873)

No doubt it may be necessary to legislate in such a manner as to correct the vices of society or to protect it against special dangers or diseases to which it is liable. Law in this case is analogous to surgery, and the rights and duties imposed by it might be compared to the irons which are sometimes contrived for the purpose of supporting a weak limb or keeping it in some particular position.

3. *The life cycle.* Metaphorical applications of the human life cycle are too various to sort by topic; it provides a convenient basis for comparison to a great range of

subjects that we can better tour at once. Birth in particular has been put to a wide variety of uses (on which see also the discussion of personification in chapter 12).

> IAGO. ...There are many events in the womb of time, which will be delivered.

Othello, I, 3

> A man should spend his life or, rather, does spend his life in being born. His life is his birth throes. But most men miscarry and never come to the true birth at all and some live but a very short time in a very little world and none are eternal.

Note Books of Samuel Butler (1912)

> A crowd of women eye a transcendent beauty entering a room, much as though a bird from Arabia had lighted on the window-sill. Say what you will, their jealousy – if any – is but an afterbirth to their open admiration.

Melville, *Pierre* (1852)

Old age:

> [A]n ancient and ever-altering constitution is like an old man who still wears with attached fondness clothes in the fashion of his youth: what you see of him is the same; what you do not see is wholly altered.

Bagehot, *The English Constitution* (1867)

> If one can depend on any season, it is on the chill suns of October, which, like an elderly beauty, are less capricious than spring or summer.

Walpole, letter to Rev. Cole (1771)

> An empty house is like a stray dog or a body from which life has departed. Decay sets in at once in every part of it, and what mould and wind and weather would spare, street boys commonly destroy.

Butler, *The Way of All Flesh* (1902)

Different stages of the life cycle can be used together to poignant effect, as when describing beginnings and endings of institutions or creative works.

Grattan, speech in the Irish
Parliament (1805)

The Parliament of Ireland – of that assembly I have a parental recollection. I sat by her cradle, I followed her hearse.

Macaulay, speech in the
House of Commons (1831)

And so it may be that infancy is a happier time than manhood, and manhood than old age. But God has decreed that old age shall succeed to manhood, and manhood to infancy. Even so have societies their law of growth.

Dickens, *David Copperfield*
(1850)

But fashions are like human beings. They come in, nobody knows when, why, or how; and they go out, nobody knows when, why, or how. Everything is like life, in my opinion, if you look at it in that point of view.

Swift, *A Tale of a Tub* (1704)

Books, like men their authors, have no more than one way of coming into the world, but there are ten thousand to go out of it, and return no more.

4. *Parts of the body.* As noted at the outset of this book, small and local things often are interesting to the practitioner of metaphor for what they epitomize – for whatever about them may be a prime instance of some larger or recurring principle or pattern. Many parts of the body are like this: hair, because it grows back; limbs, as the epitome of that which may be lost and not grow back; testicles, for the use Holmes makes of them at the end of this chapter, which is too fine for paraphrase. Let us have a brief tour of the physical self, reintroducing its elements as sources of metaphorical ideas.

a. *Eyes.*

Locke, *An Essay Concerning
Human Understanding* (1690)

[T]he understanding, like the eye, judging of objects only by its own sight, cannot but be pleased with what it discovers, having less regret for what has escaped it, because it is unknown.

[N]o characters can be admitted into the circulation of fame, but by occupying the place of some that must be thrust into oblivion. The eye of the mind, like that of the body, can only extend its view to new objects, by losing sight of those which are now before it.

Johnson, *The Rambler* no. 203 (1752)

I am not aware that any one has demonstrated how it is that a stronger capacity is required for the conduct of great affairs than of small ones. The organs of the mind, like the pupil of the eye, may be contracted or dilated to view a broader or a narrower surface, and yet find sufficient variety to occupy its attention in each.

Hazlitt, *On Great and Little Things* (1821)

I made a comparison ... of the mind of a bigot to the pupil of the eye; the more light you pour on it, the more it contracts.

Holmes, *The Autocrat of the Breakfast Table* (1858)

But there is something in corruption, which, like a jaundiced eye, transfers the color of itself to the object it looks upon, and sees everything stained and impure; for unless you were capable of such conduct yourselves, you would never have supposed such a character in us.

Paine, *The American Crisis* (1783)

b. *Hair.*

Good officers, that is, well-experienced ones, we shall soon have, and the navy of Great Britain cannot stop our whole trade. Our towns are but brick and stone, and mortar and wood. They, perhaps, may be destroyed. They are only the hairs of our heads. If sheared ever so close, they will grow again. We compare them not with our rights and liberties.

Dickinson, letter to Arthur Lee (1775)

[T]he Rhodesian power in Africa is only an external thing, placed upon the top like a hat; the Dutch power and tradition is a thing rooted and

Chesterton, *How I Met the President* (1910)

growing like a beard; we have shaved it, and it is growing again.

James Fitzjames Stephen,
Liberty, Equality, Fraternity
(1873)

Suppose that man is a mere passing shadow, and nothing else. What is he to say of his conscience? Surely a rational man holding such a theory of his own nature will be bound in consistency to try and to determine the question whether he ought not to prune his conscience just as he cuts his hair and nails.

c. *Teeth.*

Prov. 25:18

Confidence in an unfaithful man in time of trouble is like a broken tooth, and a foot out of joint.

Holmes, *The Professor at the Breakfast Table* (1859)

[I]t has fallen into sad decay, and the moss grows on the rotten shingles of the roof, and the clapboards have turned black, and the windows rattle like teeth that chatter with fear, and the walls of the house begin to lean as if its knees were shaking....

Chesterton, *The Wisdom of Father Brown* (1914)

[T]he left-hand corner of the room was lined with as complete a set of English classics as the right hand could show of English and foreign physiologists. But if one took a volume of Chaucer or Shelley from that rank, its absence irritated the mind like a gap in a man's front teeth.

Bagehot, *The First Edinburgh Reviewers* (1855)

Writers, like teeth, are divided into incisors and grinders; Sydney Smith was a molar: he did not run a long sharp argument into the interior of a question; he did not, in the common phrase, go deeply into it: but he kept it steadily under the contact of a strong, capable, heavy, jaw-like understanding, – pressing its surface, effacing its intricacies, grinding it down.

d. *Limbs.*

ARCHBISHOP. ...If we do now make our atonement well,
    Our peace will, like a broken limb united,
    Grow stronger for the breaking.

2 *Henry IV*, 4, 1

[A] disordered mind, like a broken limb, will recover its strength by the sole benefit of being out of use, and lying without motion.

Steele, *The Tatler* no. 174 (1710)

The temper of a child, misled by vice or mistake, like a dislocated bone, is easy to be reduced into its place, if taken in time; but if suffered to remain in its dislocated position, a callous substance fills up the empty space, and, by neglect, grows equally hard with the bone, and resisting the power of the surgeon's skill, renders the reduction of the joint impossible.

Defoe, *The Family Instructor* (1715)

We hear sometimes of an action for damages against the unqualified medical practitioner, who has deformed a broken limb in pretending to heal it. But, what of the hundreds of thousands of minds that have been deformed forever by the incapable pettifoggers who have pretended to form them!

Dickens, *Nicholas Nickleby* (1839)

The amputation of limbs has been put to specialized uses of its own.

In herself she regarded this passion of hers as a healthy man regards the loss of a leg or an arm. It is a great nuisance, a loss that maims the whole life, a misfortune to be much regretted. But because a leg is gone, everything is not gone. A man with a wooden leg may stump about through much action, and may enjoy the keenest pleasures of humanity. He has his eyes left to him, and his ears, and his intellect. He will not break his heart for the loss of that leg. And so it was with Lucy

Trollope, *The Eustace Diamonds* (1873)

Morris.... She had given away her heart, and yet she would do without a lover.

Hardy, *Jude the Obscure* (1895)

[I]t is said that what a woman shrinks from – in the early days of her marriage – she shakes down to with comfortable indifference in half a dozen years. But that is much like saying that the amputation of a limb is no affliction, since a person gets comfortably accustomed to the use of a wooden leg or arm in the course of time!

James Fitzjames Stephen, *Liberty, Equality, Fraternity* (1873)

The death of a friend admits of no consolation at all. Its sting to the survivors lies in the hopeless separation which it produces, and in the destruction of a world of common interests, feelings, and recollections which nothing can replace. The amount of suffering which it inflicts depends on the temperament of the survivors, but it impoverishes them more or less for the rest of their lives, like the loss of a limb or a sense.

e. *The stomach and palate; digestion.*

Locke, *An Essay Concerning Human Understanding* (1690

The mind has a different relish, as well as the palate; and you will as fruitlessly endeavor to delight all men with riches or glory (which yet some men place their happiness in), as you would to satisfy all men's hunger with cheese or lobsters; which, though very agreeable and delicious fare to some, are to others extremely nauseous and offensive; and many people would, with reason, prefer the griping of an hungry belly, to those dishes which are a feast to others.

Pope, letter to Henry Cromwell (1710)

You see 'tis with weak heads as with weak stomachs, they immediately throw out what they received last; and what they read floats upon the surface of their mind, like oil upon water, without incorporating.

Mr. Southey has not fortitude of mind, has not patience to think that evil is inseparable from the nature of things. His irritable sense rejects the alternative altogether, as a weak stomach rejects the food that is distasteful to it.

Hazlitt, *Mr. Southey* (1825)

I wish I could learn to remember that it is unjust and dishonorable to put blame upon the human race for any of its acts. For it did not make itself... it has no more mastership nor authority over its mind than it has over its stomach, which receives material from the outside and does as it pleases with it, indifferent to its proprietor's suggestions, even, let alone his commands; wherefore, whatever the machine does – so called crimes and infamies included – is the personal act of its Maker, and He, solely, is responsible.

Twain, letter to R.H. Twichell (1904)

f. *Miscellaneous.*

He entered upon a curious discussion of the difference between intuition and sagacity; one being immediate in its effect, the other requiring a circuitous process; one he observed was the eye of the mind, the other the *nose* of the mind.

Boswell, *Life of Johnson* (1791)

However useful jealousy may be in republics, yet when like bile in the natural, it abounds too much in the body politic, the eyes of both become very liable to be deceived by the delusive appearances which that malady casts on surrounding objects.

Jay, Federalist 64 (1788)

I have a little case – whether it will go or not I don't know. As originally written it had a tiny pair of testicles – but the scruples of my brethren have caused their removal and it sings in a very soft voice now.

Holmes, Jr., letter to Felix Frankfurter (1920)

Chapter Seven

EXTREME PEOPLE & STATES

We have spent several chapters looking at metaphorical uses of nature, almost all of which gave visible form to something invisible in itself. The next few chapters turn to a different type of source material: human behavior. This family of comparisons is invoked less commonly for the sake of visibility (though we will see that usage from time to time) and more often to simplify and caricature some similar feature of the subject. We observed in the chapter on animals that a metaphor can make a human quality more vivid by comparing it to a case where it exists in more pure or exaggerated form. Some types of people, and some of the situations they inhabit, are rhetorically valuable in the same general way. They lie at the margins of conventional experience, and so display familiar human attributes in extreme or simplified form.

1. *Youth.* Childhood may serve a function analogous to some strands of mythology; the attitudes and behaviors of children are purer, simpler, or more primitive versions of what appears with more complexity in adult life. Thus parallels between the psychology of the adult and a child's fear:

Bacon, *Of Death* (1625)

Men fear death, as children fear to go in the dark; and as that natural fear in children, is increased with tales, so is the other.

Fielding, *Tom Jones* (1749)

The censures of mankind will pursue the wretch, their scorn will abash him in public; and if shame drives him into retirement, he will go to it with all those terrors with which a weary child, who is afraid of hobgoblins, retreats from company to go to bed alone.

The child and its fears are caricatures of the fears of the ordinary adult. The comparisons also simplify their subjects and make them more familiar.

Similarly, the thinking of young people can epitomize a shortage of perspective.

> I do not know what I may appear to the world, but to myself I seem to have been only like a boy playing on the sea-shore, and diverting myself in now and then finding a smoother pebble or a prettier shell than ordinary, whilst the great ocean of truth lay all undiscovered before me.

Newton, at the end of his life (c.1727)

> The men to whom we owe it that we have a House of Commons are sneered at because they did not suffer the debates of the House to be published. The authors of the Toleration Act are treated as bigots, because they did not go the whole length of Catholic Emancipation. Just so we have heard a baby, mounted on the shoulders of its father, cry out, "How much taller I am than Papa!"

Macaulay, *Sir James Mackintosh* (1835)

Likewise the misjudgments of older children:

> [J]ust as a boy who has not known much of women is apt too easily to take a woman for the woman, so these practical men, unaccustomed to causes, are always inclined to think that if a thing is proved to be an ideal it is proved to be the ideal.

Chesterton, *Heretics* (1905)

> Hence it is, that although they are the very best of sea-going craft, and built in the best possible manner, and with the very best materials, yet, a few years of scudding before the wind, as they do, seriously impairs their constitutions – like robust young men, who live too fast in their teens – and they are soon sold out for a song....

Melville, *Redburn* (1849)

To epitomize impatience, irresponsibility, foolishness, etc.:

Note Books of Samuel Butler
(1912)

In the eternal pendulum swing of thought we make God in our own image, and then make him make us, and then find it out and cry because we have no God and so on, over and over again as a child has new toys given to it, tires of them, breaks them and is disconsolate till it gets new ones which it will again tire of and break.

Anne Brontë, *Agnes Grey*
(1847)

It might have pleased him, too, in some degree, to have seen how dull and dissatisfied she was throughout that week (the greater part of it, at least), for lack of her usual source of excitement; and how often she regretted having "used him up so soon," like a child that, having devoured its plumcake too hastily, sits sucking its fingers, and vainly lamenting its greediness.

Thoreau, *On the Duty of Civil Disobedience* (1849)

As they could not reach me, they had resolved to punish my body; just as boys, if they cannot come at some person against whom they have a spite, will abuse his dog.

To illustrate vulnerability to self-inflicted trouble:

Kingsley, *Two Years Ago* (1857)

I found out that I had been trying for years which was the stronger, God or I; I found out I had been trying whether I could not do well enough without Him: and there I found that I could not, Grace; – could not! I felt like a child who had marched off from home, fancying it can find its way, and is lost at once.

William James, *Pragmatism*
(1907)

[O]ne may even fear that the being of man may be crushed by his own powers, that his fixed nature as an organism may not prove adequate to stand the strain of the ever increasingly tremendous functions, almost divine creative functions, which his intellect will more and more enable him to wield. He may drown in his wealth like a child in a bath-tub, who has turned on the water and who cannot turn it off.

2. *Savagery.* Relative to the ordinary adult, the "savage," however anachronistic the word and concept, has stood in a position partly analogous to that of the child. In the literary imagination, the absence of civilization, like the absence of maturity, causes primitive people to display attributes in simpler and more extreme form than is found in the conventional human subject.

> Here are children of tender age talked to as if they were capable of understanding Calvin's "Institutes," and nobody has honesty or sense enough to tell the plain truth about the little wretches: that they are as superstitious as naked savages....

Holmes, *The Autocrat of the Breakfast Table* (1858)

But the naïveté and primitivism of the savage, at least by reputation, differ from that of the child in respects that lend them to different uses.

> Give these people the most perfect political constitution and the soundest political program that benevolent omniscience can devise for them, and they will interpret it into mere fashionable folly or canting charity as infallibly as a savage converts the philosophical theology of a Scotch missionary into crude African idolatry.

Shaw, *Man and Superman* (1903)

> You've got that mirror, your own fixed will, your immortal understanding, your own tight conscious world, and there is nothing beyond it. There, in the mirror, you must have everything. But now you have come to all your conclusions, you want to go back and be like a savage, without knowledge. You want a life of pure sensation and "passion."

Lawrence, *Women in Love* (1920)

> Those are terrible conjunctures, when the discontents of a nation, not light and capricious discontents, but discontents which have been steadily

Macaulay, *Sir William Temple* (1838)

increasing during a long series of years, have attained their full maturity. The discerning few predict the approach of these conjunctures, but predict in vain. To the many, the evil season comes as a total eclipse of the sun at noon comes to a people of savages.

The reaction to the civilized world:

Melville, *The Encantadas* (1856)

We had been broad upon the waters for five long months, a period amply sufficient to make all things of the land wear a fabulous hue to the dreamy mind. Had three Spanish custom-house officers boarded us then it is not unlikely that I should have curiously stared at them, felt of them, and stroked them, much as savages serve civilized guests.

Darwin, *On the Origin of Species* (1859)

When we no longer look at an organic being as a savage looks at a ship, as at something wholly beyond his comprehension ... how far more interesting, I speak from experience, will the study of natural history become!

Thoreau, *Walden* (1854)

I have no doubt that it is a part of the destiny of the human race, in its gradual improvement, to leave off eating animals, as surely as the savage tribes have left off eating each other when they came in contact with the more civilized.

3. *Physical disability.* Blind people provide useful sources of comparison because they labor in literal form under a limitation from which everyone suffers to some figurative extent. If the blind did not exist, the Greeks might have invented them alongside Sisyphus and Tantalus as characters who externally manifest familiar interior problems.

Isa. 59:10

We grope for the wall like the blind, and we grope as if we had no eyes: we stumble at noon day as in the night; we are in desolate places as dead men.

Thus, in a prolix, gently-growling, foolish way, did Plornish turn the tangled skein of his estate about and about, like a blind man who was trying to find some beginning or end to it; until they reached the prison gate.

Dickens, *Little Dorrit* (1857)

To treat of the effects of love to you, must be as absurd as to discourse on colours to a man born blind; since possibly your idea of love may be as absurd as that which we are told such blind man once entertained of the colour scarlet; that colour seemed to him to be very much like the sound of a trumpet: and love probably may, in your opinion, very greatly resemble a dish of soup, or a sirloin of roast-beef.

Fielding, *Tom Jones* (1749)

The inability to see color provides a kindred source of comparison.

[T]he more she saw of him, the surer she was that his courage was mere moral paralysis, and that he talked about virtue and vice as a man who is colour-blind talks about red and green; he did not see them as she saw them; if left to choose for himself he would have nothing to guide him.

Adams, *Democracy* (1880)

These two had lived in much friendship and agreement under the tyranny of their brother Peter, as it is the talent of fellow-sufferers to do, men in misfortune being like men in the dark, to whom all colours are the same.

Swift, *A Tale of a Tub* (1704)

Deafness may serve a similar purpose.

So is there many a one among us, yes, and some who think themselves philosophers too, to whom the philosophic organ is entirely wanting. To such a man philosophy is a mere play of words and notions, like a theory of music to the deaf, or like the geometry of light to the blind. The connection

Coleridge, *Biographia Literaria* (1817)

of the parts and their logical dependencies may be seen and remembered; but the whole is groundless and hollow, unsustained by living contact. . . .

Hardy, *Jude the Obscure* (1895)

"If two and two made four when we were happy together, surely they make four now? I can't understand it, I repeat!"

"Ah, dear Jude; that's because you are like a totally deaf man observing people listening to music. You say 'What are they regarding? Nothing is there.' But something is."

Defoe, *Further Adventures of Robinson Crusoe* (1719)

[A]ll the pleasant, innocent amusements of my farm, my garden, my cattle, and my family, which before entirely possessed me, were nothing to me, had no relish, and were like music to one that has no ear, or food to one that has no taste.

4. *Insanity*. Mental disability is likewise an extreme and sometimes more literal version of symptoms and tendencies found at large in human experience. In the vocabulary of rhetoric, the insane can represent unreasoned certainty as well as the absence of self-government; some of their kinships for comparative purposes are suggested by the first illustration here from de Quincey.

de Quincey, *A Brief Appraisal of the Greek Literature in its Foremost Pretensions* (1838)

[U]nfortunately, in the Athenian audience, the ignorance, the headstrong violence of prejudice, the arrogance, and, above all, the levity of the national mind – presented, to an orator the most favourite, a scene like that of an ocean always rocking with storms; like a wasp always angry; like a lunatic, always coming out of a passion or preparing to go into one.

Wells, *First and Last Things* (1908)

Reasonable fear is a sound reason for abstinence, as when a man has a passion like a lightly sleeping maniac that the slightest indulgence will arouse.

There are two classes of disputants most frequently to be met with among us. The first is of
young students just entered the threshold of science, with a first view of its outlines, not yet filled
up with the details and modifications which a further progress would bring to their knowledge.
The other consists of the ill-tempered and rude
men in society who have taken up a passion for
politics.... From both of these classes of disputants, my dear Jefferson, keep aloof, as you would
from the infected subjects of yellow fever or pestilence. Consider yourself, when with them, as
among the patients of Bedlam needing medical
more than moral counsel.

Jefferson, letter to his
grandson (1808)

5. *Intoxication.* Those who drink can be viewed as caricatures of the sober.

Young men are as apt to think themselves·wise
enough, as drunken men are to think themselves
sober enough.

Chesterfield, letter to his son
(1753)

Like men in a state of intoxication, you forget that
the rest of the world have eyes, and that the same
stupidity which conceals you from yourselves
exposes you to their satire and contempt.

Paine, *The American Crisis*
(1783)

Watch against anger; neither speak of it nor act in
it; for like drunkenness, it makes a man a beast,
and throws people into desperate inconveniences.

Penn, letter to his wife and
children (1682)

If what he said was the mere result of a temporary
excitement; if his sentiments were but the steam
of drunkenness and the vapour of debauch; if his
foul and nauseous opinions rose out of his mind
like the reekings of a drunkard's brow, I should
allow them to disperse and pass away. They should
be permitted to dissipate like the stench of revelry
which, after a night's debauch, it is sufficient to
open a window to let out.

Sheil, speech at an aggregate
meeting (1826)

Drink and opiates also produce their own distinctive byproducts that can serve as fodder for comparison. There is, first, the transition – that is, the entry into intoxication and return from it, which has no equivalent when speaking of madness or savagery.

Emerson, *Prudence* (1841)

[The scholar] resembles the pitiful drivellers whom travelers describe as frequenting the bazaars of Constantinople, who skulk about all day, yellow, emaciated, ragged, sneaking; and at evening, when the bazaars are open, slink to the opium-shop, swallow their morsel and become tranquil and glorified seers.

Poe, *The Fall of the House of Usher* (1839)

I looked upon the scene before me – upon the mere house, and the simple landscape features of the domain – upon the bleak walls – upon the vacant eye-like windows – upon a few rank sedges – and upon a few white trunks of decayed trees – with an utter depression of soul which I can compare to no earthly sensation more properly than to the after-dream of the reveler upon opium – the bitter lapse into everyday life – the hideous dropping off of the veil.

Addiction and tolerance also have their analogues, both in people and in nations.

Burke, *A Vindication of Natural Society* (1756)

When I confess that I think this notion a mistake, I know to whom I am speaking, for I am satisfied that reasons are like liquors, and there are some of such a nature as none but strong heads can bear. There are few with whom I can communicate so freely as with Pope. But Pope cannot bear every truth.

Trollope, *He Knew He Was Right* (1869)

"If you are not overwhelmed now," said Miss Spalding, "you must be so used to flattery, that it has no longer any effect upon you. You must be like a drunkard, to whom wine is as water, and who thinks that brandy is not strong enough."

Ideas are dangerous, but the man to whom they are most dangerous is the man of no ideas. The man of no ideas will find the first idea fly to his head like wine to the head of a teetotaller.

Chesterton, *Heretics* (1905)

Chapter Eight

OCCUPATIONS & INSTITUTIONS

When one wants to describe human behavior, the most common source of comparative material is found in other human behavior. Typically the behavior described is specific and less striking by itself; the behavior borrowed – the source of the comparison – is familiar to the imagination and more extreme, and serves as a caricature of the subject. We saw examples in the previous chapter in which the source of the comparison was a distinctive sort of person from the edges of ordinary humanity: a child or a lunatic or a drunk, each of whom might be considered a caricature of the ordinary man or woman. The same idea may be extended to cases in which the extremity lies not in the inherent limitations or inner condition of the people borrowed – not in their lunacy or drunkenness – but in what the people in the comparisons *do*: their occupations.

Chesterton, *Tolstoy and the Cult of Simplicity* (1903)

Thousands of modern men move quietly and conventionally among their fellows while holding views of national limitation or landed property that would have made Voltaire shudder like a nun listening to blasphemies.

Nuns stand about as far from conventional experience as drunks, at least when put to use in a simile. (Let us not confuse that usage with reality; we won't pause to consider whether nuns shudder at blasphemies in fact.) They therefore make valuable points of reference for comparisons meant to exaggerate. Many other occupations have features that make them distinctive in analogous ways. Thus lawyers or doctors may not amount to types as extreme as nuns in the popular imagination, but aspects of their work likewise epitomize elements of human experience and so provide grist for metaphor.

In this chapter we also will consider a related type of source material: institutions, such as kingdoms or other governments, that can give comparative form to subjects more modest in scale.

1. *Lawyers.* As the unhappy epitomizers of insincerity and related unsavory qualities:

> I hear a preacher announce for his text and topic the expediency of one of the institutions of his church. Do I not know that he is pledged to himself not to look but at one side, the permitted side, not as a man, but as a parish minister? He is a retained attorney, and these airs of the bench are the emptiest affectation.

Emerson, *Self-Reliance* (1841)

> He was not a thinker, for he was never in doubt. He had recourse to disputation as a means of inculcating truth, but he used it like a lawyer arguing a case. His conclusions are fixed from the start.

Chapman, *Robert Browning* (1898)

> He admits himself that it was at the special request of the compiler of the Calendar that he wrote the preface at all, and though he courteously adds that the task is agreeable to him, still he shows only too clearly that he considers it a task and, like a clever lawyer or a popular clergyman, tries to atone for his lack of sincerity by a pleasing over-emphasis.

Wilde, *A New Calendar* (1887)

> I don't think the fellows that write such criticisms as you tell me of want to correct your faults. I don't mean to say that you can learn nothing from them, because they are not all fools by any means, and they will often pick out your weak points with a malignant sagacity, as a pettifogging

Holmes, *The Poet at the Breakfast-Table* (1872)

lawyer will frequently find a real flaw in trying to get at everything he can quibble about.

Dryden, *The Wild Gallant* (1663)

Oh, the devil's the spirit, and the parson's the flesh; and betwixt those two there must be a war; yet, to do them both right, I think in my conscience they quarrel only like lawyers for their fees, and meet good friends in private, to laugh at their clients.

Cf.:

Southey, *Sir Thomas More: Or, Colloquies on the Progress and Prospects of Society* (1824)

To understand the principles of criticism is one thing; to be what is called critical, is another; the first is like being versed in jurisprudence, the other like being litigious.

The following cases qualify for inclusion under the current heading as well: the lawyerly style of reasoning and speech.

Macaulay, *Samuel Johnson* (1831)

Johnson decided literary questions like a lawyer, not like a legislator. He never examined foundations where a point was already ruled. His whole code of criticism rested on pure assumption, for which he sometimes quoted a precedent or an authority, but rarely troubled himself to give a reason drawn from the nature of things.

Dickens, *Great Expectations* (1861)

"Which I say, Sir," replied Joe, with an air of legal formality, as if he were making his will, "Miss A., or otherways Havisham."

Dickens, *Our Mutual Friend* (1865)

"The milkman said he knew of two young ladies of the highest respectability who were in search of a suitable establishment, and he took a card," interposed Mrs Wilfer, with severe monotony, as if she were reading an Act of Parliament aloud. "Tell your father whether it was last Monday, Bella."

This is also a fitting place to note the value of legal instruments and relations as sources of comparison.

She was, indeed, well convinced that Sophia possessed the first place in Jones's affections; and yet, haughty and amorous as this lady was, she submitted at last to bear the second place; or, to express it more properly in a legal phrase, was contented with the possession of that of which another woman had the reversion.

Fielding, *Tom Jones* (1749)

To suppose that Christian morals can ever survive the downfall of the great Christian doctrine of a future state of rewards and punishments is as absurd as to suppose that a yearly tenant will feel towards his property like a tenant in fee simple.

James Fitzjames Stephen, *Liberty, Equality, Fraternity* (1873)

In conveyancing the ultimately potent thing is not the deed but the invisible intention and desire of the parties to the deed; the written document itself is only evidence of this intention and desire. So it is with music, the written notes are not the main thing, nor is even the heard performance; these are only evidences of an internal invisible emotion that can be felt but never fully expressed. And so it is with the words of literature and with the forms and colours of painting.

Note Books of Samuel Butler (1912)

2. *Doctors*, as the epitomizers of professional and unfeeling disinterest with respect to the agonies of others.

He only said – "We will wait a few minutes, Jane, till you are more composed." And while I smothered the paroxysm with all haste, he sat calm and patient, leaning on his desk, and looking like a physician watching with the eye of science an expected and fully understood crisis in a patient's malady.

Charlotte Brontë, *Jane Eyre* (1847)

BOSWELL. "It is easy for you, Mr. Garrick, to talk to an author as you talked to Elphinston; you, who have been so long the manager of a theatre, rejecting the plays of poor authors. You are an old Judge,

Boswell, *Life of Johnson* (1791)

who have often pronounced sentence of death. You are a practiced surgeon, who have often amputated limbs; and though this may have been for the good of your patients, they cannot like you."

The practice of medicine on oneself provides a basis for comparisons to other self-referential performances, or the aversion to them.

Sheil, speech in the House of Commons (1837)

Who is there that shows less mercy to a political adversary? Who is so relentless in the infliction of his sarcasms, even on his old friends and associates? However, I ought not to feel much surprise that he should be so sensitive as he shows himself to be: no man fears an operation so much as a surgeon, and the drummer of a regiment trembles at the lash.

Dickens, *The Old Curiosity Shop* (1841)

[A]s Doctors seldom take their own prescriptions, and Divines do not always practise what they preach, so lawyers are shy of meddling with the Law on their own account: knowing it to be an edged tool of uncertain application, very expensive in the working, and rather remarkable for its properties of close shaving, than for its always shaving the right person.

Cf.:

Chesterfield, letter to his son (1751)

People in high life are hardened to the wants and distresses of mankind, as surgeons are to their bodily pains; they see and hear of them all day long, and even of so many simulated ones, that they do not know which are real, and which not.

The useless doctor, or the doctor who does harm, is a rhetorically useful character:

Paine, *The American Crisis* (1783)

New schemes, like new medicines, have administered fresh hopes, and prolonged the disease instead of curing it. A change of generals, like a change of physicians, served only to keep the flattery alive, and furnish new pretences for new extravagance.

It was long before William the Testy could be persuaded that his much-vaunted war measure was ineffectual; on the contrary, he flew in a passion whenever it was doubted, swearing that though slow in operating, yet when it once began to work it would soon purge the land of those invaders. When convinced at length of the truth, like a shrewd physician, he attributed the failure to the quantity, not the quality of the medicine, and resolved to double the dose.

Irving, *Knickerbocker's History of New York* (1809)

Yes, you are his sure victim: yet his work is not all to your hurt – only part of it; for he is like your family physician, who comes and cures the mumps, and leaves the scarlet-fever behind. If your man is a Lake-Borgne-relief theorist, for instance, he will exhale a cloud of deadly facts and statistics which will lay you out with that disease, sure; but at the same time he will cure you of any other of the five theories that may have previously got into your system.

Twain, *Life on the Mississippi* (1883)

A medical comparison for the sake of rejecting it:

This is the arresting and dominant fact about modern social discussion; that the quarrel is not merely about the difficulties, but about the aim.... The social case is exactly the opposite of the medical case. We do not disagree, like doctors, about the precise nature of the illness, while agreeing about the nature of health. On the contrary, we all agree that England is unhealthy, but half of us would not look at her in what the other half would call blooming health.

Chesterton, *The Medical Mistake* (1910)

3. *Painters*, and their habits of eye, can attractively illustrate the need for perspective elsewhere and ways to obtain it.

Stevenson, *Cockermouth and Keswick* (1871)

Very much as a painter half closes his eyes so that some salient unity may disengage itself from among the crowd of details, and what he sees may thus form itself into a whole; very much on the same principle, I may say, I allow a considerable lapse of time to intervene between any of my little journeyings and the attempt to chronicle them.

Chesterton, *The Man on Top* (1912)

To judge about success or failure one must see things very simply; one must see them in masses, as the artist, half closing his eyes against details, sees light and shade. That is the only way in which a just judgment can be formed as to whether any departure or development, such as Islam or the American Republic, has been a benefit upon the whole.

Johnson, *Preface to Shakespeare* (1765)

[Shakespeare's] adherence to general nature has exposed him to the censure of critics, who form their judgments upon narrower principles. Dennis and Rymer think his Romans not sufficiently Roman, and Voltaire censures his kings as not completely royal.... These are the petty cavils of petty minds; a poet overlooks the casual distinction of country and condition, as a painter, satisfied with the figure, neglects the drapery.

Compare:

Holmes, Jr., letter to Harold Laski (1917)

His and Wells's remarks led me to get Joyce, Portrait of the Artist as a Young Man, of which I have read a part. Certainly a singular picture – on the whole not carrying me away – but worth reading. Many pages are impressionist blots – you have to stand two rooms off to see the solid intended.

4. *Soldiers*. The easy applications involve the soldier's discipline and sense of duty, which are proverbial.

> A parson is like a doctor, my boy: he must face infection as a soldier must face bullets.

Shaw, *Candida* (1898)

> This summons Kant invariably obeyed without one moment's delay, as a soldier does the word of command – never, under any circumstances, allowing himself a respite, not even under the rare accident of having passed a sleepless night.

de Quincey, *The Last Days of Immanuel Kant* (1827)

> He has become a robber by profession; but like a soldier, when not in action, he can lay aside his weapon and his fierceness, and become like other men.

Irving, *Tales of a Traveller* (1824)

The more interesting cases find what is picturesque and prime in some more specific circumstance of the soldier.

> The workman of the new generation is full of distrust, the most demoralising of social influences.... He is like a private soldier obsessed with the idea that nothing can save the situation but the death of an incompetent officer. His distrust is so profound that he ceases not only to believe in the employer, but he ceases to believe in the law....

Wells, *An Englishman Looks at the World* (1914)

> This is the time that, owing to the relaxed discipline of the ship, old and almost forgotten quarrels are revived, under the stimulus of drink; and, fencing themselves up between the guns – so as to be sure of a clear space with at least three walls – the combatants, two and two, fight out their hate, cribbed and cabined like soldiers duelling in a sentry-box.

Melville, *White-Jacket* (1850)

> [T]he difference between the ideal shepherd who danced with Amaryllis and the real shepherd who thrashed her is not a scrap greater than the

Chesterton, *A Defence of China Shepherdesses* (1901)

difference between the ideal soldier who dies to capture the colours and the real soldier who lives to clean his accoutrements, between the ideal priest who is everlastingly by someone's bed and the real priest who is as glad as anyone else to get to his own. There are ideal conceptions and real men in every calling; yet there are few who object to the ideal conceptions, and not many, after all, who object to the real men.

5. *Police and watchmen* – to epitomize the deliverers of order and help, for better or worse:

Burke, *Thoughts on the Cause of the Present Discontents* (1770)

If the wealth of the nation be the cause of its turbulence, I imagine it is not proposed to introduce poverty, as a constable to keep the peace.

Dickens, *The Life and Adventures of Martin Chuzzlewit* (1844)

This mystery and loneliness engendered fancies in Tom's mind, the folly of which his common sense could readily discover, but which his common sense was quite unable to keep away, notwithstanding; that quality being with most of us, in such a case, like the old French Police – quick at detection, but very weak as a preventive power.

Holmes, *Border Lines of Knowledge in Some Provinces of Medical Science* (1861)

Arsenic-eating may seem to improve the condition of horses for a time, – and even of human beings, if Tschudi's stories can be trusted, – but it soon appears that its alien qualities are at war with the animal organization. So of copper, antimony, and other non-alimentary simple substances; every one of them is an intruder in the living system, as much as a constable would be, quartered in our household.

More elaborate applications can enlarge the cast of characters.

Emerson, *Montaigne; Or, The Skeptic* (1850)

I mean to use the occasion, and celebrate the calendar-day of our Saint Michel de Montaigne,

by counting and describing these doubts or nega-
tions. I wish to ferret them out of their holes, and
sun them a little. We must do with them as the
police do with old rogues, who are shown up to
the public at the marshal's office. They will never
be so formidable, when once they have been identified and registered.

The watchman making the rounds is a source that may
be obsolete – but was probably obsolete already, yet not
without charm, when these examples appeared:

> Never seem wiser, nor more learned, than the
> people you are with. Wear your learning, like your
> watch, in a private pocket: and do not pull it out
> and strike it; merely to show that you have one.
> If you are asked what o'clock it is, tell it; but do
> not proclaim it hourly and unasked, like the
> watchman.

Chesterfield, letter to his son (1748)

> Or is it possible that you could bring yourselves
> to say to your country, that at such a season the
> press ought to sleep upon its post, or to act like
> the perfidious watchman on his round, that sees
> the villain wrenching the door, or the flames
> bursting from the windows, while the inhabitant
> is wrapt in sleep, and cries out that "'tis past five
> o'clock, the morning is fair, and all is well."

Curran, argument in defence of Peter Finnerty (1798)

6. *Acrobats*, or others in odd bodily postures, can aptly
illustrate those who stand in remarkable postures ver-
bally or psychologically.

> BOSWELL. "But, Sir, does not affecting a warmth
> when you have no warmth, and appearing to be
> clearly of one opinion when you are in reality of
> another opinion, does not such dissimulation
> impair one's honesty? Is there not some danger
> that a lawyer may put on the same mask in

Boswell, *Life of Johnson* (1791)

common life, in the intercourse with his friends?" JOHNSON. ..."Sir, a man will no more carry the artifice of the bar into the common intercourse of society, than a man who is paid for tumbling upon his hands will continue to tumble upon his hands when he should walk on his feet."

Emerson, *Self-Reliance* (1841)

He who knows that power is inborn, that he is weak because he has looked for good out of him and elsewhere, and so perceiving, throws himself unhesitatingly on his thought, instantly rights himself, stands in the erect position, commands his limbs, works miracles; just as a man who stands on his feet is stronger than a man who stands on his head.

Holmes, *The Professor at the Breakfast Table* (1859)

[W]e may consider the mind as it moves among thoughts or events, like a circus-rider whirling round with a great troop of horses. He can mount a fact or an idea, and guide it more or less completely, but he cannot stop it.... The will does not act in the interspaces of thought, for there are no such interspaces, but simply steps from the back of one moving thought upon that of another.

The Education of Henry Adams (1918)

The mind, like the body, kept its unity unless it happened to lose balance, but the professor of physics, who slipped on a pavement and hurt himself, knew no more than an idiot what knocked him down, though he did know – what the idiot could hardly do – that his normal condition was idiocy, or want of balance, and that his sanity was unstable artifice.... His artificial balance was acquired habit. He was an acrobat, with a dwarf on his back, crossing a chasm on a slack-rope, and commonly breaking his neck.

Compare de Quincey's explanation of why Pope gave up on writing literary letters:

One reason doubtless was, that he found it too fatiguing; since in this way of letter-writing he was put to as much expense of wit in amusing an individual correspondent, as would for an equal extent have sufficed to delight the whole world. A funambulist may harass his muscles and risk his neck on the tight-rope, but hardly to entertain his own family.

de Quincey, *Pope* (1848)

7. *Gamblers* of the conventional kind can of course serve as stand-ins for those who take risks, play games, and compete on other planes.

[M]any men were undone by not going deep enough in roguery; as in gaming any man may be a loser who doth not play the whole game.

Fielding, *Life of Jonathan Wild the Great* (1743)

For the few persons, at any rate, abnormal or not, with whom my anecdote is concerned, literature was a game of skill, and skill meant courage, and courage meant honour, and honour meant passion, meant life. The stake on the table was of a special substance and our roulette the revolving mind, but we sat round the green board as intently as the grim gamblers at Monte Carlo.

Henry James, *The Figure in the Carpet* (1896)

Or the scale may be enlarged, as when a whole nation (or world) is the gambler, or the house:

Britain, like a gamester nearly ruined, has now put all her losses into one bet, and is playing a desperate game for the total.

Paine, *The American Crisis* (1783)

Next, we know that parties must ever exist in a free country. We know, too, that the emulations of such parties, their contradictions, their reciprocal necessities, their hopes, and their fears, must send them all in their turns to him that holds the balance of the state. The parties are the gamesters;

Burke, *Speech on Conciliation with America* (1775)

but government keeps the table, and is sure to be the winner in the end.

Note Books of Samuel Butler (1912)

The world is a gambling-table so arranged that all who enter the casino must play and all must lose more or less heavily in the long run, though they win occasionally by the way.

8. *Anatomists* have been representatives of a single principal idea – but a good one.

Conan Doyle, *The Five Orange Pips* (1891)

"The ideal reasoner," he remarked, "would, when he had once been shown a single fact in all its bearings, deduce from it not only all the chain of events which led up to it but also all the results which would follow from it. As Cuvier could correctly describe a whole animal by the contemplation of a single bone, so the observer who has thoroughly understood one link in a series of incidents should be able to accurately state all the other ones, both before and after."

Wilde, *The Rise of Historical Criticism* (1908)

Polybius points out that those phenomena particularly are to be dwelt on which may serve as a [paradigm] or sample, and show the character of the tendencies of the age as clearly as 'a single drop from a full cask will be enough to disclose the nature of the whole contents.' This recognition of the importance of single facts, not in themselves but because of the spirit they represent, is extremely scientific; for we know that from the single bone, or tooth even, the anatomist can recreate entirely the skeleton of the primeval horse, and the botanist tell the character of the flora and fauna of a district from a single specimen.

Compare Russell's paraphrase of Hegel, who admired Cuvier:

Just as a comparative anatomist, from a single bone, sees what kind of animal the whole must have been, so the metaphysician, according to Hegel, sees, from any one piece of reality, what the whole of reality must be – at least in its large outlines.

Russell, *The Problems of Philosophy* (1912)

9. Some attractive uses of pairs and longer combinations:

He that seeketh victory over his nature, let him not set himself too great, nor too small tasks; for the first will make him dejected by often failings; and the second will make him a small proceeder, though by often prevailings. And at the first let him practice with helps, as swimmers do with bladders or rushes; but after a time let him practise with disadvantages, as dancers do with thick shoes.

Bacon, *Of Nature in Men* (1625)

The universe is wider than our views of it. Yet we should oftener look over the tafferel of our craft, like curious passengers, and not make the voyage like stupid sailors picking oakum.

Thoreau, *Walden* (1854)

Mr Rugg's enjoyment of embarrassed affairs was like a housekeeper's enjoyment in pickling and preserving, or a washerwoman's enjoyment of a heavy wash, or a dustman's enjoyment of an overflowing dust-bin, or any other professional enjoyment of a mess in the way of business.

Dickens, *Little Dorrit* (1857)

10. *Governors* of various kinds provide an important set of sources for metaphor. Kings and other rulers, for example. are characters with familiar, extreme, and useful features.

ROBERTSON. 'Dr. Johnson, allow me to say, that in one respect I have the advantage of you; when you were in Scotland you would not come to hear any of our preachers, whereas, when I am here, I attend your public worship without scruple, and indeed, with great satisfaction.' JOHNSON. 'Why,

Boswell, *Life of Johnson* (1791)

Sir, that is not so extraordinary: the King of Siam sent ambassadors to Louis the Fourteenth; but Louis the Fourteenth sent none to the King of Siam.'

(Johnson turns out to have had his facts wrong, but who cares?)

de Quincey, *The Pagan Oracles* (1842)

And Christianity, during this era of public alarm, was so far from assuming a more winning aspect to Roman eyes, as a religion promising to survive their own, that already, under that character of reversionary triumph, this gracious religion seemed a public insult, and this meek religion a perpetual defiance; pretty much as a king sees with scowling eyes, when revealed to him in some glass of Cornelius Agrippa, the portraits of that mysterious house which is destined to supplant his own.

Chesterton, *Woman* (1915)

The average woman, as I have said, is a despot; the average man is a serf. I am for any scheme that any one can suggest that will make the average woman more of a despot.

An ironic application:

Emerson, *Compensation* (1841)

Thus the Greeks called Jupiter, Supreme Mind; but having traditionally ascribed to him many base actions, they involuntarily made amends to reason by tying up the hands of so bad a god. He is made as helpless as a king of England.

The throne itself can serve similar purposes.

Berkeley, *The Guardian* no. 55 (1713)

The thought, that our existence terminates with this life, doth naturally check the soul in any generous pursuit, contract her views, and fix them on temporary and selfish ends. It dethrones the reason, extinguishes all noble and heroic sentiments, and subjects the mind to the slavery of every present passion.

Aristotle was, and still is, the sovereign lord of the understanding; the faculty judging by the senses. He was a conceptualist, and never could raise himself into that higher state, which was natural to Plato, and has been so to others, in which the understanding is distinctly contemplated, and, as it were, looked down upon from the throne of actual ideas, or living, inborn, essential truths.

Specimens of the Table Talk of Samuel Taylor Coleridge (1835)

In contradiction to those who, having a wife and children, prefer domestic enjoyments to those which a tavern affords, I have heard him assert, that a tavern chair is the throne of human felicity.

John Hawkins, speaking of Samuel Johnson in Boswell's *Life* (1791)

Some uses of other officials:

Matters that are recommended to our thoughts by any of our passions take possession of our minds with a kind of authority, and will not be kept out or dislodged, but, as if the passion that rules were, for the time, the sheriff of the place, and came with all the posse, the understanding is seized and taken with the object it introduces, as if it had a legal right to be alone considered there.

Locke, *An Essay Concerning Human Understanding* (1690)

Even in good men, the judge within is often in danger of being corrupted by the violence and injustice of their selfish passions, and is often induced to make a report very different from what the real circumstances of the case are capable of authorizing.

Smith, *The Theory of Moral Sentiments* (1759)

Reason, it is true, is dictator in the society of mankind; from her there ought to lie no appeal: but here we want a Pope in our philosophy, to be the infallible judge of what is or is not reason.

Defoe, *An Essay Upon Public Credit* (1710)

It is but a short step from those applications to others that make use of institutions rather than individuals – to government rather than the governor. This shift brings with it a loss of visibility; the source of the metaphor is now an abstraction. But it still can provide conceptual help.

Locke, *Of the Conduct of the Understanding* (1706)

Many men firmly embrace falsehood for truth, not only because they never have thought otherwise, but because, thus blinded, they never could think otherwise; at least without a vigor of mind able to contest the empire of habit, and look into its own principles: a freedom which few men have the notion of in themselves, and fewer are allowed the practice of by others....

Hume, *A Treatise of Human Nature* (1738)

... I cannot compare the soul more properly to anything than to a republic or commonwealth, in which the several members are united by the reciprocal ties of government and subordination, and give rise to other persons who propagate the same republic in the incessant changes of its parts. And as the same individual republic may not only change its members, but also its laws and constitutions; in like manner the same person may vary his character and disposition, as well as his impressions and ideas, without losing his identity.

Thoreau, *Walden* (1854)

Simplify, simplify. Instead of three meals a day, if it be necessary eat but one; instead of a hundred dishes, five; and reduce other things in proportion. Our life is like a German Confederacy, made up of petty states, with its boundary forever fluctuating, so that even a German cannot tell you how it is bounded at any moment.

Chapter Nine

CIRCUMSTANCES

We have seen in the last two chapters how various types of people can epitomize qualities or patterns and thus serve as sources of comparison to describe human behavior (and occasionally other subjects). Thus in Chapter 7 we considered people who are caricatures of ordinary men and women because of their personal characteristics – youth, insanity, and so forth. In Chapter 8 we considered occupational roles. In this chapter we look at a final and related way that human behavior may serve as a basis for comparison: by virtue of extreme circumstances.

Desperate situations provide the best examples of extremity and will be the subject of our consideration here. They naturally can serve as exaggerated versions of ordinary human experience. Instead of a lunatic or an acrobat we have a central character who is imprisoned or shipwrecked. These situations, like the characters seen in the previous chapters, are met at the edges of life. They present caricatures, too, but of human events rather than human beings. The extreme is used to help the reader see the remarkable features of the ordinary. (Of course the reverse is possible as well: comparisons to ordinary things for the sake of making extreme situations more familiar and understandable.)

We also will see human circumstances used to give life to abstractions and inner states. The extreme cases discussed here are rhetorically versatile; bankruptcy, shipwreck, and other such disasters may happen, figuratively speaking, to a political state or to a mind, and so can provide images to make them all visible.

1. *Poverty*. The distinctive feelings and circumstances of the beggar can resemble inner insolvency.

Poe, *The Premature Burial* (1844)

Just as the day dawns to the friendless and house-less beggar who roams the streets throughout the long desolate winter night – just so tardily – just so wearily – just so cheerily came back the light of the Soul to me.

de Quincey, *Style* (1841)

Accordingly, the degrees of anxiety which sever-ally affect the two cases are best brought to the test in this one question – "What shall I say next?" – an anxiety besetting orators like that which besets poor men in respect to their children's daily bread.

As in many cases we have seen, the source material can be enlarged by considering not just the subject but the reaction to the subject.

Addison, *The Spectator* no. 280 (1712)

There is indeed something so shameless in taking all opportunities to speak of your own affairs, that he who is guilty of it towards him upon whom he depends, fares like the beggar who exposes his sores, which instead of moving compassion makes the man he begs of turn away from the object.

These examples caricature their subjects and also give a more striking visual image to something either invisible or more heard than seen.

2. *Starvation and thirst* tend to be deployed for the sake of caricature, as they are among the simplest forms of desperation.

Coleridge, letter to Humphry Davy (1800)

I will say nothing about Spring – a thirsty man tries to think of anything but the stream when he knows it to be ten miles off!

Scott, *My Aunt Margaret's Mirror* (1832)

[H]e who is dying of thirst cannot refrain from drinking poisoned water. She who suffers under suspense must seek information, even were the powers which offer it unhallowed and infernal.

The days passed slowly, and the cricket season began. Instead of being a relief, this made matters worse. The little cricket he could get only made him want more. It was as if a starving man had been given a handful of wafer biscuits.

Wodehouse, *Psmith in the City* (1910)

This next example, a lesson from Churchill, does not involve caricature; the picture brought in for the sake of comparison may be less extreme than the subject it illustrates. But the metaphor simplifies the point and makes it accessible to the senses.

The orator who wished to incite his audience to a deed of violence would follow his accumulative argument, his rhythmical periods, his vivid word-pictures, by a moderate and reasonable conclusion. The cooling drink will be withheld from the thirsty man. The safety valves will be screwed down and the people will go out into the night to find the expression of their feelings for themselves.

Churchill, *The Scaffolding of Rhetoric* (1897)

3. *Shipwreck*, unlike thirst, is not known firsthand to most readers, but it is easily accessible to the imagination. Sometimes simple images of it can make an abstraction visible:

Every man beholds his human condition with a degree of melancholy. As a ship aground is battered by the waves, so man, imprisoned in mortal life, lies open to the mercy of coming events.

Emerson, *Intellect* (1841)

In the shipwreck of the state, trifles float and are preserved; while every thing solid and valuable sinks to the bottom, and is lost forever.

Junius, Letter LIX (1771)

[O]ur country is compared to a ship of which we are all passengers, and, from thence 'tis gravely

"A Newport Man," Anti-Federalist 20 (1788).

concluded that no officer can ever betray or abuse his trust. But that men will sacrifice the public to their private interest, is a saying too well known to need repeating. And the instances of designed shipwrecks, and ships run away with by a combination of masters, supercargoes, and part owners, is so great that nothing can equal them but those instances in which pretended patriots and politicians have raised themselves and families to power and greatness, by destroying that freedom and those laws they were chosen to defend.

Shipwreck, like other headings in this chapter, is also associated with certain classic behaviors – stock images of response to scarcity or desperation that can caricature more ordinary situations.

Thoreau, *Walden* (1854)

At present men make shift to wear what they can get. Like shipwrecked sailors, they put on what they can find on the beach, and at a little distance, whether of space or time, laugh at each other's masquerade.

Bright, speech in the House of Commons (1853)

[T]he twenty-four gentlemen who are directors of the East India Company are, by a process of self-immolation, to be reduced to fifteen. I think this reduction will be one of the most affecting scenes in the history of the Government of India.... There we shall see the hon. Member for Guildford (Mr. Mangles), the hon. Member for Honiton (Sir J. W. Hogg), one of the hon. Members for the City of London, and the other directors, meeting together, and looking much like shipwrecked men in a boat casting lots who should be thrown overboard.

A spectacular extended case, which makes a financial disaster available to many of the senses at once, as well as depicting large numbers of characters and offering moral commentary – all in one sentence with a perfect ending:

> With a precursory sound of hurried breath and hurried feet, Mr Pancks rushed into Arthur Clennam's Counting-house. The Inquest was over, the letter was public, the Bank was broken, the other model structures of straw had taken fire and were turned to smoke. The admired piratical ship had blown up, in the midst of a vast fleet of ships of all rates, and boats of all sizes; and on the deep was nothing but ruin; nothing but burning hulls, bursting magazines, great guns self-exploded tearing friends and neighbours to pieces, drowning men clinging to unseaworthy spars and going down every minute, spent swimmers floating dead, and sharks.

Dickens, *Little Dorrit* (1857)

4. *Fire*, as an occasion for the most excitable of all human reactions.

> RODERIGO. Here is her father's house; I'll call aloud.
> IAGO. Do, with like timorous accent and dire yell
> As when, by night and negligence, the fire
> Is spied in populous cities.

Othello, 1, 1

> [W]hen this hell in himself yawned beneath him, a wild cry would be heard through the ship; and with glaring eyes Ahab would burst from his state room, as though escaping from a bed that was on fire.

Melville, *Moby-Dick* (1851)

> Half undrest as she was, she fled forth into the forest, she knew not whither, running as one does wrapt in fire: but the fire was not without her, but within.

Kingsley, *Hereward* (1866)

> The sudden change in her, the towering fury and intense abhorrence sparkling in her eyes and lighting up her brow, made him stop as if a fire had stopped him.

Dickens, *Dombey and Son* (1848)

5. *Drowning.* To give visibility to inner struggle:

Melville, *Pierre* (1852)

From these random slips, it would seem, that Pierre is quite conscious of much that is so anomalously hard and bitter in his lot, of much that is so black and terrific in his soul. Yet that knowing his fatal condition does not one whit enable him to change or better his condition. Conclusive proof that he has no power over his condition. For in tremendous extremities human souls are like drowning men; well enough they know they are in peril; well enough they know the causes of that peril; – nevertheless, the sea is the sea, and these drowning men do drown.

Drowning also is associated with desperate behaviors in those who are threatened with it, which can epitomize and simplify more complex patterns in how people relate to intangibles.

Macbeth, I, 2

MALCOLM. ... Say to the King the knowledge of
   the broil
   As thou didst leave it.
SERGEANT.   Doubtful it stood,
   As two spent swimmers that do cling together
   And choke their art.

Wodehouse, *Mike and Psmith* (1909)

Mr. Downing was seized with a hideous fear lest he had lost his senses. Glaring down at the crimson animal that was pawing at his knees, he clutched at his reason for one second as a drowning man clutches at a life belt.

Lincoln, speech at Springfield (1857)

If he can, by much drumming and repeating, fasten the odium of that idea upon his adversaries, he thinks he can struggle through the storm. He therefore clings to this hope, as a drowning man to the last plank.

Again, the metaphorical potential may be expanded by adding characters:

> Is not a Patron, my Lord, one who looks with unconcern on a man struggling for life in the water, and, when he has reached ground, encumbers him with help? The notice which you have been pleased to take of my labours, had it been early, had been kind: but it has been delayed till I am indifferent and cannot enjoy it; till I am solitary and cannot impart it; till I am known and do not want it.

Johnson, letter to Lord Chesterfield (1755)

Chesterfield showed Johnson's letter to those who visited his house, and complimented the high quality of its expression.

6. *Bankruptcy* – the legal analogue to an exhaustion of resources that may be found elsewhere; it may be applied to abstract features of a person, or a government, or a world.

> [T]he idea seems to be, that you and Shelley and he are to conspire together in the Examiner. I cannot believe this, – and deprecate such a plan with all my might. Alone you may do any thing; but partnerships in fame, like those in trade, make the strongest party answerable for the deficiencies or delinquencies of the rest, and I tremble even for you with such a bankrupt *Co.*

Byron, letter to Thomas Moore (c. 1822)

> Indeed, the change of Government that has just taken place is less like an ordinary transfer of power from one great party to another than the winding up of an insolvent concern which had been conducted by questionable and even shady methods to a ruinous conclusion.

Churchill, speech at Manchester (1905)

> That is what is wrong with the world at present. It scraps its obsolete steam engines and dynamos;

Shaw, *Major Barbara* (1905)

but it won't scrap its old prejudices and its old moralities and its old religions and its old political constitutions. What's the result? In machinery it does very well; but in morals and religion and politics it is working at a loss that brings it nearer bankruptcy every year.

7. *Slavery*, to epitomize domination of one by another.

Swift, *The Sentiments of a Church-of-England Man with Respect to Religion and Government* (1708)

This distinction excludes arbitrary power in whatever numbers; which notwithstanding all that Hobbes, Filmer and others have said to its advantage, I look upon as a greater evil than anarchy itself; as much as a savage is in a happier state of life than a slave at the oar.

Melville, *Mardi* (1849)

Ere this, I had regarded the ocean as a slave, the steed that bore me whither I listed, and whose vicious propensities, mighty though they were, often proved harmless, when opposed to the genius of man. But now, how changed! In our frail boat, I would fain have built an altar to Neptune.

Slavery, like drowning and like bankruptcy – perhaps like anything – has its distinctive incidental features that may also serve as a basis for comparison.

Holmes, *John Lothrop Motley—A Memoir* (1879)

The chief magistrate's responsibility to duty, to the fellow-citizen at his mercy, to his countrymen, to mankind, is in proportion to his power. His prime minister, the agent of his edicts, should feel bound to withstand him if he seeks to gratify a personal feeling under the plea of public policy, unless the minister, like the slaves of the harem, is to find his qualification for office in leaving his manhood behind him.

Imagine a competition to describe voters who are given poor choices and so are compared to slaves. Our finalists:

This, then, is the sum of the political liberty of the ordinary American or Englishman, that is the political emancipation which Englishwomen have shown themselves so pathetically eager to share. He may reject one of two undesirables, and the other becomes his "representative." ... Whatever the two party organisations have a mind to do together, whatever issue they chance to reserve from "party politics," is as much beyond the control of the free and independent voter as if he were a slave subject in ancient Peru.

Wells, *An Englishman Looks at the World* (1914)

And if the dangerous comfort and self-flattery of modern England continues much longer there will be less democratic value in an English election than in a Roman saturnalia of slaves. For the powerful class will choose two courses of action, both of them safe for itself, and then give the democracy the gratification of taking one course or the other. The lord will take two things so much alike that he would not mind choosing from them blindfold – and then for a great jest he will allow the slaves to choose.

Chesterton, *The Voter and the Two Voices* (1912)

8. *Imprisonment.* Sometimes this theme may depict a miserable but straightforward instance of confinement.

No man will be a sailor who has contrivance enough to get himself into a jail; for being in a ship is being in a jail, with the chance of being drowned.

Johnson, in Boswell's *Life* (1791)

Marriage was like a doom to him. He was willing to condemn himself in marriage, to become like a convict condemned to the mines of the underworld, living no life in the sun, but having a dreadful subterranean activity.

Lawrence, *Women in Love* (1920)

But prisons also can provide images of inner situations.

Goldsmith, *The Citizen of the World* (1760)

Why was I brought into being; for what purposes made; from whence have I come; whither strayed; or to what regions am I hastening! Reason cannot resolve. It lends a ray to show the horrors of my prison, but not a light to guide me to escape them. Ye boasted revelations of the earth, how little do you aid the inquiry!

Coleridge, *The Third Landing-Place* (1818)

[A]ny person who has witnessed the religious processions in honour of the favourite saints, both at Valetta and at Messina or Palermo ... must have been struck with the contrast between the apparent apathy, or at least the perfect sobriety of the Maltese, and the fanatical agitations of the Sicilian populace. Among the latter each man's soul seems hardly containable in his body, like a prisoner whose gaol is on fire, flying madly from one barred outlet to another; while the former might suggest the suspicion that their bodies were on the point of sinking into the same slumber with their understandings.

James Fitzjames Stephen, *Liberty, Equality, Fraternity* (1873)

It seems to me that we are spirits in prison, able only to make signals to each other, but with a world of things to think and to say which our signals cannot describe at all.

Cf.:

Defoe, *On the History and Reality of Apparitions* (1727)

For I cannot agree that the soul is in the body, as in a prison; but rather that, like a rich nobleman, he is pleased to inhabit a fine country seat or palace of his own building, where he resolves to live and enjoy himself, and does so, 'till by the fate of things his fine palace being overturned, whether by earthquake or otherwise, is buried in its own ruins, and the noble owner turned out of possession, without a house.

9. *Execution; death* – to represent confrontation with finality and the qualities it may evoke, which vary widely with the circumstances.

The defence is concluded; the judge proceeds to sum up the evidence; and the prisoner watches the countenances of the jury, as a dying man, clinging to life to the very last, vainly looks in the face of his physician for a slight ray of hope.	Dickens, *Sketches by Boz* (1836)

Among the things we may gamble away in a lazy selfish life is the capacity for truth, compunction, or any unselfish regret – which we may come to long for as one in slow death longs to feel laceration, rather than be conscious of a widening margin where consciousness once was.	Eliot, *Daniel Deronda* (1876)

Mrs Crummles trod the pavement as if she were going to immediate execution with an animating consciousness of innocence, and that heroic fortitude which virtue alone inspires.	Dickens, *Nicholas Nickleby* (1839)

The men sprang to their feet and were aligned by the company commanders. They awaited the word "forward" – awaited, too, with beating hearts and set teeth the gusts of lead and iron that were to smite them at their first movement in obedience to that word. The word was not given; the tempest did not break out. The delay was hideous, maddening! It unnerved like a respite at the guillotine.	Bierce, *One Officer, One Man* (1889)

Broadening the use of the source idea by enlarging the cast of characters or the story:

To prevent, therefore, any such malicious applications, I declare here, once for all, I describe not men, but manners; not an individual, but a species....	Fielding, *Joseph Andrews* (1742)

This places the boundary between, and distinguishes the satirist from the libeller: for the former privately corrects the fault for the benefit of the person, like a parent; the latter publicly exposes the person himself, as an example to others, like an executioner.

Henry VIII, 4, 2

KATHERINE. O my good lord, that comfort comes
    too late,
'Tis like a pardon after execution:
That gentle physic, given in time, had cur'd me;
But now I am past all comforts here, but prayers.

The usual purpose of these comparisons is to caricature feelings held by a person in a parallel but less extreme case, but they also can give visual form to an inner truth.

Melville, *Pierre* (1852)

But, as sometimes men are coffined in a trance, being thereby mistaken for dead; so it is possible to bury a tranced grief in the soul, erroneously supposing that it hath no more vitality of suffering.

Chapter Ten

THE CLASSICAL WORLD
& OTHER SOURCES OF STORY

The animal kingdom might seem, from the human vantage point, to spread out beneath us. A few animals have such dignity as to flatter those who are compared to them, but the more typical use leaves the subject humbled. Mythology tends the other way. It spreads out above rather than below. Many of its characters and creatures do not resemble earlier drafts of men and women; they are more like later drafts. Myths depict what is essential in human life in simpler terms and in colors more vivid than we are able to see ordinarily, in the same way that a painting may capture a truth better than a photograph. So mythology can function like the animal kingdom in providing exaggerated versions of the familiar in human subjects, but here the result is more likely to be elevation.

In prior times classical comparisons were easier to use with confidence because mythology and ancient history were better known to those who wrote and to the audience they cared about reaching. Today more people write, more are counted as part of the audience, and fewer in either group know much about the classical world. The reader of a classical comparison might therefore need to be helped along tactfully with some explanation of how it works. Such explanation naturally can reduce the efficiency of a metaphor or simile, but classical comparisons may have great value nevertheless. They can offer images of life that are dramatic, suggestive of the heroic, and stimulating to the reader's curiosity.

Under the heading of this chapter we will consider some uses of classical history as well as mythology. Ancient historical figures – real ones – can epitomize subjects in human life just as mythological characters do. Even the real characters from that earlier age in the life story of mankind often seem otherworldly, and in many cases our knowledge of them is bound up in legend; historical anecdotes frequently survive and retain interest because they have the same resonant quality that myths do. Their similar distance and place of origin allows them to serve similar imaginative ends.

This chapter considers just one branch of a larger category of source material: the use of story, which might today also include comparisons drawn from other periods of history, or from film, or from anecdote.

1. *Elevation generally*. We have seen that comparisons to animals typically reduce a human subject in stature. As noted a moment ago, comparisons to myth have the opposite tendency; they more often are employed to dignify their subjects, human or otherwise.

Boswell, *Life of Johnson* (1791)

I observed that Garrick, who was about to quit the stage, would soon have an easier life. JOHNSON. "I doubt that, Sir." BOSWELL. "Why, Sir, he will be Atlas with the burthen off his back." JOHNSON. "But I know not, Sir, if he will be so steady without his load."

Huxley, *On The Origin of Species* (1860)

Extinguished theologians lie about the cradle of every science as the strangled snakes beside that of Hercules....

A mythological reference point can serve as a high bar that earthly activity exceeds, figuratively or not:

Thoreau, *Walden* (1854)

The twelve labors of Hercules were trifling in comparison with those which my neighbors have undertaken; for they were only twelve, and had an end; but I could never see that these men slew or captured any monster or finished any labor.

Trollope, *Autobiography* (1883)

Nothing surely is so potent as a law that may not be disobeyed. It has the force of the water drop that hollows the stone. A small daily task, if it be really daily, will beat the labours of a spasmodic Hercules.

Not the white bull Jupiter swimming away with ravished Europa clinging to his graceful horns; his lovely, leering eyes sideways intent upon the maid; with smooth bewitching fleetness, rippling straight for the nuptial bower in Crete; not Jove, not that great majesty Supreme! did surpass the glorified White Whale as he so divinely swam.

Melville, *Moby-Dick* (1851)

Some ideas, such as proportion, can be illustrated using many of the different families of source material discussed in this book, but each family of material also has features that lack good substitutes in the others. The complexity of mythology or other human story allows comparisons more nuanced than non-sentient sources can provide. As an example of a pattern from myth that is hard to as effectively suggest using other material, consider the great figure disguised in humble attire:

After all, there is such a thing as looking like a gentleman. There are men whose class no dirt or rags could hide, any more than they could Ulysses.

Kingsley, *Alton Locke* (1849)

It was hoped that in this swelling scene in which he moved, with some of the first potentates of Europe for his fellow-actors, and with so many of the rest for the anxious spectators of a part which, as he plays it, determines forever their destiny and his own, like Ulysses in the unravelling point of the epic story, he would have thrown off his patience and his rags together, and, stripped of unworthy disguises, he would have stood forth in the form and in the attitude of an hero.

Burke, Letter on the Proposals for Peace with the Regicide Directory of France (1797)

2. *Epitomes and ultimates*. Mythology is an abundant source of comparisons to establish the ultimate form of

some condition. The point of these applications is not necessarily to elevate the subject. It is to establish the superlative form of a quality, good or bad.

Wodehouse, *A Damsel in Distress* (1919)

"I cannot understand how Maud could have come to lose her head over such a man. He seemed to me to have no attraction whatever," said Lord Belpher, a little unreasonably, for Apollo himself would hardly appear attractive when knocking one's best hat off.

Stevenson, *The Art of Writing* (1905)

I remember I used to look, in those days, upon every three-volume novel with a sort of veneration, as a feat – not possibly of literature – but at least of physical and moral endurance and the courage of Ajax.

Thoreau, *Walden* (1854) (the quotation is from a sonnet by Joseph Blanco White, *Night and Death* (1828))

Humility like darkness reveals the heavenly lights. The shadows of poverty and meanness gather around us, "and lo! creation widens to our view." We are often reminded that if there were bestowed on us the wealth of Croesus, our aims must still be the same, and our means essentially the same.

To epitomize horrors or make them seem larger than life:

Scott, *Life of Dryden* (1808)

Were an author of distinguished merit to announce his having made choice of a subject for a large poem, the writer would have more than common confidence who should venture to forestall his labours. But, in the seventeenth century, such an intimation would, it seems, have been an instant signal for the herd of scribblers to souse upon it, like the harpies on the feast of the Trojans, and leave its mangled relics too polluted for the use of genius....

Jefferson, letter to Barnabas Bidwell (1806)

I sincerely congratulate you on the triumph of republicanism in Massachusetts. The Hydra of federalism has now lost all its heads but two.

Ah, but the charm of the sea! Oh, yes, charm enough. Or rather a sort of unholy fascination as of an elusive nymph whose embrace is death, and a Medusa's head whose stare is terror. That sort of charm is calculated to keep men morally in order.

Conrad, *Well Done* (1918)

Suffering.

For although the debility of age disables me from the services and sufferings of the field, yet, by the total annihilation in value of the produce which was to give me subsistence and independence, I shall be like Tantalus, up to the shoulders in water, yet dying with thirst.

Jefferson, letter to William Short (1814)

During the last fortnight of Kant's life, he busied himself unceasingly in a way that seemed not merely purposeless but self-contradictory. Twenty times in a minute he would unloose and tie his neck handkerchief – so also with a sort of belt which he wore about his dressing-gown, the moment it was clasped, he unclasped it with impatience, and was then equally impatient to have it clasped again. But no description can convey an adequate impression of the weary restlessness with which from morning to night he pursued these labors of Sisyphus – doing and undoing – fretting that he could not do it, fretting that he had done it.

de Quincey, *The Last Days of Immanuel Kant* (1827)

God help thee, old man, thy thoughts have created a creature in thee; and he whose intense thinking thus makes him a Prometheus; a vulture feeds upon that heart for ever; that vulture the very creature he creates.

Melville, *Moby-Dick* (1851)

3. *Laws.* A myth may be invoked to suggest more than a quality or feeling; it can epitomize some greater law or pattern in human character or human affairs. Statements

of these similarities may sometimes amount to unfigurative parallels, but a chapter on comparisons that draw from the classical world can hardly pass them by.

Hume, *An Enquiry Concerning the Principles of Morals* (1751)

The quality, the most necessary for the execution of any useful enterprise, is discretion.... The greatest parts without it, as observed by an elegant writer, may be fatal to their owner; as Polyphemus, deprived of his eye, was only the more exposed, on account of his enormous strength and stature.

Emerson, *History* (1841)

Antæus was suffocated by the grip of Hercules, but every time he touched his mother earth his strength was renewed. Man is the broken giant, and in all his weakness both his body and his mind are invigorated by habits of conversation with nature.

Butler, *Life & Habit* (1878)

So, again, it is said that when Andromeda and Perseus had travelled but a little way from the rock where Andromeda had so long been chained, she began upbraiding him with the loss of her dragon who, on the whole, she said, had been very good to her. The only things we really hate are unfamiliar things.

Churchill, address to the United States (1938)

The dictator is held in the grip of his party machine. He can go forward, he cannot go back. He must blood his hounds and show them sport, or else like Actaeon of old be devoured by them.

4. *Reversals and pairings.* The complexity of stories can permit some impressive comparative stunts, such as reversal of their logic.

Boswell, letter to Johnson (1779)

I was quite enchanted at Chester, so that I could with difficulty quit it. But the enchantment was the reverse of that of Circé; for so far was there from being anything sensual in it, that I was all mind.

Yet even Sybil was startled as she rode through the gate and found herself suddenly met by the long white ranks of head-stones, stretching up and down the hill-sides by thousands, in order of baffle; as though Cadmus had reversed his myth, and had sown living men, to come up dragons' teeth.

Adams, *Democracy* (1880)

Under the penitentiary act, and the plans of management that have been grounded on it, the condition of the prisoners alternates between the two opposite extremes: a state of absolute solitude during one part of the twenty-four hours; a state of promiscuous association in crowds during the remainder. This plan, it has been shown, unites the ill effects of solitude and association, without producing the good effects obtainable from the former.... It is the history of Penelope's web reversed: the work of the night is unraveled by the day.

Bentham, *A View of the Hard-Labour Bill* (1778)

The range of characters and situations in mythology, or in other families of story, allows another attractive effect: contrasting comparisons from closely related sources. (We saw some analogous patterns in the chapter on animals.)

The ripeness, or unripeness, of the occasion (as we said) must ever be well weighed; and generally it is good, to commit the beginnings of all great actions to Argus, with his hundred eyes, and the ends to Briareus, with his hundred hands; first to watch, and then to speed.

Bacon, *Of Delays* (1625)

Mr. Flood, my rival, as the pamphlet calls him – and I should be unworthy the character of his rival, if in his grave I did not do him justice – he had his faults, but he had great powers; great public effect; he persuaded the old, he inspired the young; the Castle vanished before him. On a small subject he was miserable. Put into his hand

Grattan, *Answer to a Pamphlet of Lord Clare* (1822)

a distaff, and like Hercules he made sad work of it: but give him the thunderbolt, and he had the arm of Jupiter.

Carlyle, letter to Emerson
(1836)

Some months more, and it is ended; and I am done with French Revolution, and with Revolution and Revolt in general; and look once more with free eyes over this Earth, where are other things than mean internecine work of that kind: things fitter for me, under the bright Sun, on this green Mother's-bosom (though the Devil does dwell in it)! For the present, really, it is like a Nessus' shirt, burning you into madness, this wretched Enterprise; nay, it is also like a kind of Panoply, rendering you invulnerable, insensible, to all other mischiefs.

One sufficiently rich character may provide both ends of such a pairing:

Curtis, speech at Concord
(1875)

There is a cynicism which fondly fancies that in its beginning the American Republic moved proudly toward the future with all the splendid assurances of the Persian Xerxes descending on the shores of Greece, but that it sits to-day among shattered hopes, like Xerxes above his ships at Salamis.

Caffery, speech at Indianapolis
(1896)

We deem it wise to pursue an aggressive rather than a negative policy; to be Achilles dragging Hector around the walls of Troy rather than Achilles sulking in his tent.

5. *Biblical sources.* The Bible was until recently a common source of metaphor and allusion for the orator and author. Comparisons to its tales often lent gravity and a sense of the universal to a subject. They also served to draw the author and reader together by confirming their shared membership in a community of readers and

perhaps also a community of believers. The Bible is somewhat less rhetorically useful now because the needed familiarity with it may be lacking all the way around, and because references that even appear religious are out of fashion. But still –

a. *The eye of the needle*. Matt. 19:24:

> And again I say unto you, it is easier for a camel to go through the eye of a needle, than for a rich man to enter into the kingdom of God.

Matt. 19:24

See also Mark 10:25, Luke 18:24-25. Some applications:

> If the mode of election was what it ought to be, there would be no more difficulty in women voting for a representative in Parliament than for a director at the India House. The world will find out at some time that the readiest way to secure justice on some points is to be just on all: – that the whole is easier to accomplish than the part; and that, whenever the camel is driven through the eye of the needle, it would be simple folly and debility that would leave a hoof behind.

Bentham, *On Mill's Essays on Government* (1829)

> But the reader is aware by this time of my steadfast conviction, that more easily might a camel go through the eye of a needle, than a reporter, fresh from a campaign blazing with partisanship, and that partisanship representing ancient and hereditary feuds, could by possibility cleanse himself from the virus of such a prejudice.

de Quincey, *Autobiographic Sketches* (1853)

> He knew well how difficult it was for a camel to go through the eye of a needle. They had the highest possible authority for that. But Scriptures never said that the camel, which, as he explained it, was simply a thread larger than ordinary thread, could not go through the needle's eye. The camel which succeeded, in spite of the difficulties attending its

Trollope, *The Eustace Diamonds* (1873)

exalted position, would be peculiarly blessed. And he went on to suggest that the three ladies before him, one of whom was about to enter upon a new phase of life to-morrow, under auspices peculiarly propitious, were, all of them, camels of this description.

b. *The swallowing of the rods.* From Chapter 7 of the Book of Exodus:

Exodus ch. 7

8 And the Lord spake unto Moses and unto Aaron, saying,

9 When Pharaoh shall speak unto you, saying, Shew a miracle for you: then thou shalt say unto Aaron, Take thy rod, and cast it before Pharaoh, and it shall become a serpent.

10 And Moses and Aaron went in unto Pharaoh, and they did so as the Lord had commanded: and Aaron cast down his rod before Pharaoh, and before his servants, and it became a serpent.

11 Then Pharaoh also called the wise men and the sorcerers: now the magicians of Egypt, they also did in like manner with their enchantments.

12 For they cast down every man his rod, and they became serpents: but Aaron's rod swallowed up their rods.

13 And he hardened Pharaoh's heart, that he hearkened not unto them; as the Lord had said.

Applications:

Johnson, *Preface to Shakespeare* (1765)

Other passions have, undoubtedly, their sway, but love, when it does prevail, like Aaron's rod, swallows up every feeling beside.

Clinton, Anti-Federalist 30 (1787)

This, indeed, [the federal constitutional convention] has now done in the most unequivocal manner; nor has it stopped here, for it has fairly annihilated the constitution of each individual state. It has proposed to you a high prerogative government, which, like Aaron's serpent, is to swallow up the rest.

In fashionable life, flippancy, tepid amours, weak infidelism, small aims, or no aims at all, only to kill time. In business, (this all-devouring modern word, business,) the one sole object is, by any means, pecuniary gain. The magician's serpent in the fable ate up all the other serpents; and money-making is our magician's serpent, remaining to-day sole master of the field.

Whitman, *Democratic Vistas* (1871)

c. *Miscellaneous examples.*

Every great man nowadays has his disciples, and it is always Judas who writes the biography.

Wilde, *Intentions* (1891)

A man building up an intellectual system has to build like Nehemiah, with the sword in one hand and the trowel in the other. The imagination, the constructive quality, is the trowel, and argument is the sword.

Chesterton, *Thomas Carlyle* (1903)

Their case is this – their slaves were emancipated in 1833, and for the loss which they sustained, they consider themselves to be entitled, in the shape of exclusive privileges, to compensation. This is a plain statement, and the answer is also plain – England paid a ransom, which almost dazzles the imagination, and she is entitled to a receipt in full. No, answers the member for Newark, whose motion is insatiable, and who cries out, like the horse-leech's daughter, "More, more."

Sheil, speech in the House of Commons (1841)

6. *Aesop's fables.* Fables, defined most narrowly, are short stories with morals attached to them, often involving animals. Aesop's fables from ancient Greece are the best known; each is a short and charming epitome of some aspect of moral life. Some of them, such as the tortoise

and the hare or the boy who cried wolf, have passed into cliché. Here are a few short examples from Aesop (taken from the L'Estrange versions of 1692) that have not been beaten quite so hard, along with examples of how they have been put to comparative use.

a. *The Fly upon a Wheel.*

What a dust do I raise! says the fly, upon the Coach-Wheel; and what a rate do I drive at, says the same fly again, upon the horse's buttock.

Applications:

Hazlitt, *On Great and Little Things* (1821)

Great objects move on by their own weight and impulse; great power turns aside petty obstacles; and he who wields it is often but the puppet of circumstances, like the fly on the wheel that said, 'What a dust we raise!' It is easier to ruin a kingdom and aggrandize one's own pride and prejudices than to set up a greengrocer's stall.

Richardson, *On Egotism* (1840)

A real claim is always willingly conceded as soon as it is fairly proved. It is only when, like the fly upon the chariot-wheel, some insignificant human insect imagines he raises all the dust and turmoil of the world, that we feel disposed to be angry at his folly and presumption.

Neele, *Atlantic and American Notes* (1882)

Can it be that the Bostonians consider, like the fly on the carriage wheel, they are the cause of all the stir in the world?

b. *The Ass in the Lion's Skin.*

An Ass once found a Lion's skin which the hunters had left out in the sun to dry. He put it on and went towards his native village. All fled at his approach, both men and animals, and he was a proud Ass that day. In his delight he lifted up his voice and brayed, but then every one knew him, and his owner came up and gave him a sound cudgelling for the fright he had caused. And shortly afterwards a Fox came up to him and said: "Ah, I knew you by your voice."

Fine clothes may disguise, but silly words will disclose a fool.

Applications:

Other gentlemen, not scholars, abused "all law" for the same reason – and it occurred neither to the one party nor to the other that the law about which they were disputing might possibly be no law at all – an ass of a law in the skin of a lion.

Poe, The Rationale of Verse (1848)

I long have said there is no such thing as a hard case. I am frightened weekly but always when you walk up to the lion and lay hold the hide comes off and the same old donkey of a question of law is underneath.

Holmes, Jr., letter to Frederick Pollock (1909)

The usual state of Rome is quiet and sober. One could almost fancy the actual generation held their breath, and stole by on tiptoe, in presence of so memorable a past. But during the Carnival all mankind, womankind and childkind think it unbecoming not to play the fool. The modern donkey pokes its head out of the lion's skin of old Rome, and brays out the absurdest of asinine roundelays.

Sterling, letter to his wife (1839)

c. *The Farmer and the Snake.*

One Winter a Farmer found a Snake stiff and frozen with cold. He had compassion on it, and taking it up, placed it in his bosom. The Snake was quickly revived by the warmth, and resuming its natural instincts, bit its benefactor, inflicting on him a mortal wound. "Oh," cried the Farmer with his last breath, "I am rightly served for pitying a scoundrel."

> The greatest kindness will not bind the ungrateful.

Applications:

2 *Henry VI*, 3, 1

YORK. ...Well, nobles, well, 'tis politicly done
To send me packing with an host of men.
I fear me you but warm the starved snake,
Who, cherish'd in your breasts, will sting your hearts.

Johnson, letter to Boswell (1763)

This vanity makes one mind nurse aversion, and another actuate desires, till they rise by art much above their original state of power; and as affectation, in time, improves to habit, they at last tyrannise over him who at first encouraged them only for show. Every desire is a viper in the bosom, who, while he was chill, was harmless; but when warmth gave him strength, exerted it in poison.

Melville, *Typee* (1846)

When the inhabitants of some sequestered island first descry the 'big canoe' of the European rolling through the blue waters towards their shores, they rush down to the beach in crowds, and with open arms stand ready to embrace the strangers. Fatal embrace! They fold to their bosom the vipers whose sting is destined to poison all their joys; and the instinctive feeling of love within their breast is soon converted into the bitterest hate.

d. *Miscellaneous examples.*

Selden, *Table Talk* (1689)

Marriage is a desperate thing. The frogs in Aesop were extremely wise; they had a great mind to some water, but they would not leap into the well because they could not get out again.

Thoreau, *Walden* (1854)

He was a lucky fox that left his tail in the trap. The muskrat will gnaw his third leg off to be free. No wonder man has lost his elasticity. How often he is at a dead set!

When the exultant and long-eared animal described
in the fable reveled madly in the frog-pond, dashing about his tail and hoof among the unfortunate
inhabitants of that piece of water, it is stated that
the frogs remonstrated, exclaiming, "Why, O donkey, do you come kicking about in our habitation?
It may be good fun for you to lash out, and plunge,
and kick in this absurd manner, but it is death to
us:" on which the good-natured quadruped agreed
to discontinue his gambols; and left the frogs to
bury their dead and rest henceforth undisturbed
in their pool.

 The inhabitants of Brighton are the frogs – and
I dare say they will agree as to the applicability of
the rest of the simile. It might be good fun to *me*
to "mark their manners, and their ways survey;"
but could it be altogether agreeable to them? I am
sorry to confess it has not proved so....

Thackeray, Meditations Over
Brighton (1845)

7. *Fabulous characters generally.* Fable in the broader
sense can refer to legends from other times and places
but not very different in type from the classical mythology considered earlier. Characters familiar from fabulous stories can serve purposes similar to those we have
recently seen – visualization, exaggeration, etc.

There was a time when the vault of liberty could
hardly contain the flight of your pinion; some of
you went forth like a giant rejoicing in his
strength; and now you stand like elves, at the door
of your own pandemonium.

Grattan, speech in the Irish
Parliament (1792)

[S]talking to and fro across the Three Hills with a
fierceness which made it almost a new pestilence,
there was that mighty conqueror – that scourge
and horror of our forefathers – the small-pox. We
cannot estimate the affright which this plague

Hawthorne, Lady Eleanore's
Mantle (1838)

inspired of yore, by contemplating it as the fang-less monster of the present day.

Hazlitt, *On Patronage and Puffing* (1821)

For there is no egotism or vanity so hateful as that which strikes at our satisfaction in everything else, and derives its nourishment from preying, like the vampire, on the carcass of others' reputation.

8. *Uses of history.* As noted in the introduction to this chapter, ancient historical figures can epitomize features of life or character just as mythical creatures do. Events sometimes become prominent in the cultural memory precisely because they represent some more general pattern of life in microcosm. Thus a historical comparison may not only help describe the subject but also create a pleasing link to its antecedents. Again, in this space it will only be feasible to consider a handful of good and representative illustrations.

a. *Phalaris and the brazen bull.* Phalaris was a Sicilian tyrant, c. 570 B.C., famous for the "brazen bull" he commissioned to torment his enemies. The bull was a hollow sculpture of brass; the victim was put inside and a fire then lit underneath that would heat the bull until the victim's screams were emitted from the bull's mouth, perhaps after passing through tubes that would make them sound like music or like the animal's roar. It is said that after the bull was built and presented by Perillus of Athens, Phalaris first tested it on Perillus himself; it is also said that the subjects of Phalaris later revolted and gave Phalaris himself a turn inside the bull.

Swift, Letter to the Tradesmen, Shop-Keepers, Farmers, and Common-People in General of Ireland (c. 1722)

I have heard scholars talk of a man who told a king that he had invented a way to torment people by putting them into a bull of brass with fire under it, but the prince put the projector first into his own brazen bull to make the experiment; this very much resembles the project of Mr. Wood, and the like of this may possibly be Mr. Wood's fate, that the brass he contrived to torment this kingdom with, may prove his own torment, and his destruction at last.

Pop, Pop, Pop, Pop! green guavas, seeds, and berries were flying about in every direction, and during this dangerous state of affairs I was half afraid that, like the man and his brazen bull, I should fall a victim to my own ingenuity.

Melville, *Typee* (1846)

Any man's advancement is the capital offence to his malice; yet this envy, like Phalaris's bull, makes that a torment for himself which he had prepared for others....

Overbury, *Characters* (1614)

The fate of Phalaris is similar to that of the mythical Procrustes, who stretched the bodies of his guests, or lopped off parts of them, until they fit the bed that he provided for them. Theseus ended the practice by fitting Procrustes himself to the bed.

b. *Xerxes and his army.*

[W]hen I contemplate a modern library, filled with new works in all the bravery of rich gilding and binding, I feel disposed to sit down and weep, like the good Xerxes, when he surveyed his army, pranked out in all the splendor of military array, and reflected that in one hundred years not one of them would be in existence.

Irving, *The Mutability of Literature* (1820)

When I first entered Ranelagh, it gave an expansion and gay sensation to my mind, such as I never experienced any where else. But, as Xerxes wept when he viewed his immense army, and considered that not one of that great multitude would be alive a hundred years afterwards, so it went to my heart to consider that there was not one in all that brilliant circle, that was not afraid to go home

Johnson, in Boswell's *Life* (1791)

and think; but that the thoughts of each individual there, would be distressing when alone.

de Quincey, *Revolt of the Tartars* (1837)

The Khan, knowing how much he was individually answerable for the misery which had been sustained, must have wept tears even more bitter than those of Xerxes when he threw his eyes over the myriads whom he had assembled: for the tears of Xerxes were unmingled with compunction.

c. *The Colossus (of Rhodes)*. A colossus is any statute that is much larger than life. Several famous ones were built in ancient times, of which the best-known was the bronze statue of Helios at the harbor of the island and city of Rhodes. That statute was among the Seven Wonders of the World featured in ancient books telling the Hellenistic traveler where to visit and what to see. The statue lasted less than a century; its destruction by an earthquake in 226 B.C. left much room for artists and others to later imagine what it might have been, and it is often depicted as straddling the mouth of the harbor so that entrants would pass between its legs. (Those who have studied the case conclude that in fact the statue probably stood nearby in a manner more closely resembling the modern Statue of Liberty.) Metaphorical uses of a colossus need not mean the one at Rhodes, but that is the most usual and natural reference point.

Julius Caesar, I, 2

BRUTUS. Another general shout!
  I do believe that these applauses are
  For some new honors that are heap'd on Caesar.
CASSIUS. Why, man, he doth bestride the narrow
     world
  Like a Colossus, and we petty men
  Walk under his huge legs and peep about
  To find ourselves dishonorable graves.

Melville, *Moby-Dick* (1851)

There you stand, a hundred feet above the silent decks, striding along the deep, as if the masts were gigantic stilts, while beneath you and between your legs, as it were, swim the hugest monsters of the sea, even as ships once sailed between the boots of the famous Colossus at old Rhodes.

He not only humbles your virtues, he degrades your vices and gives them a poorer cast: so you that lose the high mettle which sometimes mixes with human infirmity, dignifies the nature of vice, and makes ambition virtue. You do not make this man a Colossus, but he makes you pigmies; and both lose your natural proportion; he his natural inferiority, and you your natural superiority in your native land.

Grattan, speech in the Irish Parliament (1791)

d. *Classical history: miscellaneous examples.*

Besides though New Bedford has of late been gradually monopolizing the business of whaling, and though in this matter poor old Nantucket is now much behind her, yet Nantucket was her great original – the Tyre of this Carthage; – the place where the first dead American whale was stranded.

Melville, Moby-Dick (1851)

Their long, stringy, slimy sentences are of that consistency that they naturally flow and run together. They read as if written for military men, for men of business, there is such a dispatch in them. Compared with these, the grave thinkers and philosophers seem not to have got their swaddling-clothes off; they are slower than a Roman army in its march, the rear camping to-night where the van camped last night.

Thoreau, A Week on the Concord and Merrimack Rivers (1849)

Lycurgus, when he promulgated his laws to the Spartans, made them swear that they would make no alterations in them until he should return from a journey which he was then about to undertake. He chose never to return, and therefore no

Anti-Federalist 49 (1787)

alteration could be made in his laws.... In like manner the proposed constitution holds out a prospect of being subject to be changed if it be found necessary or convenient to change it; but the conditions upon which an alteration can take place, are such as in all probability will never exist. The consequence will be that when the constitution is once established it never can be altered or amended without some violent convulsion or civil war.

Chapter Eleven

ARCHITECTURE
& OTHER MAN-MADE THINGS

We have seen that source material for metaphor comes from a finite number of families: from animals and from nature, animate and inanimate; from human circumstances and behavior and institutions; and from story. A last broad category remains: man-made things. The world of human invention and machinery is too endless for a full survey of its comparative uses. We will take up one important example – architecture – and see some of what can be done with it; then at the chapter's end we will glance briefly at some possibilities with technologies and inventions of other kinds

Like other non-sentient sources, buildings are used rarely for the sake of caricature. Their typical function is to give visible form to an abstraction or some other subject invisible in itself.

1. *Political order and institutions*. Prior chapters showed how these subjects may be lent visibility by images from nature or from human biology. They also may be compared to dwellings, so as to emphasize their man-made character, and that they are built over time, and that we live in them. The first part of the initial example here is familiar from Chapter 8.

> To judge about success or failure one must see things very simply; one must see them in masses, as the artist, half closing his eyes against details, sees light and shade. That is the only way in which a just judgment can be formed as to whether any departure or development, such as Islam or the American Republic, has been a benefit upon the whole. Seen close, such great erections always

Chesterton, *The Man on Top* (1912)

abound in ingenious detail and impressive solidity; it is only by seeing them afar off that one can tell if the Tower leans.

Carlyle, *The New Downing Street* (1850)

Alas, wise men do exist, born duly into the world in every current generation; but the getting of them regimented is the highest pitch of human polity, and the feat of all feats in political engineering: – impossible for us, in this poor age, as the building of St. Paul's would be for Canadian Beavers, acquainted only with the architecture of fish-dams, and with no trowel but their tail.

Paine, *The Rights of Man* (1791)

When once such a vicious system is established it becomes the guard and protection of all inferior abuses. The man who is in the receipt of a million a year is the last person to promote a spirit of reform, lest, in the event, it should reach to himself. It is always his interest to defend inferior abuses, as so many outworks to protect the citadel....

Applied to constitutions:

Pitt, speech in the House of Commons (1770)

A breach has been made in the Constitution – the battlements are dismantled – the citadel is open to the first invader – the walls totter – the Constitution is not tenable. What remains, then, but for us to stand foremost in the breach, and repair it, or perish in it?

Grattan, speech in the Irish Parliament (1800)

Well, the minister has destroyed this constitution; to destroy is easy; the edifices of the mind, like the fabrics of marble, require an age to build, but ask only minutes to precipitate; and, as the fall of both is an effort of no time, so neither is it a business of any strength; a pick-axe and a common labourer will do the one – a little lawyer, a little pimp, a wicked minister, the other.

Architectural images are used powerfully for other ends in scripture, and have then been borrowed for purposes of statesmanship later. An example from Churchill:

> In my Father's house are many mansions: if it were not so, I would have told you. I go to prepare a place for you.

John 14:1–2

> Let the great cities of Warsaw, of Prague, of Vienna banish despair even in the midst of their agony. Their liberation is sure. The day will come when the joybells will ring again throughout Europe, and when victorious nations, masters not only of their foes but of themselves, will plan and build in justice, in tradition, and in freedom a house of many mansions where there will be room for all.

Churchill, London radio broadcast (1940)

From Lincoln:

> And knowing their thoughts he said unto them, Every kingdom divided against itself is brought to desolation; and every city or house divided against itself shall not stand:
>   And if Satan casteth out Satan, he is divided against himself; how then shall his kingdom stand?

Matt. 12:23–28

> "A house divided against itself cannot stand." I believe this government cannot endure permanently half slave and half free. I do not expect the Union to be dissolved – I do not expect the house to fall – but I do expect it will cease to be divided. It will become all one thing, or all the other.

Lincoln, speech at Springfield (1858)

2. *Books, art, and ideas.* We have likewise seen products of the mind described by reference to natural sources. Again, comparisons to the works of man have the advantage of suggesting not only properties of the subject (such as its complexity and structure) but also where the subject came from (e.g., nuances of how it was planned and built). To begin with literature:

Specimens of the Table Talk of
Samuel Taylor Coleridge (1835)

Poetry is certainly something more than good sense, but it must be good sense, at all events; just as a palace is more than a house, but it must be a house, at least.

Chapman, *Robert Browning*
(1898)

Browning, on the other hand, loved pictures, places, music, men and women, and his works are like the house of a rich man, – a treasury of plunder from many provinces and many ages, whose manners and passions are vividly recalled to us.

Chesterton, *The Position of Sir*
Walter Scott (1903)

Scott was very far indeed from being a perfect writer, but I do not think that it can be shown that the large and elaborate plan on which his stories are built was by any means an imperfection. He arranged his endless prefaces and his colossal introductions just as an architect plans great gates and long approaches to a really large house.

Scaffolding and unfinished buildings:

Hazlitt, *Jeremy Bentham* (1825)

[B]ooks of reference are chiefly serviceable for facilitating the acquisition of knowledge, and are constantly liable to be superseded and to grow out of fashion with its progress, as the scaffolding is thrown down as soon as the building is completed.

Melville, *Moby-Dick* (1851)

But I now leave my cetological System standing thus unfinished, even as the great Cathedral of Cologne was left, with the cranes still standing upon the top of the uncompleted tower.

de Quincey, *Confessions of an*
English Opium Eater (1821)

I had devoted the labour of my whole life, and had dedicated my intellect, blossoms and fruits, to the slow and elaborate toil of constructing one single work, to which I had presumed to give the title of an unfinished work of Spinoza's – viz., *De Emendatione Humani Intellectus*. This was now lying locked up, as by frost, like any Spanish bridge or aqueduct, begun upon too great a scale for the resources of the architect....

As this last example suggests, ideas not reduced to books and the like can also be given visible form by comparison to architecture. A set of ideas may themselves be viewed as a dwelling.

> But he never fell into the error of arresting his intellectual development by any formal acceptance of creed or system, or of mistaking, for a house in which to live, an inn that is but suitable for the sojourn of a night, or for a few hours of a night in which there are no stars and the moon is in travail.

Wilde, *The Picture of Dorian Gray* (1890)

> Man was indeed screwed up, by mood and figure, into a logical machine, that was to forward the public good with the utmost punctuality and effect, and it might go very well on smooth ground and under favourable circumstances; but would it work up-hill or against the grain? It was to be feared that the proud Temple of Reason, which at a distance and in stately supposition shone like the palaces of the New Jerusalem, might (when placed on actual ground) be broken up into the sordid styes of sensuality, and the petty huckster's shops of self-interest!

Hazlitt, *William Godwin* (1825)

> The knowledge, if knowledge it be, of the mystic is not transmissible. It is not cumulative; it begins and ends with the solitary dreamer, and the next who follows him has to build his own cloud-castle as if it were the first aerial edifice that a human soul had ever constructed.

Holmes, *Ralph Waldo Emerson* (1891)

Or the mind itself may be regarded as an architectural production – a variation that will serve as a transition to our next topic.

Hazlitt, *On Coffee-House Politicians* (1821)

His ideas lie like square pieces of wood in his brain, and may be said to be piled up on a stiff architectural principle, perpendicularly, and at right angles. There is no inflection, no modification, no graceful embellishment, no Corinthian capitals.

Irving, *Bracebridge Hall* (1822)

There is an odd mixture of eccentricity and good sense in all the opinions of my worthy host. His mind is like modern Gothic, where plain brick-work is set off with pointed arches and quaint tracery. Though the main ground-work of his opinions is correct, yet he has a thousand little notions, picked up from old books, which stand out whimsically on the surface of his mind.

3. *Architecture and the self.* Various sorts of physical structures can give a perceptible form to mind and character.

Matt. 23:27

Woe unto you, scribes and Pharisees, hypocrites! for ye are like unto whited sepulchres, which indeed appear beautiful outward, but are within full of dead men's bones, and of all uncleanness.

Mandeville, *The Fable of the Bees (Part II)* (1732)

The soul, whilst in the body, cannot be said to think, otherwise than an architect is said to build a house, where the carpenters, bricklayers, &c. do the work, which he chalks out and superintends.

Macaulay, *Machiavelli* (1850)

Like an ancient temple deformed by the barbarous architecture of a later age, his character acquires an interest from the very circumstances which debase it. The original proportions are rendered more striking by the contrast which they present to the mean and incongruous additions.

Henry James, *The Europeans* (1878)

In his younger years he had been – or he had tried to be – of the opinion that it would be a good deal "jollier" not to marry, and he had flattered himself that his single condition was something of a citadel. It was a citadel, at all events, of which he had long since leveled the outworks. He had removed the guns from the ramparts; he had lowered the draw-bridge across the moat. The draw-bridge had swayed lightly under Madame Munster's step; why should he not cause it to be raised again, so that she might be kept prisoner?

Capture; ruin.

Not to tire the reader, by leading him through every scene of this courtship (which, though in the opinion of a certain great author, it is the pleasantest scene of life to the actor, is, perhaps, as dull and tiresome as any whatever to the audience), the captain made his advances in form, the citadel was defended in form, and at length, in proper form, surrendered at discretion.

Fielding, *Tom Jones* (1749)

Her unconsciousness of the evil which lives in the secret thoughts and therefore in the open acts of mankind, whenever it happens that evil thought meets evil courage; her unconsciousness was to be broken into with profane violence with desecrating circumstances, like a temple violated by a mad, vengeful impiety.

Conrad, *Chance* (1913)

A mental system may be undermined or weakened by this interstitial alteration just as a building is, and yet for a time keep upright by dead habit. But a new perception, a sudden emotional shock, or an occasion which lays bare the organic alteration, will make the whole fabric fall together. . . .

William James, *The Varieties of Religious Experience* (1902)

Cf.:

He that hath no rule over his own spirit is like a city that is broken down, and without walls.

Prov. 25:28

Architecture sometimes makes a good source of comparison because the details of a structure may be lined up with details of the self. Thus windows:

Locke, *An Essay Concerning Human Understanding* (1690)

I pretend not to teach, but to inquire; and therefore cannot but confess here again, – that external and internal sensation are the only passages I can find of knowledge to the understanding. These alone, as far as I can discover, are the windows by which light is let into this dark room.

Melville, *Moby-Dick* (1851)

"In of that tempestuous wind called Euroclydon," says an old writer – of whose works I possess the only copy extant – "it maketh a marvellous difference, whether thou lookest out at it from a glass window where the frost is all on the outside, or whether thou observest it from that sashless window, where the frost is on both sides, and of which the wight Death is the only glazier." True enough, thought I, as this passage occurred to my mind – old black-letter, thou reasonest well. Yes, these eyes are windows, and this body of mine is the house.

Or the attic:

Lamb, letter to Bernard Barton (1824)

[M]y brains are gone out to see a poor relation in Moorfields, and they did not say when they'd come back again; my skull is a Grub Street attic to let, – not so much as a joint-stool left in it; my hand writes, not I, from habit, as chickens run about a little when their heads are off.

Emerson, *Intellect* (1841)

Each truth that a writer acquires is a lantern, which he turns full on what facts and thoughts lay already in his mind, and behold, all the mats and rubbish which had littered his garret become precious. Every trivial fact in his private biography becomes an illustration of this new principle, revisits the day, and delights all men by its piquancy and new charm. Men say, Where did he get this? and think there was something divine in his life. But no; they have myriads of facts just as good, would they only get a lamp to ransack their attics withal.

I consider that a man's brain originally is like a little empty attic, and you have to stock it with such furniture as you choose. A fool takes in all the lumber of every sort that he comes across, so that the knowledge which might be useful to him gets crowded out, or at best is jumbled up with a lot of other things so that he has a difficulty in laying his hands upon it. Now the skilful workman is very careful indeed as to what he takes into his brain-attic. He will have nothing but the tools which may help him in doing his work, but of these he has a large assortment, and all in the most perfect order.

Conan Doyle, *A Study in Scarlet* (1887)

Cf.:

The most important events, when they become familiar, are no longer considered with wonder or solicitude; and that which at first filled up our whole attention, and left no place for any other thought, is soon thrust aside into some remote repository of the mind, and lies among other lumber of the memory, overlooked and neglected.

Johnson, *The Rambler* no. 78 (1750)

Depths.

His best moments are with an intimate acquaintance or two, when he gossips in a fine vein about old authors, Clarendon's History of the Rebellion, or Burnet's History of his own Times; and you perceive by your host's talk, as by the taste of seasoned wine, that he has a cellarage in his understanding!

Hazlitt, *William Godwin* (1825)

I wish I could make you see how much my mind is at this moment like a rayless dungeon, with one

Charlotte Brontë, *Jane Eyre* (1847)

shrinking fear fettered in its depths – the fear of being persuaded by you to attempt what I cannot accomplish!

Melville, *Pierre* (1852)

Deep, deep, and still deep and deeper must we go, if we would find out the heart of a man; descending into which is as descending a spiral stair in a shaft, without any end, and where that endlessness is only concealed by the spiralness of the stair, and the blackness of the shaft.

Melville, in a journal entry from his visit to France in December 1849, wrote this:

Thence to the Hotel de Cluny. A most unique collection. The house is just the house I should like to live in. Glorious old cabinets – ebony, ivory carving. – Beautiful chapel. Tapestry, old keys. Leda & the Swan. Descended into the vaults of the old Roman palace of Thermes. Baths, &c.

A year later he was drafting *Moby-Dick*, and wrote:

Melville, *Moby-Dick* (1851)

This is much; yet Ahab's larger, darker, deeper part remains unhinted. But vain to popularise profundities, and all truth is profound. Winding far down from within the very heart of this spiked Hotel de Cluny where we here stand – however grand and wonderful, now quit it; – and take your way, ye nobler, sadder souls, to those vast Roman halls of Thermes; where far beneath the fantastic towers of man's upper earth, his root of grandeur, his whole awful essence sits in bearded state; an antique buried beneath antiquities, and throned on torsoes!

Thus does a prodigious mind turn the grist of ordinary observation into material for metaphor.

4. *People as buildings; exteriors.* We have seen how correspondences between people and buildings can be used

to describe human interiors. They can be used to caricature human exteriors as well.

> Unconscious of this prediction, Mr. Dick contin-
> ued to occupy precisely the same ground in refer-
> ence to the Doctor and to Mrs. Strong. He seemed
> neither to advance nor to recede. He appeared to
> have settled into his original foundation, like a
> building; and I must confess that my faith in his
> ever moving, was not much greater than if he had
> been a building.

Dickens, *David Copperfield* (1850)

> He was an old gentleman, one side of whose face
> was no match for the other. The eyelid drooped
> and hung down like an unhinged window shutter.
> Indeed, the whole side of his head was dilapidated,
> and seemed like the wing of a house shut up and
> haunted.

Irving, *Tales of a Traveller* (1824)

> As when, drawing nigh unto old Rome, amid the
> crowd of sculptured columns and gables, St. Peter's
> grand dome soars far aloft, serene in the upper air;
> so, showed one calm grand forehead among those
> of this mob of chieftains.

Melville, *Mardi* (1849)

Columns, towers, and pillars as images of human
stature:

> It is true, the mind, as well as the eye, can take in
> objects larger than itself; but this is only true of
> great minds: for a man of low capacity, who con-
> siders a consummate genius, resembles one, who
> seeing a column for the first time, and standing at
> too great a distance to take in the whole of it, con-
> cludes it to be flat.

More, *Miscellaneous Observations on Genius, Good Taste, Good Sense, &c.* (1777)

> One of the company mentioned his having seen a
> noble person driving in his carriage, and looking
> exceedingly well, notwithstanding his great age.
> JOHNSON. 'Ah, Sir; that is nothing. Bacon observes,

Boswell, *Life of Johnson* (1791)

that a stout healthy old man is like a tower undermined?'

Melville, *Bartleby, the Scrivener* (1853)

But he answered not a word; like the last column of some ruined temple, he remained standing mute and solitary in the middle of the otherwise deserted room.

Cf.:

Chesterfield, letter to his son (1749)

I would wish you to be a Corinthian edifice upon a Tuscan foundation; the latter having the utmost strength and solidity to support, and the former all possible ornaments to decorate. The Tuscan column is coarse, clumsy, and unpleasant; nobody looks at it twice; the Corinthian fluted column is beautiful and attractive; but without a solid foundation, can hardly be seen twice, because it must soon tumble down.

5. *Other man-made things*. The most familiar sources of experience become the deepest funds of material for comparison. We draw from what we know best. If humans dealt as much with the hippopotamus as they do with the dog, uses of the former might be as common as the latter; alas, the hippo is invoked for figurative purposes but rarely. In the world of invention we find the same general pattern. The comparative uses of man-made items are too vast to survey, but some common and familiar ones are pressed into metaphorical service with versatility – houses and other sorts of architecture, as we have just seen, but also some other things and technologies that we will sample just a bit to suggest the range of possibilities they offer.

a. *Books*. As a way to describe people:

Wilde, *Intentions* (1891)

When people talk to us about others they are usually dull. When they talk to us about themselves they are nearly always interesting, and if one could shut them up, when they become wearisome, as easily as one can shut up a book of which one has grown wearied, they would be perfect absolutely.

"Well," the young man after a moment returned, "I'm not sure he was really meant by nature to be quite so good. It's like the new edition of an old book that one has been fond of – revised and amended, brought up to date, but not quite the thing one knew and loved."

Henry James, *The Ambassadors* (1903)

As a way to describe nature, or life – the book to represent the subject of study:

[T]he path of science and of letters is not the way into nature. The idiot, the Indian, the child and unschooled farmer's boy stand nearer to the light by which nature is to be read, than the dissector or the antiquary.

Emerson, *History* (1841)

I have read the book of life for a long time, and I have read other books a little. Nothing has happened to me, but what has happened to men much better than me, and in times and in nations full as good as the age and country that we live in.

Burke, speech at Bristol (1780)

The mind:

HAMLET. ...Yea, from the table of my memory
I'll wipe away all trivial fond records,
All saws of books, all forms, all pressures past,
That youth and observation copied there;
And thy commandment all alone shall live
Within the book and volume of my brain,
Unmix'd with baser matter....

Hamlet, 1, 5

b. *Clocks*. The inexorable advance of time lends itself to comparisons to social progress.

Unless a man is prepared to say that all the existing evils of society are due to our having moved too slowly – that the clock is wrong solely because

James Fitzjames Stephen, *Liberty, Equality, Fraternity* (1873)

it has a pendulum, and that to take off the pendulum and allow the weights to pull the wheels round with no restriction at all will ensure universal happiness – he has no right to regard the forward impulse as an unmixed good.

Chesterton, *The Fear of the Past* (1910)

There is one metaphor of which the moderns are very fond; they are always saying, "You can't put the clock back." The simple and obvious answer is "You can." A clock, being a piece of human construction, can be restored by the human finger to any figure or hour. In the same way society, being a piece of human construction, can be reconstructed upon any plan that has ever existed.

Timepieces tell their keepers something about the world, accurately or not, and so allow people to coordinate their joint activities. This aspect of a clock's purpose allows for comparisons to humanity.

Specimens of the Table Talk of Samuel Taylor Coleridge (1835)

A philosopher's ordinary language and admissions, in general conversation or writings *ad populum*, are as his watch compared with his astronomical timepiece. He sets the former by the town-clock, not because he believes it right, but because his neighbours and his cook go by it.

Melville, *Pierre* (1852)

[I]n an artificial world like ours, the soul of man is further removed from its God and the Heavenly Truth, than the chronometer carried to China, is from Greenwich. And, as that chronometer, if at all accurate, will pronounce it to be 12 o'clock high-noon, when the China local watches say, perhaps, it is 12 o'clock midnight; so the chronometric soul, if in this world true to its great Greenwich in the other, will always, in its so-called intuitions of right and wrong, be contradicting the mere local standards and watch-maker's brains of this earth.

Circumstances do the planning for us all, no doubt, by help of our temperaments. I see no great difference between a man and a watch, except that the man is conscious and the watch isn't, and the man *tries* to plan things and the watch doesn't. The watch doesn't wind itself and doesn't regulate itself – these things are done exteriorly. Outside influences, outside circumstances, wind the *man* and regulate him. Left to himself, he wouldn't get regulated at all, and the sort of time he would keep would not be valuable. Some rare men are wonderful watches, with gold case, compensation balance, and all those things, and some men are only simple and sweet and humble Waterburys.

Twain, *The Turning-Point of My Life* (1910)

A comparative use that is famous, if not figurative:

[S]uppose I had found a watch upon the ground, and it should be inquired how the watch happened to be in that place; I should hardly think of the answer I had before given, that for anything I knew, the watch might have always been there.... There must have existed, at some time, and at some place or other, an artificer or artificers, who formed it for the purpose which we find it actually to answer; who comprehended its construction, and designed its use.... Every indication of contrivance, every manifestation of design, which existed in the watch, exists in the works of nature; with the difference, on the side of nature, of being greater or more, and that in a degree which exceeds all computation.

Paley, *Natural Theology* (1802)

c. *Clothing*. Clothes cover the body like a skin, but unlike a skin they come off. This makes them natural analogues to states of the self that may come and go.

To instance no more, is not religion a cloak, honesty a pair of shoes worn out in the dirt, self-love

Swift, *A Tale of a Tub* (1704)

a surtout, vanity a shirt, and conscience a pair of breeches, which, though a cover for lewdness as well as nastiness, is easily slipped down for the service of both?

Dickens, *A Tale of Two Cities* (1859)

But, perhaps the confidential bachelor clerks in Tellson's Bank were principally occupied with the cares of other people; and perhaps second-hand cares, like second-hand clothes, come easily off and on.

Shoes, the pinching of which may illustrate individual or social misery:

James Fitzjames Stephen, *Liberty, Equality, Fraternity* (1873)

To try to get out of this by telling those who disagree with you that their notion of happiness is wrong and yours right is a mere evasion. It is the shoemaker telling the wearer of the shoe that it does not pinch. It may be quite right that it should pinch, but on the question whether it pinches or not the feelings of the wearer are the only possible test.

Mill, *Principles of Political Economy* (1848)

Experience having obtruded these evils on the notice of Parliament, the sort of compromise took place, of which English legislation affords so many instances, and which helps to make our laws and policy the mass of inconsistency that they are. The law was reformed as a person reforms a tight shoe, who cuts a hole in it where it pinches hardest, and continues to wear it. Retaining the erroneous principle as a general rule, Parliament allowed an exception in the case in which the practical mischief was most flagrant.

d. *Machinery*, the workings of which can be used to describe a remarkable range of life – history, governments, economics, families, individuals, etc.

[A]s the greater weight will always carry up the
less, and as all the wheels of a machine are put in
motion by one, it only remains to know which
power in the constitution has the most weight, for
that will govern; and though the others, or a part
of them, may clog, or, as the phrase is, check the
rapidity of its motion, yet so long as they cannot
stop it, their endeavours will be ineffectual; the
first moving power will at last have its way, and
what it wants in speed, is supplied by time.

Paine, *Common Sense* (1776)

There cannot, in short, be intrinsically a more
insignificant thing, in the economy of society,
than money; except in the character of a contrivance for sparing time and labour. It is a machine
for doing quickly and commodiously, what would
be done, though less quickly and commodiously,
without it: and like many other kinds of machinery, it only exerts a distinct and independent influence of its own when it gets out of order.

Mill, *Principles of Political
Economy* (1848)

Though in one sense, our family was certainly a
simple machine, as it consisted of a few wheels; yet
there was thus much to be said for it, that these
wheels were set in motion by so many different
springs, and acted one upon the other from such
a variety of strange principles and impulses – that
though it was a simple machine, it had all the
honour and advantages of a complex one, – and a
number of as odd movements within it, as ever
were beheld in the inside of a Dutch silk-mill.

Sterne, *Tristram Shandy* (1759)

e. *Lenses and mirrors* are tools to allow and enhance perception; viewed this way, they allow comparisons to the
internal capacity to perceive.

A strong mind sees things in their true proportions; a weak one views them through a magnify-
ing medium, which, like the microscope, makes

Chesterfield, letter to his son
(1749)

an elephant of a flea: magnifies all little objects, but cannot receive great ones.

Chesterton, *A Dead Poet* (1915)

Any common Imperialist can have large ideas so long as he is not called upon to have small ideas also. Any common scientific philosopher can have small ideas so long as he is not called upon to have large ideas as well. But great poets use the telescope and also the microscope.

Lenses also may describe whatever else in the world reflects and makes visible some larger or smaller thing.

Ruskin, *The Queen of the Air* (1869)

So that when once you have learned how to spell these most precious of all legends, – pictures and buildings, – you may read the characters of men, and of nations, in their art, as in a mirror; nay, as in a microscope, and magnified a hundredfold; for the character becomes passionate in the art, and intensifies itself in all its noblest or meanest delights.

As mirrors show what is in front of them, but not always accurately, they too suggest comparisons to the mind.

Bacon, *The Great Instauration* (1620)

For let men please themselves as they will in admiring and almost adoring the human mind, this is certain: that as an uneven mirror distorts the rays of objects according to its own figure and section, so the mind, when it receives impressions of objects through the sense, cannot be trusted to report them truly, but in forming its notions mixes up its own nature with the nature of things.

Poe, *Review of* The Quacks of Helicon (1841)

He as often tilts at what is true as at what is false; and thus his lines are like the mirrors of the temples of Smyrna, which represent the fairest images as deformed.

Chesterton, *Manalive* (1912)

Animals have no second thoughts; man alone is able to see his own thought double, as a drunkard sees a lamp-post; man alone is able to see his own thought upside down as one sees a house in a puddle. This duplication of mentality, as in a mirror, is (we repeat) the inmost thing of human philosophy.

Prisms might reasonably be considered a part of this family of sources.

In very many subjective exercises of the mind, – as, for instance, in that class of poetry which has been formally designated by this epithet (meditative poetry, we mean, in opposition to the Homeric, which is intensely objective), the problem before the writer is to project his own inner mind; to bring out consciously what yet lurks by involution in many unanalyzed feelings; in short, to pass through a prism and radiate into distinct elements what previously had been even to himself but dim and confused ideas intermixed with each other.

de Quincey, *Style* (1841)

He views man as he does colors in Sir Isaac Newton's prism, where only the capital ones are seen; but an experienced dyer knows all their various shades and gradations, together with the result of their several mixtures. Few men are of one plain, decided color. . . .

Chesterfield, letter to his son (1752)

But the thing of which we must divest our minds is to look partially upon others; all is to be viewed; and the creature judged, as he must be by his Creator, not dissected through a prism of morals, but in the unrefracted ray.

Stevenson, letter to his father (1883)

Cf.:

We learn that it is not the rays which bodies absorb, but those which they reject, that give them the colours they are known by; and in the same way people are specialized by their dislikes

Hardy, *Far from the Madding Crowd* (1874)

and antagonisms, whilst their goodwill is looked upon as no attribute at all.

f. *Ships* have an immense range of comparative uses. We have seen some of them already, as when people or institutions in earlier chapters have suffered shipwreck. Here it is convenient to add notice of how ships may describe humans making their way through life.

Addison, *The Spectator* no. 62 (1711)

Sometimes the poet's heart is frozen in every breast, and sometimes scorched in every eye. Sometimes he is drowned in tears and burnt in love, like a ship set on fire in the middle of the sea.

Emerson, *Spiritual Laws* (1841)

Each man has his own vocation. The talent is the call. There is one direction in which all space is open to him. He has faculties silently inviting him thither to endless exertion. He is like a ship in a river; he runs against obstructions on every side but one, on that side all obstruction is taken away and he sweeps serenely over a deepening channel into an infinite sea.

Emerson, *Self-Reliance* (1841)

[O]f one will, the actions will be harmonious, however unlike they seem. These varieties are lost sight of at a little distance, at a little height of thought. One tendency unites them all. The voyage of the best ship is a zigzag line of a hundred tacks. See the line from a sufficient distance, and it straightens itself to the average tendency.

Irving, *John Bull* (1820)

It is not, therefore, fighting that he ought so much to be on his guard against as making friends. It is difficult to cudgel him out of a farthing; but put him in a good humor and you may bargain him out of all the money in his pocket. He is like a stout ship which will weather the roughest storm uninjured, but roll its masts overboard in the succeeding calm.

Chapter Twelve

PERSONIFICATION

Human behavior typically is invoked by metaphor or simile to illustrate the doings and traits of other humans. Personification is an exception to those tendencies. It assigns human behavior and human qualities to an abstraction or other non-human subject. Or at least the source is usually human; despite the limits of the word, however, "personification" is often, and here, considered to include the attribution of animal and mythical personalities, as well as human ones, to something inanimate.

Like other uses of metaphor, personification is a powerful resource partly on account of its economy. A well-chosen word or two can cause a picture to appear in place of a flatter and lengthier effort at literal description.

In all very numerous assemblies, of whatever character composed, passion never fails to wrest the sceptre from reason.

Madison, Federalist 55 (1788)

"If the law supposes that," said Mr. Bumble, squeezing his hat emphatically in both hands, "the law is a ass – a idiot."

Dickens, *Oliver Twist* (1838)

With only a bit more elaboration, the device can generate little movies rather than still photographs.

Death, to be sure, has a mouth as black as a wolf's, and to be thrust into his jaws is a serious thing. But true it most certainly is – and I speak from no hearsay – that to sailors, as a class, the grisly king seems not half so hideous as he appears to those who have only regarded him on shore, and at a deferential distance.

Melville, *Mardi* (1849)

1. *Classic cases; degrees.* Personification may be considered a matter of degree. It can be used with a light touch, as in these cases where a well-chosen noun by itself gives brief human form to a concept.

Hazlitt, *Lord Byron* (1825)

Death is the great assayer of the sterling ore of talent.

Holmes, *The Autocrat of the Breakfast Table* (1891) (preface)

Now it is the grandchildren who are still turning to these pages, which I might well have thought would be voted old-fashioned, outworn, an unvalued bequest to posterity with Oblivion as residuary legatee.

As the example from Holmes shows, personification works attractively at the end of a claim. The words roll along in the ordinary two-dimensional way; then comes an unexpected shift in perspective and gain in visibility. It provides punctuation of a conceptual kind.

The device may be intensified in increments as the author drives home the identity between the subject and its personification. This pattern occurs naturally when the device is used not just to give identity to an abstraction but to assign it traits or behaviors.

Hamlet, 4, 5

CLAUDIUS. ...When sorrows come, they come not
         single spies,
But in battalions.

Dickens, speech at Boston (1842)

I believe that Virtue shows quite as well in rags and patches, as she does in purple and fine linen.

Melville, *Billy Budd* (1891)

The retaliation is apt to be in monstrous disproportion to the supposed offense; for when in anybody was revenge in its exactions aught else but an inordinate usurer?

At greater rhetorical risk, a still heavier effect is possible: the extended case, in which the personality of the abstract subject is described in some detail. Here the goal is not just to lend temporary visual form to a point. Personification instead becomes a vehicle to fully describe the workings of an abstraction or invisible human tendency.

"Affection," said Miss Lavinia, glancing at her sister for corroboration, which she gave in the form of a little nod to every clause, "mature affection, homage, devotion, does not easily express itself. Its voice is low. It is modest and retiring, it lies in ambush, waits and waits."

Dickens, *David Copperfield* (1850)

Guilt and misery shrink, by a natural instinct, from public notice: they court privacy and solitude: and even in their choice of a grave will sometimes sequester themselves from the general population of the churchyard, as if declining to claim fellowship with the great family of man, and wishing (in the affecting language of Mr. Wordsworth) humbly to express a penitential loneliness.

de Quincey, *Confessions of an English Opium Eater* (1821)

Fortune, in fact, is a pestilent shrew, and, withal, an inexorable creditor; and though for a time she may be all smiles and courtesies, and indulge us in long credits, yet sooner or later she brings up her arrears with a vengeance, and washes out her scores with our tears.

Irving, *Knickerbocker's History of New York* (1809)

2. *Offspring*. Personification helps to describe causal relationships, as when an invisible force begets an intangible consequence. Procreation provides images for such a case.

MESSALA. Mistrust of good success hath done
  this deed.
O hateful error, melancholy's child,
Why dost thou show to the apt thoughts of men
The things that are not? O error, soon conceived,

Julius Caesar, 5, 3

Thou never comest unto a happy birth,
But kill'st the mother that engender'd thee!

Conrad, *Lord Jim* (1900)

The fear grows shadowy; and Imagination, the enemy of men, the father of all terrors, unstimulated, sinks to rest in the dullness of exhausted emotion.

Melville, *Pierre* (1852)

The brightest success, now seemed intolerable to him, since he so plainly saw, that the brightest success could not be the sole offspring of Merit; but of Merit for the one thousandth part, and nine hundred and ninety-nine combining and dovetailing accidents for the rest.

Those examples involved the production of inner states or otherwise local results – error, fear, and success. Some cases in which the causes and effects illustrated by personification are social or general:

Ames, speech in the House of Representatives (1796)

Such a nation might truly say to corruption, thou art my father, and to the worm, thou art my mother and my sister.

Hawthorne, *American Notebooks* (1836)

Then proceed to generalize and classify the whole world together, as none can claim utter exemption from either sorrow, sin, or disease; and if they could, yet Death, like a great parent, comes and sweeps them all through one darksome portal, – all his children.

Churchill, speech in the House of Commons (1955)

[I]t may well be that we shall by a process of sublime irony have reached a stage in this story where safety will be the sturdy child of terror, and survival the twin brother of annihilation.

An interesting branch of this usage depicts a person as the parent – or one parent – of personified offspring, as when describing creative work.

But who these Meddlers are, or where the judicious leaders have picked them up, I shall never go about to conjecture: factious rancour, false wit, abandoned scurrility, impudent falsehood, and servile pedantry, having so many fathers, and so few to own them, that curiosity herself would not be at the pains to guess.

Swift, *The Examiner* no. 42 (1711)

Mr. Coleridge has flirted with the Muses as with a set of mistresses: Mr. Godwin has been married twice, to Reason and to Fancy, and has to boast no short-lived progeny by each.

Hazlitt, *Mr. Coleridge* (1825)

Riley says that sometimes he is so afflicted with a yearning to write a sparkling and absorbingly readable letter that he simply cannot resist it, and so he goes to his den and revels in the delight of untrammeled scribbling; and then, with suffering such as only a mother can know, he destroys the pretty children of his fancy and reduces his letter to the required dismal accuracy.

Twain, *Riley—Newspaper Correspondent* (1870)

The reverse is possible as well – the human offspring of an abstraction:

But whatever he is, he is not a realist. Or rather I would say that he is a child of realism who is not on speaking terms with his father.

Wilde, *Intentions* (1891)

You had but to look in the faces of these twelve hundred, and despair, for most part, of ever "commanding" them at all. Miserable distorted blockheads, the generality; ape-faces, imp-faces, angry dog-faces, heavy sullen ox-faces; degraded underfoot perverse creatures, sons of *in*docility, greedy mutinous darkness, and in one word, of STUPIDITY, which is the general mother of such.

Carlyle, *Model Prisons* (1850)

3. *Animals.* Personification sounds like a device that necessarily involves human qualities. As noted at the

start of the chapter, however, it may also refer to traits of animals assigned to concepts or other inanimate things.

Greene, *Pandosto* (1588)

Conscience is a worm that ever biteth, but never ceaseth.

Macaulay, *Milton* (1825)

Such a spirit is Liberty. At times she takes the form of a hateful reptile. She grovels, she hisses, she stings. But woe to those who in disgust shall venture to crush her!

Eliot, *The Mill on the Floss* (1860).

For there is nothing more widely misleading than sagacity if it happens to get on a wrong scent, and sagacity persuaded that men usually act and speak from distinct motives, with a consciously proposed end in view, is certain to waste its energies on imaginary game.

Ingersoll, *Ernest Renan* (1892)

How the snake of superstition writhes when he finds that his fangs have lost their poison.

The comparison may also take a less direct form than any of those shown thus far; it can rely just on adjectives derived from animals. These cases sometimes veer from full personification into more modest cases of comparison.

Melville, *Moby-Dick* (1851)

Human madness is oftentimes a cunning and most feline thing. When you think it fled, it may have but become transfigured into some still subtler form.

Emerson, letter to Carlyle (1856)

One book, last summer, came out in New York, a nondescript monster which yet had terrible eyes and buffalo strength, and was indisputably American, – which I thought to send you; but the book throve so badly with the few to whom I showed it, and wanted good morals so much, that I never did. Yet I believe now again, I shall. It is called *Leaves of Grass....*

4. *Mythical creatures*, like animals or humans, can give life to abstractions.

> IAGO. O, beware, my lord, of jealousy!
> It is the green-eyed monster, which doth mock
> The meat it feeds on.

Othello, 3, 3

> It is the most painful of all their types of any benef-
> icent power, and even among those of evil influ-
> ences, none can be compared with it, except its
> opposite, the tortoise-headed demon of indolence.

Ruskin, *The Ethics of the Dust* (1866)

> All I mean by this senseless interrupted tale is,
> that by my central situation I am a little over-com-
> panied. Not that I have any animosity against the
> good creatures that are so anxious to drive away
> the harpy Solitude from me. I like 'em, and cards,
> and a cheerful glass. . . .

Lamb, letter to Mrs. Wordsworth (1818)

> The fame I had won, such as it was, seemed to
> attend me, – not going before me in the shape of
> a woman with a trumpet, but rather following me
> like one of Actæon's hounds, his throat open,
> ready to pull me down and tear me. What a fierce
> enemy is that which bays behind us in the voice
> of our proudest bygone achievement!

Holmes, *A Mortal Antipathy* (1885)

5. *Personified pairs*, like the pairs considered in the earlier discussion of mythology, allow the portrayal of relations more complicated than cause and effect. This
pattern is notably useful when two forces or abstractions
are opposite in character and may be thought to compete. Thus truth and falsehood:

> And though all the winds of doctrine were let
> loose to play upon the earth, so Truth be in the
> field, we do injuriously, by licensing and prohibit-
> ing, to misdoubt her strength. Let her and False-
> hood grapple; who ever knew Truth put to the
> worse, in a free and open encounter?

Milton, *Areopagitica* (1660)

Swift, *The Examiner* no. 15 (1710)	Falsehood flies, and Truth comes limping after it; so that when men come to be undeceived, it is too late, the jest is over, and the tale has had its effect....
Burke, letter to the Earl Fitzwilliam (1795)	He supposes (to use his own expression) "that the salutary truths which he inculcates are making their way into their bosoms." Their bosom is a rock of granite, on which Falsehood has long since built her stronghold. Poor Truth has had a hard work of it, with her little pickaxe. Nothing but gunpowder will do.

Cf.:

Johnson, in Boswell's *Life* (1791)	Hume, and other sceptical innovators, are vain men, and will gratify themselves at any expense. Truth will not afford sufficient food to their vanity; so they have betaken themselves to error. Truth, Sir, is a cow which will yield such people no more milk, and so they are gone to milk the bull.

Good and evil, and virtue and vice, invite similar usage.

Julius Caesar, 3, 2	ANTONY. ...The evil that men do lives after them, The good is oft interred with their bones.
Chesterfield, letter to his son (1748)	Vice, in its true light, is so deformed, that it shocks us at first sight; and would hardly ever seduce us, if it did not at first wear the mask of some virtue.
Melville, *White-Jacket* (1850)	[W]hen Virtue rules by compulsion, and domineers over Vice as a slave, then Virtue, though her mandates be outwardly observed, bears little interior sway.

Some miscellaneous other personified pairings:

Bentham, *An Introduction to the Principles of Morals and Legislation* (1789)	Nature has placed mankind under the governance of two sovereign masters, *pain* and *pleasure*.

Desert and reward, I can assure her, seldom keep company together.

Richardson, *Clarissa* (1748)

Conscience, like every other judge, may be misled, and there is no advocate so eloquent as self-interest before that high, but not infallible tribunal.

Sheil, *The Solicitor-General, Mr. Joy* (1823)

[I]t is not among the least of the mischiefs that the Christian system has done to the world, that it has abandoned the original and beautiful system of theology, like a beautiful innocent, to distress and reproach, to make room for the hag of superstition.

Paine, *The Age of Reason* (1795)

Liberty (the philosopher's and the poet's bride) had fallen a victim, meanwhile, to the murderous practices of the hag, Legitimacy.

Hazlitt, *Mr. Coleridge* (1825)

Voltaire must be criticized; besides, every man's favorite is attacked: for every prejudice is exposed, and our prejudices are our mistresses; reason is at best our wife, very often heard indeed, but seldom minded.

Chesterfield, letter to his son (1752)

Our current idea need not be limited to pairs. One may wish to speak of several abstractions, and they may have relations more complex than the rivalries just shown.

O Vanity! how little is thy force acknowledged, or thy operations discerned! ... All our passions are thy slaves. Avarice itself is often no more than thy handmaid, and even Lust thy pimp. The bully Fear, like a coward, flies before thee, and Joy and Grief hide their heads in thy presence.

Fielding, *Joseph Andrews* (1742)

Invention is exhausted; reason is fatigued; experience has given judgment; but obstinacy is not yet conquered.

Burke, Speech on American Taxation (1774)

Chapter Thirteen

THE CONSTRUCTION OF SIMILES

This chapter looks at various ways that similes may be presented – where they can be placed and how they can be expressed within a sentence, or in a set of sentences, and to what effect. The chapter after this one explores the same questions with respect to metaphor and examines differences between the two types of comparisons. Much of what follows here might be considered technical in character, as it involves little choices in word order; but then good writing often consists of nothing but many small decisions made well.

A simile is a figurative comparison that is explicit, or announced: not referring to one's enemy as an insect, but saying that one's enemy is *like* an insect. Most people recall hearing in school that a simile is a comparison starting with *like* or *as*, but those are merely the most common ways to announce a comparison. Here are some examples of similes without those words:

Fielding, *Tom Jones* (1749)

Such histories as these do, in reality, very much resemble a newspaper, which consists of just the same number of words, whether there be any news in it or not. They may likewise be compared to a stage coach, which performs constantly the same course, empty as well as full.

Addison, *The Spectator* no. 476 (1712)

There is not one dispute in ten which is managed in those Schools of Politicks, where, after the three first sentences, the question is not entirely lost. Our disputants put me in mind of the cuttle-fish, that when he is unable to extricate himself, blackens all the water about him till he becomes invisible.

[F]or any poetic purposes, metre resembles, (if the aptness of the simile may excuse its meanness), yeast, worthless or disagreeable by itself, but giving vivacity and spirit to the liquor with which it is proportionally combined.

Coleridge, *Biographia Literaria* (1832)

1. *Simple similes*. The subject in the most basic sort of simile is a noun. The comparison makes its qualities or circumstances more vivid. The easiest pattern for the purpose explains the subject and then appends a *like* clause with a brief comparison. The best of these are notable for their compression; they squeeze a good deal of meaning and imagery into fewer than a dozen words.

I do believe that feeling is the deeper source of religion, and that philosophic and theological formulas are secondary products, like translations of a text into another tongue.

William James, *The Varieties of Religious Experience* (1902)

But Unitarianism is, in effect, the worst of one kind of Atheism, joined to the worst of one kind of Calvinism, like two asses tied tail to tail.

Specimens of the Table Talk of Samuel Taylor Coleridg (1835)

In short, Mr. Bentham writes as if he was allowed but a single sentence to express his whole view of a subject in, and as if, should he omit a single circumstance or step of the argument, it would be lost to the world for ever, like an estate by a flaw in the title-deeds.

Hazlitt, *Jeremy Bentham* (1825)

It had a black canal in it, and a river that ran purple with ill-smelling dye, and vast piles of building full of windows where there was a rattling and a trembling all day long, and where the piston of the steam-engine worked monotonously up and down, like the head of an elephant in a state of melancholy madness.

Dickens, *Hard Times* (1854)

The most emphatic spot in a sentence is typically the end. Finishing with the comparison thus calls attention to it and leaves it as the last impression in the reader's mind. Putting it last may also allow the simile to serve as a pithier summary of what the rest of the sentence said.

A more extreme form of this pattern makes the comparison still shorter and later, so that it arrives as the last word.

Chapman, *Robert Browning* (1898)

The force of his feelings is so much greater than his intellect that his mind serves his soul like a valet.

Johnson, in Boswell's *Life* (1791)

The savages have no bodily advantages beyond those of civilised men. They have not better health; and as to care or mental uneasiness, they are not above it, but below it, like bears.

Poe, *The Murders in the Rue Morgue* (1841)

Nevertheless, that he failed in the solution of this mystery, is by no means that matter for wonder which he supposes it; for, in truth, our friend the Prefect is somewhat too cunning to be profound. In his wisdom is no stamen. It is all head and no body, like the pictures of the Goddess Laverna, – or, at best, all head and shoulders, like a codfish.

This structure can add punch to a simile, as when a subject is set forth at some length and then hit hard by the notably short comparison at the end. Putting the important word last allows it to resonate.

An *as* clause can serve in similar fashion to a *like* clause:

Dryden, *The Spanish Friar* (1681)

And pity still foreruns approaching love,
As lightning does the thunder!

Hazlitt, *Mr. Brougham—Sir F. Burdett* (1825)

[H]e is led away by the headstrong and over-mastering activity of his own mind. He is borne along, almost involuntarily, and not impossibly against his better judgment, by the throng and restlessness of his ideas as by a crowd of people in motion.

Starting a simile with *as* – or with *just as*, or *even as*, or *as if* – often signals the start of a more substantial comparison. Those little words have an advantage over *like*: they can easily be followed by entire independent clauses – in other words, by complete thoughts that resemble (or could have been) whole sentences. This allows the source of the comparison to be explained in more detail.

> A man will not reach eloquence if he is afraid of bombast, just as a man will not jump a hedge if he is afraid of a ditch.

Chesterton, *The Position of Sir Walter Scott* (1903)

> [I]nstead of protesting against the conditions they protest against the man, the other victim; just as a woman in a crowd will abuse the man who crushes against her, when he is only the helpless transmitter of the pressure put upon him.

Hardy, *Jude the Obscure* (1895)

> Often it was only the smallest trace, Watson, the faintest indication, and yet it was enough to tell me that the great malignant brain was there, as the gentlest tremors of the edges of the web remind one of the foul spider which lurks in the centre.

Conan Doyle, *The Adventure of the Norwood Builder* (1903)

Since *like* cannot easily be followed by an ordinary sentence (subject-verb-object), starting an involved comparison with that word tends to require a more imaginative sentence structure – usually beginning with a noun and then using commas or parenthetical structures to insert or tack on dependent clauses that describe it.

> [T]here is no doubt that a man may appear very gay in company who is sad at heart. His merriment is like the sound of drums and trumpets in a battle, to drown the groans of the wounded and dying.

Boswell, *Life of Johnson* (1791)

> The time had been when the Father himself had wept, in the shades of that yard, as his own poor wife had wept. But it was many years ago; and now he was like a passenger aboard ship in a long

Dickens, *Little Dorrit* (1857)

voyage, who has recovered from sea-sickness, and is impatient of that weakness in the fresher passengers taken aboard at the last port.

Melville, *Moby-Dick* (1851)

[Y]ou must be sure and take the exact intersecting latitude and longitude of your first stand-point, else so chance-like are such observations of the hills, that your precise, previous stand-point would require a laborious re-discovery; like the Solomon islands, which still remain incognita, though once high-ruffled Mendanna trod them and old Figuera chronicled them.

If one can summon Lincoln's gift for the arrangement of words, the same degree of complexity may be expressed with a *like* comparison that uses no commas at all.

Lincoln, telegram to Gen. Hooker (1863)

If he should leave a rear force at Fredericksburg, tempting you to fall upon it, it would fight in entrenchments and have you at advantage, and so, man for man, worst you at that point, while his main force would in some way be getting an advantage of you northward. In one word, I would not take any risk of being entangled up on the river like an ox jumped half over a fence and liable to be torn by dogs front and rear without a fair chance to gore one way or to kick the other.

We will examine some more patterns of this kind below. Before closing this section, however, notice the pleasure and force that can be produced by a succession of simple similes to describe the same subject:

Defoe, *A Discourse Upon Occasional Conformity* (1698)

All the histories of religion in the world do not show such a case; 'tis like a ship with her sails hauled some back and some full; 'tis like a workman that builds with one hand and pulls down with the other; 'tis like a fisherman who catches fish with one hand, and throws them into the sea with the other; 'tis like everything which signifies nothing. To say a man can be of two religions is a contradiction, unless there be two Gods to worship, or he has two souls to save.

This is fine reasoning. To what shall I compare it? Shall I liken it to children in the market-place, or shall I liken it to children making bubbles with a pipe? Shall I not rather compare it to two boys upon a balanced board? One goes up, the other down; and so they go up and down, down and up, till the sport is over, and the board is left exactly on the balance in which they found it.

Livingston, speech at New York Ratifying Convention (1788)

This pattern can be conveniently joined with the rhetorical device known as polysyndeton (the repeated use of conjunctions):

[T]hat which most afflicted him was to observe his brother's coat so well reduced into the state of innocence, while his own was either wholly rent to his shirt, or those places which had escaped his cruel clutches were still in Peter's livery. So that he looked like a drunken beau half rifled by bullies, or like a fresh tenant of Newgate when he has refused the payment of garnish, or like a discovered shoplifter left to the mercy of Exchange-women, or like a bawd in her old velvet petticoat resigned into the secular hands of the mobile.

Swift, A Tale of a Tub (1704)

The man of genius, like a dog with a bone, or the slave who has swallowed a diamond, or a patient with the gravel, sits afar and retired, off the road, hangs out no sign of refreshment for man and beast, but says, by all possible hints and signs, I wish to be alone – good-by – farewell.

Thoreau, The Landlord (1843)

2. *Fresh sentences.* We have mostly been occupied with comparisons in which the subject and source are

contained in the same sentence. Putting the simile into a sentence of its own is an additional option and can simplify its expression. The types of constructions that can follow the word *like* are no different here than before, but starting fresh relieves the pressure on both the writer and the reader to keep a long sentence aloft.

Wells, *War and the Future* (1917)

Quietly perhaps and unobtrusively, everyone I know is trying to find the way out of the war, and I am convinced that the same is the case in Germany. That is what makes the Peace-at-any-price campaign so exasperating. It is like being chased by clamorous geese across a common in the direction in which you want to go.

James Fitzjames Stephen, *Liberty, Equality, Fraternity* (1873)

Nay, the attempt, even the successful attempt, to put into words thoughts not too deep for them has its inconveniences. It is like selling out stock which might have risen in value if it had been left alone.

Conrad, *Nostromo* (1904)

A man of his sort has never contemplated remaining indefinitely at the mercy of ignorance and corruption. It was like being a prisoner in a cavern of banditti with the price of your ransom in your pocket, and buying your life from day to day.

Of course the same can be done with *as if* clauses and similar expressions, which make possible a slightly different set of usages, just as before: the writer can follow those words with a subject and verb, making a full explanation easy to express.

Holmes, *The Autocrat of the Breakfast-Table* (1858)

Some persons seem to think that absolute truth, in the form of rigidly stated propositions, is all that conversation admits. This is precisely as if a musician should insist on having nothing but perfect chords and simple melodies, – no diminished fifths, no flat sevenths, no flourishes, on any account.

Beware when the great God lets loose a thinker on this planet. Then all things are at risk. It is as when a conflagration has broken out in a great city, and no man knows what is safe, or where it will end.

Emerson, *Circles* (1841)

He has broken the conventions, but he has kept the commandments. It is as if a man were found gambling wildly in a gambling hell, and you found that he only played for trouser buttons. It is as if you found a man making a clandestine appointment with a lady at a Covent Garden ball, and then you found it was his grandmother.

Chesterton, *Manalive* (1912)

These structural ideas are useful in efforts to make a claim seem foolish by comparing it to another that is parallel and more foolish: "That is like saying...." Sometimes these uses can suggest a strict logical equivalency rather than a figurative one.

It is stupid to say that "most people" are stupid. It is like saying "most people are tall," when it is obvious that "tall" can only mean taller than most people.

Chesterton, *The Red Town* (1910)

Johnson was present when a tragedy was read, in which there occurred this line: "Who rules o'er freemen should himself be free." The company having admired it much, "I cannot agree with you," said Johnson; "it might as well be said: 'Who drives fat oxen must himself be fat.'"

Boswell, *Life of Johnson* (1791)

3. *Explaining the sense of the comparison.* In the examples shown so far, the reader of the comparison is expected to grasp the sense of the similarity once it is presented. Another family of constructions provides more help: the comparison is announced and then explained. The explanatory clause at the end states a proposition that applies to both the source and the subject. It may resemble a punch line.

Burke, *Observations on a Late Publication on the Present State of the Nation* (1769)

One of his projects depends for success upon another project, and this upon a third, all of them equally visionary. His finance is like the Indian philosophy; his earth is poised on the horns of a bull, his bull stands upon an elephant, his elephant is supported by a tortoise! and so on forever.

Sumner, speech at Boston (1845)

The mind which trains the child is like the hand which commands the end of a long lever: a gentle effort at that time suffices to heave the enormous weight of succeeding years.

Note Books of Samuel Butler (1912)

But my unseen world is to be bona fide unseen and, in so far as I say I know anything about it, I stultify myself. It should no more be described than God should be represented in painting or sculpture. It is as the other side of the moon; we know it must be there but we know also that, in the nature of things, we can never see it.

The explanations in the cases above were signaled with a colon or semicolon. Those forms of punctuation have the advantage of lifting the expectation in the reader's ear before satisfying it with the words that follow. But the payoff can also be appended more informally.

Taylor, *Rule and Exercises of Holy Dying* (1651)

[T]he last words of a dying man are like the tooth of a wounded lion, making a deeper impression in the agony, than in the most vigorous strength.

Shaw, *Saint Joan* (preface) (1923)

When Abernethy, the famous doctor, was asked why he indulged himself with all the habits he warned his patients against as unhealthy, he replied that his business was that of a direction post, which points out the way to a place, but does not go thither itself.

Irving, *Knickerbocker's History of New York* (1809)

The reader will now witness the manner in which a peaceful community advances towards a state of war; which is apt to be like the approach of a horse to a drum, with much prancing and little progress, and too often with the wrong end foremost.

Notice the rhythmic similarity of most of these examples. Another venerable use of this idea, also notably rhythmic and sometimes attractive for its wit, follows the statement of the simile with an explanation that displays two sides of the comparison.

> Laws are like cobwebs, which may catch small flies, but let wasps and hornets break through.

Swift, *A Critical Essay Upon the Faculties of the Mind* (1707)

> Certainly fame is like a river, that beareth up things light and swollen, and drowns things weighty and solid.

Bacon, *Of Praise* (1625)

> Dictionaries are like watches, the worst is better than none, and the best cannot be expected to go quite true.

Johnson, letter to Francesco Sastres (1784)

In some cases an explanation must be offered not just to make clear the sense of the comparison but because the reader's familiarity with the source of the simile cannot be assumed. A case of this kind involves peculiar challenges. The source invoked may be helpful because it simplifies the subject elegantly; yet the reader might need to be swiftly educated if the simile is to do its work. The art lies in keeping the explanation compact. Some examples where it is provided in a few strokes:

> If we began stickling for proof in this way, our opponents would not be long in letting us know that absolute proof is unattainable on any subject, that reasonable presumption is our highest certainty, and that crying out for too much evidence is as bad as accepting too little. Truth is like a photographic sensitized plate, which is equally ruined by over and by under exposure, and the just exposure for which can never be absolutely determined.

Butler, *The Deadlock in Darwinism* (1890)

Melville, *Pierre* (1852)

For indeed the democratic element operates as a subtle acid among us; forever producing new things by corroding the old; as in the south of France verdigris, the primitive material of one kind of green paint, is produced by grape-vinegar poured upon copper plates.

Lincoln, debate with Stephen Douglas at Charleston (1858)

I would then like to know how it comes about that when each piece of a story is true the whole story turns out false. I take it these people have some sense; they see plainly that Judge Douglas is playing cuttle-fish, a small species of fish that has no mode of defending itself when pursued except by throwing out a black fluid, which makes the water so dark the enemy cannot see it, and thus it escapes. Ain't the Judge playing the cuttle-fish?

Comparisons that use mythology commonly call for explanation of this kind, as we also saw in the chapter discussing that topic.

Boswell, *Journal of a Tour to the Hebrides* (1773)

After having been shut up so long in Col, the sight of such an assemblage of moving habitations, containing such a variety of people, engaged in different pursuits, gave me much gaiety of spirit. When we had landed, Dr Johnson said, "Boswell is now all alive. He is like Antæus; he gets new vigour whenever he touches the ground."

Melville, *White-Jacket* (1850)

There is a fable about a painter moved by Jove to the painting of the head of Medusa. Though the picture was true to the life, yet the poor artist sickened at the sight of what his forced pencil had drawn. Thus, borne through my task toward the end, my own soul now sinks at what I myself have portrayed.

Sometimes explanation must be added not because obscure knowledge is needed to understand the comparison, but because the author has in mind an involved alignment that has to be established point by point.

> Religious ideas have the fate of melodies, which, once set afloat in the world, are taken up by all sorts of instruments, some of them woefully coarse, feeble, or out of tune, until people are in danger of crying out that the melody itself is detestable.

Eliot, *Janet's Repentance* (1857)

> Man little knows what calamities are beyond his patience to bear till he tries them; as in ascending the heights of ambition, which look bright from below, every step we rise shews us some new and gloomy prospect of hidden disappointment; so in our descent from the summits of pleasure, though the vale of misery below may appear at first dark and gloomy, yet the busy mind, still attentive to its own amusement, finds as we descend something to flatter and to please. Still as we approach, the darkest objects appear to brighten, and the mental eye becomes adapted to its gloomy situation.

Goldsmith, *The Vicar of Wakefield* (1766)

> A transition from an author's book to his conversation is too often like an entrance into a large city, after a distant prospect. Remotely, we see nothing but spires of temples and turrets of palaces, and imagine it the residence of splendour, grandeur, and magnificence; but when we have passed the gates, we find it perplexed with narrow passages, disgraced with despicable cottages, embarrassed with obstructions, and clouded with smoke.

Johnson, *The Rambler* no. 14 (1750)

Johnson's simile works because it is as good as familiar by the time he is done narrating it; the images are vivid enough to make the feelings about it easy to imagine even if never experienced firsthand. He strengthens the effect by writing the comparison in the first person, as though walking with the reader and pointing out things equally visible to both. Parts of the technique in use here – piling up details about the source of a comparison to make it convincing and affecting – will be considered further in the section below on the Homeric simile.

4. *Parenthetical introduction of similes*. A similar idea to one just discussed: the speaker interrupts the statement of the subject to introduce the comparison, then finishes both at the same time. These amount to further cases in which the simile is stated and then explained.

Coleridge, *On the Principles of Political Knowledge* (1809)

Hence it is that human experience, like the stern-lights of a ship at sea, illumines only the path which we have passed over.

Fielding, *Tom Jones* (1749)

A single bad act no more constitutes a villain in life, than a single bad part on the stage. The passions, like the managers of a playhouse, often force men upon parts without consulting their judgment, and sometimes without any regard to their talents.

Specimens of the Table Talk of Samuel Taylor Coleridge (1834)

I would recommend an advocate to devote a part of his leisure time to some study of the metaphysics of the mind, or metaphysics of theology... Some such studies are wanted to counteract the operation of legal studies and practice, which sharpen, indeed, but, like a grinding-stone, narrow whilst they sharpen.

The basis of the similarity is stated in language that applies to both elements, so that the application of the unifying idea to the two halves comes into view simultaneously. It resembles a riddle: how are the passions like managers of a playhouse? Then comes the explanation, in words that fit both.

The part of the simile offered in this parenthetical style cannot be too long, for the rest of the sentence has been paused for the sake of it. The reader has to hold the original subject in mind while the comparative idea is introduced, so the introduction should be quick. Besides, the parenthetical is only supposed to get the comparison started. The rest is left to the revelation clause that follows (narrow whilst they sharpen, etc.). But one can get away with packing a bit more into the parenthetical, as here:

> I have already observed, in examining the foundation of mathematics, that the imagination, when set into any train of thinking, is apt to continue even when its object fails it, and, like a galley put in motion by the oars, carries on its course without any new impulse.

Hume, *A Treatise of Human Nature* (1738)

> An aristocratic body, like the screw in mechanics, working its way by slow degrees, and holding fast whatever it gains, should ever be suspected of an encroaching tendency.

George Mason, speech at Federal Ratifying Convention (1787)

5. *The simile to strengthen a modifier.* Another use of the simile employs it to intensify an adjective. Most common adjectives have ready-made similes of this kind associated with them – flat as a pancake, clear as a bell, stubborn as a mule, quiet as a mouse, with others the reader can easily supply for lightness, heaviness, coldness, hardness, and so on: an entire vocabulary of clichés. One wants to avoid those and think of something fresh.

> LEWIS. ...Life is as tedious as a twice-told tale Vexing the dull ear of a drowsy man.

King John, 3, 4

> I should like to write a novel certainly, a novel that would be as lovely as a Persian carpet and as unreal.

Wilde, *The Picture of Dorian Gray* (1890)

> How could the Prince occupy himself, what interests could he create, and what faculties, gracious heaven, did he possess? He was as ignorant as a fish, and as narrow as his hat-band.

Henry James, *The Princess Casamassima* (1886)

The example from James suggests the fun that can be had in combining uses of this pattern. A succession of brief similes has a force of its own; it lends itself naturally to the rhetorical scheme known as isocolon, or parallel structure. The cumulative force of such comparisons – the sense of onrush they create – may compensate for the familiarity of them, as in these cases.

Kingsley, *Westward Ho!* (1855)

Slander? Ask Leigh here, who has but known me a fortnight, whether I am not as vain as a peacock, as selfish as a fox, as imperious as a bona roba, and ready to make a cat's paw of him or any man, if there be a chestnut in the fire....

Lamb, letter to Bernard Barton (1824)

I have not a thing to say; nothing is of more importance than another; I am flatter than a denial or pancake; emptier than Judge Parke's wig when the head is in it; duller than a country stage when the actors are off it; a cipher, an o!

Dickens, *A Christmas Carol* (1843)

"I don't know what to do!" cried Scrooge, laughing and crying in the same breath; and making a perfect Laocoön of himself with his stockings. "I am as light as a feather, I am as happy as an angel, I am as merry as a schoolboy. I am as giddy as a drunken man. A merry Christmas to everybody!"

It is a short distance from the constructions just shown to comparisons in which the subject exceeds the source: not *as sharp as*, but *sharper than*:

King Lear, 1, 4

LEAR. ...How sharper than a serpent's tooth it is
To have a thankless child! Away, away!

As You Like It, 4, 1

ROSALIND. ...I will be more jealous of thee than a Barbary cock-pigeon over his hen, more clamorous than a parrot against rain, more new-fangled than an ape, more giddy in my desires than a monkey.

Melville, *Mardi* (1849)

Now, one of these boats was to be made way with. No facile matter, truly. Harder than for any dashing young Janizary to run off with a sultana from the Grand Turk's seraglio.

Adverbs can be the subject of the same approach just shown. They have not been burdened with clichés to the same extent as adjectives; usually the simile is more precisely tailored to its circumstances.

> [A] man may grow a new reputation as easily as a lobster grows a new claw, or, if he have health and money, may thrive in great peace of mind without any reputation at all.

Butler, *The Way of All Flesh* (1902)

> [H]e was a most acute reasoner, who could unfold a proposition into its consequences as patiently, as convincingly, as a palaeontologist extorts its confession from a fossil fragment.

Holmes, *The Pulpit and the Pew* (1881)

> Whatever of value, interest, or meaning our respective worlds may appear endued with are thus pure gifts of the spectator's mind. The passion of love is the most familiar and extreme example of this fact. If it comes, it comes; if it does not come, no process of reasoning can force it. Yet it transforms the value of the creature loved as utterly as the sunrise transforms Mont Blanc from a corpse-like gray to a rosy enchantment....

William James, *The Varieties of Religious Experience* (1902)

6. *Nouns.* The miniature similes just shown embellish modifiers. A similar idea may be used with nouns: the subject is said to have a quality, and is compared to a source that also has it, using *of* rather than *as* to introduce the comparison. An example will be clearer than a description:

> But I may as well tell you that I can find nothing the matter with Mr Merdle. He has the constitution of a rhinoceros, the digestion of an ostrich, and the concentration of an oyster.

Dickens, *Little Dorrit* (1857)

As the illustration shows, uses of this form can be multiplied in a manner parallel to the cases seen a moment ago. The triplet is a satisfying pattern.

Prior, *Life of the Right Hon. Edmund Burke* (1824)

> When Croft's "Life of Dr. Young" was spoken of as a good imitation of Dr. Johnson's style, "No, no," said he, "it is not a good imitation of Johnson; it has all his pomp without his force; it has all the nodosities of the oak, without its strength; it has all the contortions of the sibyl, without the inspiration."

Poe, *Mellonta Tauta* (1850)

> He was a giant in stature – insolent, rapacious, filthy, had the gall of a bullock with the heart of a hyena and the brains of a peacock.

An instance, finally, of how various of the ideas just reviewed may be used attractively alongside each other:

Dickens, *Great Expectations* (1861)

> He'd no more heart than a iron file, he was as cold as death, and he had the head of the Devil afore mentioned.

7. *The comparison comes first.* We have considered similes that appear after the subjects they describe. But the comparison can also be moved to the start of the sequence, and so appear before the thing described. This works a few changes in rhetorical effect. It creates a little suspense; since the comparison is stated before the point of it comes fully into view, the reader has to put up with a brief delay in understanding that is relieved by the arrival of the subject. Second, the subject of the comparison receives more emphasis, since it is the culminating thought left in the mind's eye and ear when the sentence is done. The simile then has to be recalled and reflected upon.

Yet in a different sense the early placement of a simile makes it more conspicuous. When a simile comes after its subject, it can have the flavor of an afterthought that occurred to the speaker after making the claim that it illustrates. Not so when the simile is stated first; the speaker then has made an unmistakable decision in advance to speak figuratively. This may help explain why such usages are less common now than they once were. It is not fashionable to make an utterance that openly reflects planning. The construction nevertheless has charm when the comparison is good. Examples with *like* clauses:

> Like a rejected lover making merry at the wedding of his rival, the president felicitates himself hugely over the late Presidential election.

Lincoln, speech at Chicago (1856)

(Lincoln was speaking of Franklin Pierce, the incumbent, who had been denied the nomination of his party to run again; his rival, Buchanan, had just gone on to win the general election.) Or the *as* clause in advance, which, as ever, takes an independent clause afterwards:.

> As a selfish man will impoverish his family and often bring them to ruin, so a selfish king brings ruin on his people and often plunges them into war.

Thackeray, *Vanity Fair* (1848)

This early placement of a simile especially invites the use of parallel structure between the clause stating the source of the comparison and the clause stating the subject of it – again, isocolon. Thus the first and second clauses in the examples just shown have almost the same number of words. In Lincoln's case they mostly contain the same parts of speech in the same order; in the case from Thackeray the structure is partly parallel (*a selfish man...*; *a selfish king...*) and partly reversed: the first clause ends with *ruin* and the second one starts with it (a case of chiasmus, or perhaps anadiplosis). Letting the clauses mirror each other in these ways helps to reinforce the similarity between the things compared.

Consider some examples in which the initial statement of the simile is more elaborate, with little sub-clauses;

and notice that in each case the second half – the clause explaining the subject – tends toward a similar level of complexity as the first half.

Dickens, *David Copperfield* (1850)

As a man upon a field of battle will receive a mortal hurt, and scarcely know that he is struck, so I, when I was left alone with my undisciplined heart, had no conception of the wound with which it had to strive.

Melville, *Pierre* (1852)

And as the mariner, shipwrecked and cast on the beach, has much ado to escape the recoil of the wave that hurled him there; so Pierre long struggled, and struggled, to escape the recoil of that anguish, which had dashed him out of itself, upon the beach of his swoon.

de Quincey, *Alexander Pope* (1848)

Like a hornet, who is said to leave his sting in the wound, and afterwards to languish away, Pope felt so greatly exhausted by the efforts connected with the Dunciad, (which are far greater, in fact, than all his Homeric labors put together,) that he prepared his friends to expect for the future only an indolent companion and a hermit.

The examples just seen have all involved single similes that arrive in advance of their subjects. But a *like* or *as* clause can also include a second round of comparison before coming to the point. In effect the subject is made the target of two similes. Both of them are stated before arriving at the claim that ties all three of the points together. This extends the suspense a little and gives the reader more matter for reflection once the subject arrives.

Thoreau, *A Week on the Concord and Merrimack Rivers* (1849)

As polishing expresses the vein in marble, and grain in wood, so music brings out what of heroic lurks anywhere.

Like the great dome of St. Peter's, and like the great whale, retain, O man! in all seasons a temperature of thine own.

Melville, *Moby-Dick* (1851)

8. *The separate sentence.* We saw earlier that a simile can be split off from the end of a sentence and made a sentence of its own. The same can happen at the front: the source idea can be stated by itself, then the comparison announced afterwards. This manner of expression allows the source to be explained at leisure. It edges toward the Homeric style of simile.

If prize-fighters were allowed to give foul blows and hit or kick a man when he is down, they would hurt each other more than they do, but their relative strength and endurance would be less effectually tested. So with religions; what is wanted is not peace, but fair play.

James Fitzjames Stephen, *Liberty, Equality, Fraternity* (1873)

Who in the rainbow can draw the line where the violet tint ends and the orange tint begins? Distinctly we see the difference of the colors, but where exactly does the one first blendingly enter into the other? So with sanity and insanity.

Melville, *Billy Budd* (1891)

A witty Irish soldier, who was always boasting of his bravery when no danger was near, but who invariably retreated without orders at the first charge of an engagement, being asked by his captain why he did so, replied: "Captain, I have as brave a heart as Julius Caesar ever had; but, somehow or other, whenever danger approaches, my cowardly legs will run away with it." So with Mr. Lamborn's party.

Lincoln, speech at Springfield (1839)

The "so with" constructions just shown are classic, but the same idea can be invoked less formally, as here:

It is not enough for the knight of romance that you agree that his lady is a very nice girl – if you do not

Holmes, Jr., *Natural Law* (1918)

admit that she is the best that God ever made or will make, you must fight.... It seems to me that this demand is at the bottom of the philosopher's effort to prove that truth is absolute and of the jurist's search for criteria of universal validity which he collects under the head of natural law.

9. *The Homeric simile.* The Homeric or "epic" simile is distinctive for its long, specific, and picturesque description of the source material, which is described in more detail than the function of the comparison seems to require and typically comes in advance of what it illustrates. It is epitomized by these examples from Samuel Butler's translation of the *Iliad* (1898):

> As a lion or wild boar turns fiercely on the dogs and men that attack him, while these form a solid wall and shower their javelins as they face him – his courage is all undaunted, but his high spirit will be the death of him; many a time does he charge at his pursuers to scatter them, and they fall back as often as he does so – even so did Hector go about among the host exhorting his men, and cheering them on to cross the trench.

> Ajax son of Oileus never for a moment left the side of Ajax son of Telamon, but as two swart oxen both strain their utmost at the plough which they are drawing in a fallow field, and the sweat steams upwards from about the roots of their horns – nothing but the yoke divides them as they break up the ground till they reach the end of the field – even so did the two Ajaxes stand shoulder to shoulder by one another.

More recent applications often have a whiff of parody about them.

Fielding, *Life of Jonathan Wild the Great* (1743)

As the generous bull who, having long depastured among a number of cows, and thence contracted

an opinion that these cows are all his own property, if he beholds another bull bestride a cow
within his walks, he roars aloud, and threatens
instant vengeance with his horns, till the whole
parish are alarmed with his bellowing; not with
less noise nor less dreadful menaces did the fury
of Wild burst forth and terrify the whole gate.

As two pigs may be seen at the same trough, each
striving to take the delicacies of the banquet from
the other, and yet enjoying always the warmth of
the same dunghill in amicable contiguity, so had
these young ladies lived in sisterly friendship, while
each was striving to take a husband from the other.

Trollope, *He Knew He Was Right* (1869)

As in the hurricane that sweeps the plain, men fly
the neighborhood of some lone, gigantic elm,
whose very height and strength but render it so
much the more unsafe, because so much the more
a mark for thunderbolts; so at those last words of
Ahab's many of the mariners did run from him in
a terror of dismay.

Melville, *Moby-Dick* (1851)

As though a criminal should be chained in a stationary boat on a deep clear river, condemned,
whatever countless leagues of water flowed past
him, always to see the body of the fellow-creature
he had drowned lying at the bottom, immovable,
and unchangeable, except as the eddies made it
broad or long, now expanding, now contracting
its terrible lineaments; so Arthur, below the shift-
ing current of transparent thoughts and fancies
which were gone and succeeded by others as soon
as come, saw, steady and dark, and not to be stirred
from its place, the one subject that he endeavoured with all his might to rid himself of, and that
he could not fly from.

Dickens, *Little Dorrit* (1857)

The full-scale Homeric simile is not often seen now. Our
age is more literal, and the Homeric form runs against

that sensibility by openly lavishing energy on the comparison; in Homeric similes it is common for the account of the comparison's source – the pigs, the bull – to be longer than the statement of the subject being described, which seems outlandish and out of date to the modern ear. But there are reasons why Homeric similes have been enjoyed for millennia. One is that the details of the comparison's source are not really extraneous. They accumulate to create a stronger and more specific image and feeling, which are then transferred to the subject. Homeric similes, when artfully written, also appeal to the natural appetite for well-drawn pictures. Still, their effective use now probably requires a sense of humor to carry off.

Chapter Fourteen

THE CONSTRUCTION
OF METAPHORS

The difference between metaphor and simile is a well-known but crude tool for analysis of comparisons. A simile, as we have seen, is said to be a comparison introduced with a signaling word such as "like" or "as"; a metaphor treats the subject of the comparison and the source as the same – the one *is* the other, not merely *like* the other. The distinction is worthwhile, and we will explore it in this chapter. But sometimes that issue is less interesting than the placement of a comparison, its length, the extent to which it is explained, and the extent to which it is explicit or implied (an issue that the distinction between metaphor and simile only sometimes captures).

> JAQUES. All the world's a stage,
> And all the men and women merely players:
> They have their exits and their entrances;
> And one man in his time plays many parts,
> His acts being seven ages.

As You Like It, 2, 7

> The ugly and the stupid have the best of it in this world. They can sit at their ease and gape at the play.

Wilde, *The Picture of Dorian Gray* (1890)

Both comparisons are metaphors; the subject is treated as the source without a signaling word (*like, as*, etc.). Yet they differ in significant ways. The first is declared openly, it appears at the start, it is extended, and its details are explained. In the second example the equivalence is assumed, it appears at the end of the sentence, it is short, and it is not explained. These differences in approach can have consequences that are subtle but worth an author's attention. This chapter thus means to examine more closely some differences not just between metaphor and simile but between different kinds of metaphors.

1. *The equation.* Some metaphors are simple statements that one thing is another. Metaphors of this type are just as explicit as similes; they differ because they announce a different relationship between the source and subject.

Hazlitt, *On Nicknames* (1818)

A nickname is the heaviest stone that the devil can throw at a man.

This example is a metaphor rather than a simile only because Hazlitt omits the word *like* after the word *is* (and perhaps a bit of other rephrasing). The omission makes the claim stronger; it becomes an equation rather than a mere statement of similarity. Stronger isn't always better, of course. Sometimes one wants the bit of distance between subject and source that is supplied by *like* or *as*.

Two more metaphors that are separated from similes, and probably made more forceful, by the omission of *like*:

Byron, *Journal* (1814)

More notes from Madame de Staël unanswered – and so they shall remain. I admire her abilities, but really her society is overwhelming – an avalanche that buries one in glittering nonsense – all snow and sophistry.

Dickens, *Oliver Twist* (1838)

"You're a rough speaker, my friend, but you look an honest, open-hearted man," said the old gentleman: turning his spectacles in the direction of the candidate for Oliver's premium, whose villainous countenance was a regular stamped receipt for cruelty.

One can rewrite these examples mentally with *like* and feel what is lost. To say that a face *is* a receipt for cruelty is not the same as saying it is *like* one. The constructions call for different imaginative acts. Saying the one is like the other invites the reader to put them side by side and see the similarity. Saying the one *is* the other invites the reader to imagine the one with the characteristics of the other – to combine them, so that one pictures the face and sees the receipt.

Sometimes the equation stated by a metaphor also gains force by raising the possibility, even if half-conscious, that the subject is an instance of the source in more than a figurative sense.

> MACBETH. ... Life's but a walking shadow, a poor player
> That struts and frets his hour upon the stage
> And then is heard no more. It is a tale
> Told by an idiot, full of sound and fury,
> Signifying nothing.

Macbeth, 5, 5.

If one says that life is like a tale told by an idiot, the *like* provides a reassuring bit of insulation between the source and subject. Leaving out the word blurs the line between them and suggests deeper affinities. (Maybe it *isn't* figurative.)

Now let us see how the simple equation might be extended. The examples just shown involved nouns. One thing is said to be another. But suppose one wants to describe a practice or activity, or refer to one.

> This was one of those strokes that denote superior genius, and constitute the sublime of war. 'Twas Scipio leaving Hannibal in Italy, to overcome him at Carthage!

Hamilton, Eulogium on Nathanael Greene (1789)

Hamilton's passage uses a gerund – that is, a verb turned into a noun by adding "ing": *leaving*. Adding modifying words around it creates a gerund phrase. The gerund phrase is useful when building metaphors because it allows easy elaboration after the word "is" (or "was"). Johnson made memorable use of this pattern.

Johnson, in Boswell's *Life* (1791)

Placing him at a public school is forcing an owl upon day.

Johnson, in Boswell's *Life* (1791)

What influence can Mr. Sheridan have upon the language of this great country by his narrow exertions? Sir, it is burning a farthing candle at Dover to show light at Calais.

Boswell, *Life of Johnson* (1791)

His Lordship mentioned a charitable establishment in Wales, where people were maintained, and supplied with everything, upon the condition of their contributing the weekly produce of their labour; and he said they grew quite torpid for the want of property. JOHNSON: "They have no object for hope. Their condition cannot be better. It is rowing without a port."

Most of the examples to this point have also been self-explanatory: one thing is said to be another thing, and the reader is left to grasp the likeness and work out the implications. But just as some similes are expanded a bit after their announcement, metaphors can be expanded after they are invoked without announcement. The illustration a moment ago from *Macbeth* is an example; here is another that dispenses with *like* and then follows its comparison with a postscript that elaborates.

Boswell, *Life of Johnson* (1791)

"Let your boy learn arithmetic, dear madam," was his advice to the mother of a rich young heir: "he will not then be a prey to every rascal which this town swarms with. Teach him the value of money, and how to reckon it; ignorance to a wealthy lad of one-and-twenty is only so much fat to a sick sheep: it just serves to call the rooks about him."

This structure makes the metaphor a slightly different kind of event for the reader. As with some cases we saw in the previous chapter, the initial statement of the comparison serves as a brief riddle; it raises a question in the reader's mind about the basis of the resemblance, which is then swiftly answered. With the explanation extended and offset more gently:

> Society is a joint-stock company, in which the members agree, for the better securing of his bread to each shareholder, to surrender the liberty and culture of the eater.

Emerson, *Self-Reliance* (1841)

2. *The – (source) of – (subject)*. A certain useful construction is epitomized by phrases (from the examples below) such as "the spectacles of books" or "the furnace of adversity." "Furnace" is the source; "adversity" is the subject. "Spectacles" are the source; "books" are the subject.

> For gold is tried in the fire, and acceptable men in the furnace of adversity.

Ecclesiasticus 2:5

> Those who accuse [Shakespeare] to have wanted learning, give him the greater commendation: he was naturally learn'd; he needed not the spectacles of books to read nature; he look'd inwards, and found her there.

Dryden, *Essay of Dramatic Poesie* (1668)

This pattern creates metaphors, not similes; the subject is said to be an instance of the source (books are spectacles), not "like" the source.

> It is by distortedly exalting some men, that others are distortedly debased, till the whole is out of nature. A vast mass of mankind are degradedly thrown into the back-ground of the human picture, to bring forward, with greater glare, the puppet-show of state and aristocracy.

Paine, *The Rights of Man* (1791)

> The late House of Commons has been punished for its independence.... If these examples take root in the minds of men, what members hereafter will be bold enough not to be corrupt, especially as the king's highway of obsequiousness is so very broad and easy?

Burke, *A Representation to His Majesty, Moved in the House of Commons* (1784)

Henry James, *The Turn of the Screw* (1898)

I could only get on at all by taking "nature" into my confidence and my account, by treating my monstrous ordeal as a push in a direction unusual, of course, and unpleasant, but demanding, after all, for a fair front, only another turn of the screw of ordinary human virtue.

This style of metaphor strongly invites the creation of a hybrid picture in the mind's eye. The reader is called upon to see a furnace of adversity, a puppet-show of state and aristocracy, a highway of obsequiousness.

Sometimes these "X of Y" constructions benefit from a bit of explication or expansion after they are stated – for example, what follows "tooth of remorse" here:

Hawthorne, *The Scarlet Letter* (1850)

Others, again, – and those best able to appreciate the minister's peculiar sensibility, and the wonderful operation of his spirit upon the body, – whispered their belief, that the awful symbol was the effect of the ever active tooth of remorse, gnawing from the inmost heart outwardly, and at last manifesting Heaven's dreadful judgment by the visible presence of the letter.

Churchill, speech at Fulton, Missouri (1946)

Why cannot they share their tools and thus increase each other's working powers? Indeed they must do so or else the temple may not be built, or, being built, it may collapse, and we shall all be proved again unteachable and have to go and try to learn again for a third time in a school of war, incomparably more rigorous than that from which we have just been released.

A set to compare with each other:

Dickens, *A Tale of Two Cities* (1859)

Growling, in addition, such phrases as "Ah! yes! You're religious, too. You wouldn't put yourself in opposition to the interests of your husband and child, would you? Not you!" and throwing off other sarcastic sparks from the whirling grindstone of his indignation, Mr. Cruncher betook himself to his boot-cleaning and his general preparation for business.

> To adorn themselves with flowers, to dance, to sing in the sunlight: so much was left of the artistic spirit, and no more. Even that would fade in the end into a contented inactivity. We are kept keen on the grindstone of pain and necessity, and, it seemed to me, that here was that hateful grindstone broken at last!

Wells, *The Time Machine* (1898)

Double cases of this pattern:

> All quarrels ought to be avoided studiously, particularly conjugal ones, as no one can possibly tell where they may end; besides that lasting dislike is often the consequence of occasional disgust, and that the cup of life is surely bitter enough without squeezing in the hateful rind of resentment.

Johnson, in Piozzi's *Anecdotes* (1786)

> I would sooner die tomorrow beneath the dagger of your hate, than live in the infectious leprosy of your friendship.

Phillips, speech at Sligo (1820)

3. *Implied comparisons.* We have seen one respect in which metaphors differ from similes: the source and subject are equated, not just set next to one another. The comparisons we have considered in this chapter nevertheless have been explicit in a limited sense. The subject is named and is said directly to be an instance of the source. Society is a joint-stock company; books are spectacles. But metaphors are most distinct from similes when they are not explicit in this way – when the act of equating the one and the other occurs out of view, with their sameness assumed by the author and inferred by the reader. The author just starts talking about the subject in terms taken from the source. To start with small examples:

Pitt, speech in the House of
Lords (1770)

It is not a ceremonious recommendation from the Throne that can bring back peace and harmony to a discontented people. That insipid annual opiate has been administered so long that it has lost its effect. Something substantial, something effectual must be done.

Jefferson, letter to William
Johnson (1823)

The States supposed that by their tenth amendment, they had secured themselves against constructive powers. They were not lessoned yet by Cohen's case, nor aware of the slipperiness of the eels of the law.

In Pitt's example the subject is named and then redescribed as an opiate. We have subtracted an *is* or comparable words, and the subtraction causes the comparison to slide into view with its accuracy assumed. The comparison also is formidable in economy: the use of a single word evokes a rich set of associations. In the passage from Jefferson the subject of the comparison is not quite named at all; the reader is invited to help by supplying the identity of the eels. The comparison arrives with the equivalence established offstage. When the subject is implied but unstated, all the visual emphasis is on the source of the metaphor.

Those first examples were simple because they involved nouns renamed as other nouns: a recommendation is referred to as an opiate. But a metaphor can also arise just by implication from the verbs the author uses.

Huxley, *Biogenesis and
Abiogenesis* (1870)

[T]he great tragedy of Science – the slaying of a beautiful hypothesis by an ugly fact...

Johnson, in Piozzi's *Anecdotes*
(1786)

He is a scholar undoubtedly, Sir, but remember that he would run from the world, and that it is not the world's business to run after him. I hate a fellow whom pride, or cowardice, or laziness drives into a corner, and does nothing when he is

there but sit and growl; let him come out as I do,
and *bark.*

Notice what compactness these examples achieve. They
don't encumber the discourse with a statement of the
comparison. They imply it, sometimes just with a single
word. Most of the work is moved off the page and into
the reader's imagination.

A metaphor becomes more elaborate as it reiterates
the comparison with additional nouns and verbs borrowed from the source.

> MACBETH. ...I am in blood
> Stepp'd in so far that, should I wade no more,
> Returning were as tedious as go o'er.

Macbeth, 3, 5

> [L]ittleminded people's thoughts move in such
> small circles that five minutes' conversation gives
> you an arc long enough to determine their whole
> curve.

Holmes, *The Autocrat of the Breakfast Table* (1858)

> The amount of new knowledge which one age,
> certainly which one man, can add to the common
> store is small, and it argues stupidity or dishonesty,
> besides ingratitude, to ignore the heap while vaunt-
> ing the few grains which it may have been our
> privilege to add to it.

Frazer, *The Golden Bough* (1922)

These examples take the accuracy of the comparison for
granted. It is presented as a fait accompli, not set forth as
a proposition, and so suppresses argument.

4. *The separated statement; aphorisms.* An attractive pattern puts the comparison into a sentence of its own.
Some of these cases might be considered other than metaphorical in the strict sense we have been using to this
point in the chapter. They do not quite say that the one
thing is the other. They lay two images next to each other,
implying an identity between them or possibly a less figurative parallel.

Piozzi, *Anecdotes of the Late Samuel Johnson* (1786)

I pitied a friend before him, who had a whining wife that found every thing painful to her, and nothing pleasing – "He does not know that she whimpers (says Johnson); when a door has creaked for a fortnight together, you may observe – the master will scarcely give sixpence to get it oiled."

Johnson, in Boswell's *Life* (1791) (on a passage in Congreve's *The Mourning Bride*)

Sir, this is not comparing Congreve on the whole with Shakespeare on the whole; but only maintaining that Congreve has one finer passage than any that can be found in Shakespeare. Sir, a man may have no more than ten guineas in the world, but he may have those ten guineas in one piece; and so may have a finer piece than a man who has ten thousand pounds: but then he has only one ten guinea piece.

The sentence afterwards may be offered as a rhetorical question.

Burke, letter to the Earl Fitzwilliam (1795)

They are always considering the formal distributions of power in a constitution: the moral basis they consider as nothing. Very different is my opinion: I consider the moral basis as everything, – the formal arrangements, further than as they promote the moral principles of government, and the keeping desperately wicked persons as the subjects of laws and not the makers of them, to be of little importance. What signifies the cutting and shuffling of cards, while the pack still remains the same?

Macaulay, speech in the House of Commons (1831)

But is it not strange that men of real ability can deceive themselves so grossly, as to think that any change in the government of a foreign nation, or the rejection of any single motion, however popular, could all at once raise up a great, rich, enlightened nation, against its ancient institutions? Could such small drops have produced an overflowing, if the vessel had not already been filled to the very brim?

The late and isolated statement often takes the form of an aphorism. In skilled hands this construction can seem conclusive. If the aphorism itself sounds true, its fit to the subject is likely to feel true as well; the reader who nods at half the author's claim is on the way to nodding at both parts.

> There is one drawback, however, attending this mode of proceeding, which attaches generally, indeed, to all originality of composition; namely, that it has a tendency to a certain degree of monotony. He who draws upon his own resources, easily comes to an end of his wealth.

Hazlitt, *William Godwin* (1825)

> Publicly and privately, it were much better for the age in which he lived, that he and the legion of whom he was one were designedly bad, than indifferent and purposeless. It is the drifting icebergs setting with any current anywhere, that wreck the ships.

Dickens, *Hard Times* (1854)

> Our political vagueness divides men, it does not fuse them. Men will walk along the edge of a chasm in clear weather, but they will edge miles away from it in a fog.

Chesterton, *The New Hypocrite* (1910)

The aphoristic form of metaphor lends itself to statements of animal lore.

> BRUTUS. ...He would be crown'd:
> How that might change his nature, there's
>   the question.
> It is the bright day that brings forth the adder
> And that craves wary walking.

Julius Caesar, 2, 1

> TANNER. Talk! Talk! It means nothing to you but talk.
> Well, go back to your mother, and help her to

Shaw, *Man and Superman* (1903)

poison Rhoda's imagination as she has poisoned yours. It is the tame elephants who enjoy capturing the wild ones.

Carlyle, *The French Revolution* (1837)

Not from over France only are the unrestful flocking towards Paris; but from all sides of Europe. Where the carcase is, thither will the eagles gather.

Thoreau, *Walden* (1854)

It is same whether a man eat, or drink, or cohabit, or sleep sensually. They are but one appetite, and we only need to see a person do any one of these things to know how great a sensualist he is. The impure can neither stand nor sit with purity. When the reptile is attacked at one mouth of his burrow, he shows himself at another.

As we have seen elsewhere, it is interesting to observe how some writers return to both the same families of source material and the same patterns of expression on different occasions and for different purposes, as in these examples from Burke:

Burke, *Speech on American Taxation* (1774)

But if, intemperately, unwisely, fatally, you sophisticate and poison the very source of government, by urging subtle deductions, and consequences odious to those you govern, from the unlimited and illimitable nature of supreme sovereignty, you will teach them by these means to call that sovereignty itself in question. When you drive him hard, the boar will surely turn upon the hunters.

Burke, *Letter to a Member of the National Assembly* (1791)

It is in the relaxation of security, it is in the expansion of prosperity, it is in the hour of dilatation of the heart, and of its softening into festivity and pleasure, that the real character of men is discerned. If there is any good in them, it appears then or never. Even wolves and tigers, when gorged with their prey, are safe and gentle.

And Johnson:

> [T]he Colonists could with no solidity argue from
> their not having been taxed while in their infancy,
> that they should not now be taxed. We do not put
> a calf into the plow; we wait till he is an ox.

Johnson, *Taxation no Tyranny* (draft) (1775)

> JOHNSON. "Sir, they were examined, and found to
> be mighty ignorant fellows." BOSWELL. "But, was
> it not hard, Sir, to expel them, for I am told they
> were good beings?" JOHNSON. "I believe they
> might be good beings; but they were not fit to be in
> the University of Oxford. A cow is a very good ani-
> mal in the field; but we turn her out of a garden."

Boswell, *Life of Johnson* (1791)

The comparative and aphoristic statement also, though
less commonly, can come before its subject. Reversing the
order in this way makes a mild demand on the reader's
patience because the comparative statement is put forward
before the reason for offering it can be seen. The reader
is invited to acknowledge the sense of the claim in the
abstract and then to bear with the speaker as its rele-
vance gradually appears. The sequence offers the pleasure of a mystery momentarily created and then solved.

> Solitary trees, if they grow at all, grow strong: and
> a boy deprived of a father's care often develops, if
> he escape the perils of youth, an independence
> and vigour of thought which may restore in after
> life the heavy loss of early days.

Churchill, *The River War* (1899)

> The hues of the opal, the light of the diamond, are
> not to be seen if the eye is too near. To my friend I
> write a letter and from him I receive a letter. That
> seems to you a little. It suffices me.

Emerson, *Friendship* (1841)

> He is a bold surgeon, they say, whose hand does
> not tremble when he performs an operation upon
> his own person; and he is often equally bold who
> does not hesitate to pull off the mysterious veil of

Smith, *The Theory of Moral Sentiments* (1759)

self-delusion, which covers from his view the deformities of his own conduct.

5. *Successive cases.* We saw in the last chapter how similes may be stacked, one after the other, to good effect. The same may be done with metaphors. To begin with cases that multiply the aphoristic pattern just reviewed:

Dickens, *Hunted Down* (1859)

An observer of men who finds himself steadily repelled by some apparently trifling thing in a stranger is right to give it great weight. It may be the clue to the whole mystery. A hair or two will show where a lion is hidden. A very little key will open a very heavy door.

Beerbohm, *No. 2 The Pines* (1914)

Not philosophy, after all, not humanity, just sheer joyous power of song, is the primal thing in poetry. Ideas, and flesh and blood, are but reserves to be brought up when the poet's youth is going. When the bird can no longer sing in flight, let the nest be ready. After the king has dazzled us with his crown, let him have something to sit down on. But the session on throne or in nest is not the divine period.

William James, *Pragmatism* (1907)

The most primitive ways of thinking may not yet be wholly expunged. . . . Our ancestors may at certain moments have struck into ways of thinking which they might conceivably not have found. But once they did so, and after the fact, the inheritance continues. When you begin a piece of music in a certain key, you must keep the key to the end. You may alter your house ad libitum, but the ground-plan of the first architect persists – you can make great changes, but you cannot change a Gothic church into a Doric temple. You may rinse and rinse the bottle, but you can't get the taste of the medicine or whiskey that first filled it wholly out.

Or return to metaphors of the more conventional kind – identities and equations, the piling up of which can restate a claim or elaborate a description in a series of images.

> EDGAR. ...Wine loved I deeply, dice dearly, and in woman outparamoured the Turk. False of heart, light of ear, bloody of hand – hog in sloth, fox in stealth, wolf in greediness, dog in madness, lion in prey.

King Lear, 3, 4

> He got into a restless habit of strolling about when the cause was on, or expected, talking to the little shopkeepers and telling 'em to keep out of Chancery, whatever they did. "For," says he, "it's being ground to bits in a slow mill; it's being roasted at a slow fire; it's being stung to death by single bees; it's being drowned by drops; it's going mad by grains."

Dickens, *Bleak House* (1853)

> If we look wider, things are all alike; laws and letters and creeds and modes of living seem a travesty of truth. Our society is encumbered by ponderous machinery, which resembles the endless aqueducts which the Romans built over hill and dale and which are superseded by the discovery of the law that water rises to the level of its source. It is a Chinese wall which any nimble Tartar can leap over. It is a standing army, not so good as a peace. It is a graduated, titled, richly appointed empire, quite superfluous when town-meetings are found to answer just as well.

Emerson, *Spiritual Laws* (1841)

Stacking of this kind may consist of metaphor and simile in alternation.

> Nothing can be imagined more idle, in a general way, than talking about a century as if it were some kind of animal with a head and tail, instead of an arbitrary length cut from an unending scroll. Nor

Chesterton, *G. F. Watts* (1904)

is it less erroneous to assume that even if a period
be definitely vital or disturbing, art must be a mirror of it; the greatest political storm flutters only a
fringe of humanity; poets, like brick-layers, work
on through a century of wars, and Bewick's birds,
to take an instance, have the air of persons unaf-
fected by the French Revolution.

A vigorous instance of such alternation is found in H.L.
Mencken's assessment of the speechwriting of Warren
Harding.

Mencken, *Gamalielese* (1921)
(on Warren Harding)

[H]e writes the worst English that I have ever
encountered. It reminds me of a string of wet
sponges; it reminds me of tattered washing on the
line; it reminds me of stale bean soup, of college
yells, of dogs barking idiotically through endless
nights. It is so bad that a sort of grandeur creeps
into it. It drags itself out of the dark abysm of pish,
and crawls insanely up to the topmost pinnacle of
tosh. It is rumble and bumble. It is flap and doo-
dle. It is balder and dash.

When used in the second person, stacked metaphors can
serve as a tool for relentless insult.

1 *Henry IV*, 2, 2

FALSTAFF. Away, you starveling, you elf-skin, you
dried neat's tongue, you bull's pizzle, you stock-
fish! O for breath to utter what is like thee! you
tailor's-yard, you sheath, you bowcase; you vile
standing-tuck!

Richard II, 3, 2

KING RICHARD. O villains, vipers, damn'd without
redemption!
Dogs, easily won to fawn on any man!
Snakes, in my heart-blood warm'd, that sting
my heart!
Three Judases, each one thrice worse than Judas!

"You're a brimstone idiot. You're a scorpion – a brimstone scorpion! You're a sweltering toad. You're a chattering clattering broomstick witch that ought to be burnt!" gasps the old man, prostrate in his chair.

Dickens, *Bleak House* (1853)

Successive metaphors may serve, finally, a pedagogical purpose, as they can illustrate different aspects of a subject, and sometimes a progression from one of them to the next.

Thus, then, though Time be the mightiest of Alarics, yet is he the mightiest mason of all. And a tutor, and a counselor, and a physician, and a scribe, and a poet, and a sage, and a king.

Melville, *Mardi* (1849)

[W]isdom is a fox, who, after long hunting, will at last cost you the pains to dig out; it is a cheese, which, by how much the richer, has the thicker, the homelier, and the coarser coat; and whereof, to a judicious palate, the maggots are the best: it is a sack-posset, wherein the deeper you go, you will find it the sweeter. Wisdom is a hen, whose cackling we must value and consider, because it is attended with an egg; but then lastly, it is a nut, which, unless you choose with judgment, may cost you a tooth, and pay you with nothing but a worm.

Swift, *A Tale of a Tub* (1704)

Writing a book is an adventure. To begin with it is a toy, then an amusement. Then it becomes a mistress, and then it becomes a master, and then it becomes a tyrant and, in the last stage, just as you are about to be reconciled to your servitude, you kill the monster and fling him to the public.

Churchill, speech at London (1949)

A NOTE ON THE TYPE

FARNSWORTH'S CLASSICAL ENGLISH METAPHOR has been set in Sabon Next, a type with a distinguished and complex history. Originally commissioned in the 1960s from the master tyopographer, designer, and calligrapher Jan Tschichold, Sabon is a contemporary interpretation of a roman type attributed to Claude Garamond and an italic attributed to Robert Granjon. It was named in honor of Jacques Sabon, a punchcutter who worked for the printer who created the specimen on which Tschichold based his design. Because the types were initially intended for machine composition on both Linotype and Monotype as well as for cold-metal composition, the design was carefully drawn and modified to accommodate the limitations imposed by the various methods of composition. This process resulted in a widely popular type that was somewhat compromised by its lack of kerns, a feature that limited the appeal of the italic in particular. Sabon Next was drawn in 2002 by Jean François Porchez, who set out to harmonize Tschichold's type and the types that inspired it with the possibilities that the OpenType platform offered to the contemporary type designer. The result is an elegant, highly readable type with a complete range of characters (including a generous selection of ligatures, swash characters, and ornaments) that is beautifully suited to book work.

DESIGN & COMPOSITION BY CARL W. SCARBROUGH